Elena Poniatowska

Elena Poniatowska

An Intimate Biography

Michael K. Schuessler

Foreword by Carlos Fuentes

The University of Arizona Press
Tucson

The University of Arizona Press
© 2007 Michael K. Schuessler

Library of Congress Cataloging-in-Publication Data
Schuessler, Michael Karl.
  [Elenísima. English]
  Elena Poniatowska : an intimate biography / Michael K.
Schuessler ; foreword by Carlos Fuentes.
    p. cm.
  Includes bibliographical references and index.
  ISBN-13: 978-0-8165-2501-0 (pbk. : alk. paper)
  ISBN-10: 0-8165-2501-3 (pbk. : alk. paper)
    1. Poniatowska, Elena. 2. Authors, Mexican—20th century
—Biography. I. Title.
PQ7297.P63Z8413 2007
868'.6409–dc22
[B]
2006030298

This book is a translation, with modifications, of *Elenísima:
Ingenio y figura de Elena Poniatowska*, by Michael K. Schuessler.
© Editorial Diana, Mexico, DF, 2003.

Publication of this book is made possible in part by the proceeds of a permanent endowment created with the assistance
of a Challenge Grant from the National Endowment for the
Humanities, a federal agency.

Manufactured in the United States of America on acid-free,
archival-quality paper containing a minimum of 50% post-
consumer waste and processed chlorine free.

12 11 10 09 08 07   6 5 4 3 2 1

Contents

Illustrations

Foreword

"La Poni"

I first met Elena at a ball held at Mexico City's Jockey Club. She was disguised as a charming kitty cat, all in white; a true blonde, she wore a mask that covered only the top part of her face, and very light-colored jewels. She looked like some lovely and adorable creature dreamed up by Jean Cocteau. Like other nice little kitties, she had small whiskers that peeped out from under her mask. On her, however, those little hairs required on all cats' faces were not aggressive, like Frida Kahlo's savage moustache, but merely an intimation of several antennas already pointing in multiple directions towards the various aspects of her future work, which would include stories, novels, chronicles, newspaper reports, memoirs, etc. We made our literary debut at the same time, many years ago, I with a volume of stories, *Masked Days*, and Elena with a singular exercise of childish innocence, *Lilus Kikus*. The irony, the perversity of her first text was not immediately understood. Like one of Balthus' little girls, like a Shirley Temple without dimples, Elena finally revealed herself as an "Alice in Testimonial Land." Without ever abandoning her make-believe game of feigned astonishment when faced with the kind of eccentricity that those who seriously believe themselves eccentric conceive to be logical, Elena started achieving a personal stance of seriousness alongside her natural grace. She created a great biographical gallery of Mexico's feminine side through her portraits of famous and infamous women, some of them anonymous and others who would become famous. I may assume that the award she has just received in Madrid for her most recent novel, *La piel del cielo*, is the culmination of this imaginary and documentary exploration of the female condition. Elena gives women a central but not sanctified role in our society, as few other writers have done. And yet she has not excluded—thank you for that, Elena—us men, who love, accompany, are loved by, and are supported by women. However that may be, no one can deny that Elena Poniatowska has contributed greatly toward giving women a unique position amidst the deprivation, prejudice, and exclusion that surrounds them in our world, which is still male-dominated but has become ever more human: not only feminist, but human and all-inclusive. "Silly, you men so very adept—at wrongly faulting womankind . . . " the insignia of Sor Juana Inés de la Cruz is not only an echo in Sor Elena of the Cross-and-Fiction, it is an all-encompassing embrace, a sort of all-inclusive compassion: "Silly, you men, united to my work, to my struggle, to my own stubbornness." *La noche de Tlatelolco* is the great and definitive chronicle of the ominous dawn of a crime that also marked the twilight of the authoritarian regime of the PRI in Mexico. On that terrible night of October 2, 1968, began the transformation of Princess Poniatowska, descendant of María Lesczinska, Louis XV of France's second wife, descendant also of King Stanislaus I of Poland and of Napoleon's heroic marshal Josef Poniatowski, into a smiling and serene champion of leftist causes. I don't always agree with her positions, but I always admire the conviction and the courage with which she upholds them. Fortunately, today Mexican democracy is being forged with agreements and disagreements that are lawful, respectful, and respected. What is important about Elena is that the positions she takes in public do not reduce nor do they supplant her devotions at home: love for her children, dedication to her friends, and devotion to her writing. Having been a friend of Elena's for more years than I want—or am able—to recall, today, I send her an enormous embrace, as youthful as our first.

Carlos Fuentes

Preface

Elena Poniatowska requires no introduction. She is the author of more than thirty books that encompass almost every literary genre: interview, short story, drama, chronicle, testimony, novel, essay, and biography. Notwithstanding her wide-ranging literary corpus, she is best known for the genres she reinvented in Mexico: the interview and the testimonial novel. An outstanding example of the latter, *La noche de Tlatelolco* (1971) (*Massacre in Mexico*, 1975), is a collective account of a tragic confrontation between students and soldiers reflected in a collage of desperate voices that are at the same time the work's content and form. *Hasta no verte Jesús mío* (1969) (*Here's to You, Jesusa!*, 2001), a neorealist novel, is the testimony of a cantankerous and admirable woman who fought in the Mexican Revolution and lived more adventures than the *Periquillo Sarniento* (*The Itching Parrot*) or *La Pícara Justina* (Roguish Justine).

Although Elena has enjoyed enormous success as a journalist and writer, she has always been somewhat forsaken by elite Mexican literary circles. As a journalist, she tracked the news, and because she was reporting day and night, Elena never found time to participate in the activities of Mexican literary "café society." Moreover, Elena was quite young when she became convinced that the only books worth writing were useful ones, books meaningful to her country, which led Carlos Fuentes to exclaim: "Look at poor little Poni! There she goes in her beat-up VW Bug on her way to interview the head of the slaughterhouse." Apparently, the price of onions and tomatoes, as well as reports of evictions and land takeovers, were much more significant to her than the often fleeting ideas of the contemporary literary vanguard. Perhaps that is why one day she confessed to me that some writers consider her "the cook, the street sweep, the janitor in charge of cleaning out the toilets of the great manor of literature."

Far from belonging to this world that so fascinates her, Poniatowska is descended from the last king of Poland, Stanislaus Augusto Poniatowski, and from the marshal of France, Prince Josef Ciolek Poniatowski. Her family includes among its illustrious ancestors an archbishop, a musician, and several writers, including her Aunt Pita—Guadalupe Amor—the infamous and extraordinary poet who baptized herself "the absolute Queen of Hell." Given her royal pedigree and strong leftist inclinations, her European relatives, who treasure their royal past, dubbed Elena "La Princesse Rouge"—"The Red Princess."

Elena Poniatowska was born in Paris in 1932 and immigrated to Mexico when she was ten years old, along with her mother and sister, Kitzia, all three fleeing the dangers of Western Europe, which was at that time in the throes of the Second World War. Her mother, Paula Amor de Ferreira Iturbe, who passed away in March 2001 at age ninety-two, was a Mexican whose ancestors had left Mexico after the execution of Emperor Maximilian and the celebrated insanity of his beloved and manipulative Empress Charlotte. Born in France, Doña Paulette met her future husband, Prince Jean E. Poniatowski Sperry, during a ball held at the Rothschilds' family home in Paris, and they married shortly thereafter, in 1931. The couple had three children: Elena, Kitzia, and Jan, the youngest, who died in an automobile accident in 1968, when he was only twenty-one years old.

Elena began her education in France, where her grandfather gave her her first lessons in French and mathematics. Upon her arrival in Mexico City, she continued her elementary schooling at the British-sponsored Windsor School 'and concluded her formal education at the Convent of the Sacred Heart (Eden Hall) in Torresdale, near Philadelphia. There she completed "Academic Classes": four years of general studies as well as lessons in dance, religion, and etiquette. Although her teachers encouraged her to continue her studies at Manhattanville College, a sudden devaluation of Mexico's currency left her parents unable to finance her

university education, and Elena returned to Mexico, a land of volcanoes and pyramids, haciendas and palaces, but also of huts and
huaraches, *pulque*, and *chuitlacoche*.

Once back in Mexico, Elena studied shorthand and planned
to find work as a bilingual secretary, but she never pursued a bach-
elor's degree. In her own words, she "never even came close to
a university, not even by night," although she has been awarded several honorary doctorates by universities in Mexico and
abroad—the most recent being that conferred upon her by Mexico's national university, the Universidad Nacional Autónoma de
México (UNAM), in September 2001. Although Elena is the first
to point out that her higher education was less than conventional,
the subjects of her interviews—including Alfonso Reyes, Luis Buñuel, Octavio Paz, Diego Rivera, Juan Rulfo, André Malraux, and
Rosario Castellanos, among many others—became the generous
teachers of a young woman who was always curious and occasionally impertinent.

I first met Elena Poniatowska almost fifteen years ago when
I gave a lecture dedicated to the poetry of Guadalupe Amor. Although we had just met, Elena immediately invited me to her
house in Mexico City; upon my arrival there several months later,
she allowed me to pore over many interviews she had conducted
with her eccentric Aunt "Pita." Much of the material for my book
La undécima musa, Guadalupe Amor (1995) (The Eleventh Muse, Guadalupe Amor) was the direct result of this first meeting in Mexico.
At that moment, surrounded by innumerable photo albums, scrapbooks, newspaper clippings, and other materials that bore witness
to an extraordinary life, I decided to devote my next biographical
project to Elena. *Elena Poniatowska* is the result of more than five
years of dedicated research, many interviews, several revisions,
and more than a few mishaps.

This book has a dual purpose. On one hand, it presents the
talent and personality of one of Mexico's foremost living writers
to a general English-speaking public, to those individuals, for example, who might think that Elena Poniatowska—given her last
name—is a Russian ballerina. On the other hand, I have attempted
to create a living kaleidoscope, a mosaic composed of hundreds

of tiles—the voices of her mother, nanny, fellow writers, literary critics and, most important, herself. I hope this mosaic will be accessible to the general reader and useful for literary critics who, having direct access to the unpublished documents included in this book (some of which have remained hidden in her archives for more than fifty years), will now be able to identify and analyze the multiple literary qualities of her oeuvre, one that moves almost imperceptibly between journalism and literature, testimony and novel. This book renders unspoken homage to Elena Poniatowska through its construction as a collage, which I believe to be the best medium to reflect—albeit fleetingly—the cardinal points of her life and work. Throughout the nine chapters of *Elena Poniatowska*, I pay special attention to her most outstanding works, while recognizing that to attempt to include more than the essentials of the life and work of such a prolific author is, in the words of Mexican baroque poet Sor Juana Inés de la Cruz, "a foolish presumption, an enterprise destined for failure." Nonetheless, and perhaps in imitation of the daring Phaeton, who plunged from heaven's highest spheres to the dark depths of the ocean when he attempted to drive the carriage of the sun, I am conscientiously determined to bring her eternal fame or die trying.

The book begins with an anecdotal introduction, in which I describe my impressions of "la señora Elena," the result of a sincere and fruitful friendship that was born more than a decade ago and is still going strong. I recall our experiences together in Mexico and abroad while also describing her domestic surroundings: her home, her children, and her eternal state of disarray. I also make reference to her daily life in Mexico and share some humorous stories that lead into the first chapter of the book: a brief but detailed description of Elena's childhood, her education in France during the first half of the Second World War, her voyage to the Americas aboard the steamship *Marqués de Comillas*, and her arrival in Mexico, accompanied by her mother and younger sister, Kitzia. In this chapter I unravel the mystery of her royal title and what happened to her crown, among other family matters. Chapter 1 ends with the revelations—linguistic and personal—shared by her nanny, Magdalena Castillo, as well as a description of her sorrowful departure to Eden Hall, where she first tested her literary talents with a brief text entitled "On Nothing," published in English in *The Current Literary Coin* and reproduced here for the first time.

Chapter 2, entitled "University of the Street," explores Elena's activities upon her return to Mexico; the shorthand classes aimed at turning her into an executive secretary, her theatrical excursion, and, finally, her first journalistic endeavors in the society pages of the Mexico City daily *Excélsior* in 1953, thanks to the generosity of a girlfriend's uncle. During this first year, Elena conducted daily interviews with some of the most distinguished figures of national and international culture, besides publishing columns devoted to beauty tips for women, local gossip, the latest trends in women's fashion, and the activities of Mexico City's upper classes. These articles are signed with only her first name, Hélène or the Americanized Helen. To document this little-known period in her professional development, I have included several selections from these long-forgotten articles and interviews.

Chapter 3, "'Elenita': The Young Writer," recounts Elena's first job at the Mexican daily *Novedades*, where she established a professional relationship that lasted until the publication's demise in 2002. In that context she met some of the most outstanding Mexican intellectuals of the twentieth century, among them Fernando Benítez, director of the influential literary supplement *La Cultura en México* (Culture in Mexico). In this chapter, I also examine her literary destiny, which began in 1954 with the publication of her first book, a collection of short stories entitled *Lilus Kikus*, and, two years later, her only attempt at playwriting with the publication of her satirical play *Melés y Teléo* (Youreadme and Ireadyou).

Chapter 4 documents and interprets the circumstances surrounding the publication of *Todo empezó el domingo* (1963) (It All Started on Sunday), a series of sketches of local customs illustrated by the recently deceased graphic artist Alberto Beltrán and the first indication that Elena would eventually become Mexico's paladin of the disenfranchised. Through the ethnographic experiences of researching this book, Elena came into close contact with Mexico's working class, which she had discovered as a child through the eyes of her *nana*, Magdalena. Inspired by what she had observed during these excursions and at the request of her friend, the Spanish filmmaker Luis Buñuel, Elena began visiting Mexico City's Lecumberri Prison to interview political prisoners. On the way to one of her weekly visits to the "Black Palace of Lecumberri," as it had been known since its completion during the dictatorship of Porfirio Díaz, she discovered her soul mate and lifetime spiritual guide, Josefina Bórquez, whose gruff and inimitable persona attracted the young writer and whose unforgettable presence fills the pages of Elena's first novel, *Hasta no verte Jesús mío* (1969) (*Here's to You, Jesusa!*), one of her most significant works to date, which is the topic of chapter 5, entitled "Unknown Mexico."

Chapter 6 documents the tragic events of October 1968, a turning point in Mexico's modern history and also in Elena's development as an individual and as a writer. Her literary response to this confrontation, which resulted in the death or imprisonment of hundreds of Mexican students and lives in the Mexican consciousness like the Kent State riots do in that of the United States, is to be found in *La noche de Tlatelolco: testimonios de historia oral* (1971) (*Massacre in Mexico*). Her courageous account was awarded the coveted Xavier Villaurrutia Prize, which Elena refused with a devastating question: "Who will award prizes to those who fell in Tlatelolco?" Throughout these years of conflict, Elena never abandoned the world of women, reconstructing female voices born from their "capacity of indignation," including those of Jesusa Palancares and of Angelina Beloff through her epistolary supplications in *Querido Diego, te abraza Quiela* (1976) (*Dear Diego*, 1986), a poignant novella that explores the Russian painter's obsession with Diego Rivera, the father of her dead baby. This chapter also recounts Elena's interest in the life experiences of *Gaby Brimmer* (1979), a young woman with cerebral palsy, and the latter's astounding disavowal of Elena's participation in her biography; in fact, Elena's authorship was never recognized by Luis Mandoki, who directed a movie based on the book. Chapter 7 traces Elena's professional achievements during the decade of the eighties. As a logical outcome of her personal and literary experiences, Elena became Mexico's "Widow of Disaster" when she turned her attention to the forsaken heirs of the Mexican Revolution in *Fuerte es el silencio* (1980) (Silence Is Strong) and later, when giving a voice to the victims and anonymous heroes of the earthquake that shook Mexico City in 1985 in her chronicle of admonition and altruism, *Nada, nadie: las voces del temblor* (1988) (*Nothing, Nobody: The Voices of the Mexico City Earthquake*, 1995). The chapter concludes with an intimate self-portrait of the writer found in *La "Flor de Lis"* (1988), a semi-autobiographical novel which was the result of Elena's attempt to heal herself from her traumatic experiences during the months and years following the Mexico City earthquake.

Elena's literary career flourished in the nineties with *Tinísima* (1992) (*Tinisima*, 1996), not only a fictionalized biography of the Italian photographer and communist militant Tina Modotti, but also a political and cultural fresco of the first decades of the twentieth century in Mexico and in Europe. In Modotti, Elena discovered a persona whose life and work nearly covered the gamut of topics found in her previous books: the human condition, passionate love, and ideological conviction, in addition to the experiences of a foreigner immersed in the ancestral mysteries of the brave new American world, the same world that Modotti re-created in her sometimes delicate, sometimes dogmatic photographs. Chapter 8 relates Elena's support of the Ejército Zapatista de Liberación Nacional (Zapatista Army of National Liberation) that burst into San Cristóbal de las Casas on January 1, 1994, and relates her epistolary and personal exploits with the rebel leader, Subcomandante Marcos, deep in the mountains of Chiapas.

For Elena, this decade was also a period of reflection upon her literary and journalistic odyssey of nearly half a century, and the interviews collected in eight volumes entitled *Todo México* (1991–1999)(All of Mexico) is evidence of this inclination, as are her biographies of two key figures of the Mexican cultural world whom Elena met in the fifties when she first interviewed them: *Octavio Paz: las palabras del árbol* (Octavio Paz: The Words of the Tree) and *Juan Soriano: niño de mil años* (Juan Soriano: Child of a Thousand Years), both published in 1998. The chapter ends with Elena winning the Alfaguara Prize for Literature in 2001 for her novel *La piel del cielo*, 2001 (*The Skin of the Sky*, 2004), a literary voyage through sidereal space and black holes inhabited by white dwarfs, some of the astronomical phenomena that fired the intellectual passion of her late husband, the astrophysicist Guillermo Haro, and his novelistic alter ego, Lorenzo de Tena.

Chapter 9, "Elena: An International Treasure," documents the growing globalization of her literary work, considered required reading in universities in the United States, where many of her books and essays have been translated into English and where more and more researchers devote articles, reviews, and essays to the multiple themes encompassed in her voluminous and heterogeneous literary production.

To facilitate consultation of the works mentioned in this book, an annotated bibliography of her works is included at the end of the book, listing both Spanish-language editions and English translations and noting any other languages into which the works have been translated.

Manhattan and Coyoacán,
August–December 2001

Elena Poniatowska

Introduction: "I Am Moved by Desire"

Meeting in Chimalistac

The petite woman who greeted me on a July afternoon in 1991—wearing green sweats that matched her face, covered in a facial mask (which at first I thought might be guacamole)—was the celebrated writer, Polish princess, and reigning "Queen of Mexican Intellectuals": Hélène Elizabeth Louise Amelie Paula Dolores Poniatowska Amor, otherwise known as "Elenita." Seeing her thus, with a face resembling that of a precious little frog—just like those that live forever in the stories of the brothers Grimm—something in me changed forever. Upon our first encounter, Elena bewitched me with her carefree and innocent soul, her unique presence which is at once consoling and disquieting, and above all with her profound and visionary sensibility, an echo of the sibyl which she undoubtedly incarnated in a previous life on earth.

I greeted her with a peck on the cheek, covering my lips and chin with that greenish paste which, combined with my own sheepish blush, matched my emotions. Elena laughed and led me inside through a small garden full of roses, azaleas, camellias, and bougainvilleas that flourished under the shade of an enormous *tabachín* tree, from whose branches hung bottles of sweetened water for the hummingbirds—iridescent fugitives from an Alexandrine verse that Nezahualcóyotl, prince of Texcoco, unwittingly composed centuries ago. The notes of Felix Mendelssohn's *Wedding March* floated in the air, proceeding from the neighboring chapel of Chimalistac where, according to certain chroniclers, La Malinche, lover and translator of Hernán Cortes, was baptized. Later

I was to learn that half of Mexico wants to get married there, and that the music—so pleasant in small doses—is an everyday occurrence, as are the constant traffic and the ensuing crowds. The problem is so bad that one day Elena, extremely irritated at being unable to park her car full of grocery bags, "keyed" the front door of an automobile whose driver had found it convenient to occupy the space directly in front of her gate. She immediately repented, sought out the vehicle's owner, and paid for the damage.

Domestic Charm

Books and more books are the first things that catch one's eye upon entering Elena's modest home. They are everywhere, not only in the bookshelves that line the walls, but scattered on the floor, stuffed into shopping bags, piled on the dining room table, and lost among the foliage of some potted plant. As I took a seat in the living room, I discovered one under the cushion of the sofa that I was sitting on: it was the latest book by her dear friend José Emilio Pacheco, the very book she had been desperately looking for as she was to lecture on it the next day. The few empty spaces on the bookshelves contain family photos and daguerreotypes: her father, Prince Jean Evremont Poniatowski, in full military regalia; her mother, Doña Paula Amor de Ferreira Iturbe, Princess Poniatowska—a portrait by Edward Weston; her daughter, Paula, hugging a cat and flashing a toothy grin; several paintings by her friend, the Oaxacan painter Francisco Toledo; and a clay figurine of the "Blue Demon," a Mexican wrestler wearing blue tights and a red cape, given to her by her friend, the performance artist Jesusa Rodríguez. More than anything else, images of the Santo Niño de Atocha appear throughout the house—a spiritual legacy of her beloved Josefina Bórquez, immortalized as Jesusa, the protagonist and heroine of *Hasta no verte Jesús mío* and now the patron saint of the house and of its owner. Among the jumble of books, plants, pictures, and curios accumulated haphazardly over many years, two cats, Silvana and Gazpacho, prowl about, the former a tabby and the latter looking as if he had donned a black tie and dinner jacket. Both pets were inherited from her daughter, Paula, and are always eager to be caressed. One must be wary, however, because should one become careless, they are fully capable of meting out an unexpected bloody scratch. They are the house's only remaining pets, for Loba, the Samoyed that Paula found one morning abandoned on the freeway, got lost or was stolen, leaving a real void in the Haro-Poniatowska family. The house is not large or luxurious, but its charm evokes warmth and tranquility. It seems to be forever in a process of transformation, as it is full of all kinds of odds and ends, some quite bizarre, such as the autographed calendars of the embattled Mexican "Madonna," Gloria Trevi, or the enormous painting of the marshal of France, Josef Poniatowski, with his handlebar moustache and severe expression, surely one of her many noble ancestors. Combined, these diverse objects give an impression of generating new forms and creating altered spaces, which gives Elena's home a dynamic and ever-changing identity.

My "Mamita Mexicana"

My first meeting with Elena took place during a conference on women's literature organized by the University of California, Los Angeles, where I presented a paper on her Aunt Pita—Guadalupe Amor—the self-appointed "Doyenne of Mexican Poetry." This is the same poet who, many years ago during a gala evening, upon seeing her niece chatting with Octavio Paz, accosted her with a litany of insults that in their elaborate language were worthy of the Spanish baroque poet Francisco de Quevedo: "Don't you dare compare yourself with your aunt, who is a true firebrand! Don't you dare come close to my gale force winds, to my tempests, to my rivers! I am the sun, little girl, and if you get too close, my rays shall burn you to ashes!"

Months later, I was fortunate to have Elena put me in contact with Mexico's Editorial Diana, where she took me one day—almost by the hand—to meet Fausto Rosales Ortiz, one of the firm's editors. Elena told him marvelous things about my book manuscript about her Aunt Pita and requested that it be considered for publication. I really do not know what would have become of my literary career without Elena's support, as she took charge of supervising my incipient writings with a dedication and care that seemed almost maternal: on one occasion she even confessed that she considered herself my "mamita mexicana." I told her proudly: "Yes, you are my mamacita mexicana," but she corrected me, saying that "mamita mexicana" sounded much better, for in Spanish, "mamacita" has other connotations. Although it might seem strange, when we go out together to a restaurant or cultural event, someone always asks me: "Are you Mrs. Poniatowska's son?" Elena laughs and exclaims: "I would love to have such a great big son!"

Sometimes it is not very enjoyable to accompany her in public, because people are always pestering us, wanting to greet her. One afternoon, while we were eating at the Fonda de Santa Clara in Puebla, and Elena had gone to the restroom, a lady came out of nowhere and asked: "Are you a friend of Doña Elena's?" I answered, "No, my name is Michael." When Elena reappeared, she was smiling mischievously. I think she liked my attitude. That was fine by me, because people sometimes asked questions for which I simply had no answers. Once, several producers from the British Broadcasting Corporation came to her house for an interview. She was still getting ready, so they decided to ask me questions, which I tried my best to answer. When she heard some of my rather vague replies, Elena called out from her room: "No, Michael, that's not the way it happened! I'll be right down." Since in the same interview she mistakenly confessed to being a *work-alcoholic*, instead of a workaholic, I felt less remorse about having provided apocryphal information.

Chabeeeelaaaaa!

Chabela, Elena's housekeeper, is the house's alter ego, or at least its commander in chief, as she knows infinitely more of what goes on than does Elena herself. Chabela reminds Elena about her upcoming trips, who called for the umpteenth time, and what she will be doing next weekend. With a very down-to-earth sense of humor and a strong character, she both attracts and repels from the get-go and is always making fun of the guests and of the innumerable personages who call at all hours, day and night. Often they are extraordinary characters, some of them quite memorable: Chuchito, the man who claims to be the same age as Christ, sleeps in a crypt at the Dolores cemetery and washes trailers at the city's main market. Once in a while Diana, a native of the state of Morelos and a feminist through and through, appears at the house. Once, there arrived on Elena's doorstep "Diablito," a nine-year-old street urchin who spends his days begging and occasionally sells chewing gum. He came to love bathing and eating at the "blonde lady's" house. But the day his mother realized that Diablito was not begging at his usual street corner, she sought him out and furiously attempted to extricate him from Elena's house. Hearing her screams and threats, Elena went to see what was going on. Diablito's mother received her with a string of insults: "You damned snob, you! Let my son go or you'll pay for it!" Obviously, Elena is much more interested in the real-life stories that appear on her doorstep than in the people of her own social standing. As she puts it, she knows the latter like the palm of her hand; they will never surprise her nor impress her with their French, much less enlighten her with their daily observations. But the former do exert a strange power over her, and she never misses an opportunity to engage them.

For some reason, the people who call on the telephone are likely to be victims of Chabela's temper. One afternoon we were in the kitchen, trying to recall the song "Sabor de engaño" as interpreted by Chelo Silva, when the phone rang: "Helloooo . . . ?" Chabela answered rather wearily, as the phone rings constantly day and night. "Who? . . . Now look, Sir, I will not put her on, because every time you call she gets all upset . . . So, good-bye now!" She hung up brusquely and resumed her tasks as if nothing had happened. When I asked for an explanation, she quipped, "Someone has to take charge here, as God only knows the lady of the house is off her rocker." Some time back, Chabela threatened to pour squash blossom soup all over the Chanel dress worn by a stuck-up friend of the family's who had come for lunch, and another day she hung up on former Mexican president Carlos Salinas de Gortari because he didn't know the national anthem by heart.

Worldly Inspiration?

It is curious how my idea of literary creation changed after several years' acquaintance with an author such as Elena. I had imagined entering her study one day to find her in the midst of heavenly inspiration, in the style of the Spanish mystic poet Santa Teresa de Avila, who would enter a trancelike state when composing her verses addressed to God and the heavens, a practice that would lead to the birth of a brilliant line or the insertion of the precise word. But no, at least not in this case. For Elena, writing is work, just like that of a cobbler or a bricklayer. This attitude regarding her profession comes from her training as a journalist, with the constant deadlines, daily interviews, and quick composition that are the hallmarks of this profession. Such training proved to be very useful later in her career as a writer, for Elena is capable of constant production, and, as she puts it, "always fulfilling her commitments to others." This is true: she is neither irresponsible nor egotistical and is very simply a very hard worker. As she herself admits, however, her one great flaw is being incapable of saying no. The word simply has no place in her vocabulary. Magda, her beloved nanny, recalls how, when she was a little girl, Elenita would often empty the clay piggy bank where she kept her weekly savings, in order to distribute her pennies to the paupers who came to the door of her house begging for alms. This Magdalena recalls with a mixture of indifference and consternation; she never thought it was a good idea for a little princess to hand out money in the streets like a young Mother Teresa. On the contrary, her idea of a well-brought-up little girl would be a Marie Antoinette: if they have no bread, let them eat cake, or in this case, at least *capirotada*.

TACA-TACA-TACA-TACA

In one of her many articles published each Sunday in the now-defunct Mexican daily *El Nacional*, Elena Poniatowska admits that, for her, to write is to bear witness. In her case, however, living is a type of bearing witness and writing, a luxury. As a head of household, writer, professional, and celebrated figure of the Mexican cultural world, life for her is not always a bed of roses: so many engagements, so many calls, so many conferences, so many presentations. When does she find time to write? Like her admired, long-deceased friend, the celebrated poet and feminist Rosario Castellanos—whom she resembles in many ways—Elena only succeeds in allowing her literary imagination to flow in the wee hours of the night, while the rest of the family sleeps and the telephone is silent. Nonetheless, Elena is always working on something, and when she finally reaches the small bedroom she has converted into her study, the monotonous *taca-taca-taca-taca* of the keyboard can be heard as she types away. There is Elena, leaning over the screen, her eyes fixed upon the web of words she has just spun, embroidered with an intricate trimming of nouns nearly always ending in the diminutive form. Her computer is not the most up to date, but it seems to serve her quite well. The only problem is that she has saved all her texts on innumerable diskettes, and trying to locate the correct one may prove to be impossible. Her e-mail is always on the fritz, and she seems comfortable with a gigantic laser printer that takes up a large part of her tiny study.

When writing, Elena never looks back, nor does she make any corrections until she has finished composing. It used to bother her that when I make a mistake while typing a word, I prefer to erase it and rewrite it immediately. "Why do you do that?" she asked me, rather intrigued. "Well, it seems easier to me," I answered. Evidently, she was not very convinced. Often, according to her, the text she is working on comes out too long and is terribly bad, but nevertheless it is the material she will transform into a story, an article, a foreword, or an interview. Only after she has finished a rough draft will Elena go back to the beginning and make corrections.

Sometimes she gets impatient if I can't find what she is looking for in the disorganization of her small study. I particularly recall the time she asked me to find a text she had written years ago on Octavio Paz. To my surprise, upon reaching the closet where she stores her file boxes—in the room that used to be Paula's—I saw that the majority of them had small adhesive stickers which read

"Interviews and Miscellaneous Items." Fifty boxes with the same label! Obviously, I never found what I was looking for and Elena became visibly annoyed. Honestly, Elena can be a bit unnerving when she becomes impatient—in that way she resembles her formidable Aunt Pita—and on such occasions, her assistants become the targets of her wrath.

"Daughter of La Malinche"

Although it is difficult for Elena to recognize her many triumphs, she is the first to admit all of her failures. Sometimes I have even pointed out that accompanying her to the innumerable conferences she has held at various universities in Mexico and the United States is like going out with Madonna: people do not leave her alone for a single minute and even follow her to the ladies' room; at her book signings they crowd in so closely in search of an autograph that they almost knock her off her chair. Nonetheless, in her opinion, everything she does, both in Mexico and abroad, is a disaster. In fact, what hurts the most is her apparent failure in the United States, where she claims that Chicano/a and African American writers such as Sandra Cisneros and Toni Morrison are able to devote themselves to their writing without distractions and have marvelous literary agents besides. Furthermore, they are excellent businesswomen. Elena, in contrast, has to receive the delivery men, go to the bank, and do her own shopping at the local supermarket. The latter is an excursion that she rather enjoys, as she loves to hunt for bargains in the tent sales that local stores sometimes set up in their parking lots. The straw that broke the camel's back, according to Elena, was when a distinguished American publishing house wanted to charge her for the unsold copies of *Massacre in Mexico*. Nonetheless, she admits that many of her colleagues take themselves too seriously; an example is the time when her daughter, Paula—a professional photographer—wanted to take a picture of the Nobel Prize winner Toni Morrison. Both mother and daughter were astounded when the author of *Jazz* stipulated that the photo would have to be from a ten-meter distance, and only one shot.

Elena always wants to "shoot a hole in her head" because her conference papers disappear at the last moment, or she reads them in Spanish where hardly anyone is proficient in that language, or because she is attacked in New York by Israeli extremists convinced that she is anti-Semitic—this based on the attitudes of the seamstresses who gave firsthand testimonials in *Nothing, Nobody: The Voices of the Mexico City Earthquake*, claiming that the owners of the infamous sweatshops that collapsed during the earthquake of 1985 were Jewish, or because she "lies" about what really happened during the *Massacre in Mexico*. In response I observed (wishing to comfort her) that these were nothing but expressions of envy, pure and simple, as in the words of Marcial, brought to mind by Sor Juana Inés de la Cruz: *rarus est qui vedit cedere ingenio* (rare is the man willing to admit superiority of another). Evidently, Elena prefers to be a "Daughter of La Malinche," a title invented by her friend, the writer and university professor Margo Glantz.

"I Am Old and Wise . . . "

With all the work she has to do, all the requests heaped upon her to which she commits herself, Elena never gets herself organized and says that she is always "bumbling" in her jobs, spiraling down towards the abyss, faster and faster each day. And although she has embarked on a Dantesque voyage that will end in her total professional ruin, her business affairs are in still worse condition. One day I mentioned to her that someone did not want to pay me for a translation I had completed, and she warned me in a resigned tone, "I've been an idiot, Michael. Don't let them take advantage of you the way they have done with me." I asked her exactly what she meant by this, and she began to list all her failed projects: the movie about Gaby Brimmer for which she did not receive a single penny; her experience with Margaret Hooks, who at the time was writing a book about Tina Modotti and whom Elena helped out by lending her all the materials she had accumulated on the Italian photographer: interviews with the recently deceased Vittorio Vidali and with Tina's relatives, everything. To Elena's astonishment, Hooks signed a movie deal on the subject with Mick Jagger a few years later.

Notwithstanding all these disappointments, Elena truly loves her work. Once, when we both happened to be in San Diego at the same time, Elena gave a talk on Tina Modotti and Frida Kahlo to some five hundred people. Hers was the grand finale of the annual meeting of the Modern Language Association, a kind of meat market attended by thousands of recent PhDs seeking that elusive university position. An enormous flock of aspiring scholars, they were all dressed in tweed jackets with leather patches on the elbows. That day I observed rejected candidates crying in the hotel corridors, desperation painted on the faces of almost all, and a downcast atmosphere of dejection and nervous activity. After her conference, and attempting to be gracious toward all those wishing to greet her, Elena approached me with some words of wisdom: "Listen, Michael, don't you think it would be more fun for all these people to study you and your work than for you to study me?"

Visibly moved, I answered: "Of course it would, but it happens that I'm not you, and obviously I don't have your poise, much less your successful career."

"It doesn't matter," she answered with her motherly smile. "You already started with the book about Pita which came out so nicely. Believe me, I'm old and wise. Stay in Mexico; after all, you're not doing all that badly."

"Ten Years Later"

For more than ten years I have been a frequent visitor to Elena's house. Observing the insurmountable chaos that reigns in her home, I offered to help her in any way I could with her interminable articles, translations, screenplays, and books. For me it has been a great opportunity to work and collaborate with her, as she has taught me much, and not only in the areas of journalism, literature, and politics. She has been an example in the most basic sense of the word: she has taught me the art of being a human being; how to be generous with others, even when you feel that you are drowning in your own work; how to be modest in the midst of so much attention, fuss, and endless praise; how to appreciate the small surprises in life. One day, we arrived at Mexico City's Palace of Fine Arts and discovered that there were no seats. Almost childishly I quipped, "But Elena, as soon as they see you, we'll be assigned the best seats in the house."

She spun around, wrinkled her nose at me, and asked me in all sincerity, "How can they possibly see me if I'm about the size of a Chihuahua?"

This is Elena Poniatowska: unassuming and intelligent, ingenious and brilliant.

1   To Live a Fairy Tale

Ancestry in C Major

Many people are aware that Elena, although unassuming and modest, is an authentic princess, right out of a fairy tale. Nonetheless, when I inquired about her crown one day, she informed me with a mischievous smile and ceremonious tone that she had heard that some years back it had been pawned at the Monte de Piedad. I hope they kept the receipt. I wonder if it is the same tiara that young Pita Amor obsessively dreamed about from her earliest childhood, until in the same dream she succeeded in doing away with all the direct descendants of the Poniatowski line, in order to keep it for herself.

Elena's maternal great-grandfather, José María Amor y Escandón, left Mexico in 1863, after the death of his first wife, Leonor Subervielle, but before the arrival of Maximilian of Habsburg and his empress, Charlotte. As his youngest son would later recall, when Amor y Escandón abandoned his beloved Mexico forever, aboard a train on the first leg of a journey that would eventually take him to France, the rich landowner intoned a plaintive *Te Deum*. On his departure from Mexico, he left behind the Hacienda de San Gabriel, an enormous tract that almost encompassed the modern state of Morelos and was originally part of the enormous Marquesado de Oaxaca. José María immigrated to northern France because his second wife, Adelaide Subervielle, Leonor's younger sister, was from that region. She never liked the climate of Puente de Ixtla, much less its tropical fauna: mosquitoes, scorpions, and other exotic insects conspired to keep her awake, even if she tried to sleep slightly above the ground in the hammock that stretched from wall to wall in her luxurious suite.[1]

Elena's maternal grandfather, Pablo Amor Escandón, was a gentleman of Mexico's aristocracy. He was educated, like the majority of the men in his family, in Stoneyhurst, England, and was an expert golf player. He died in Paris in 1918, "physically and morally ill," as his daughter Paulette recalls. His illness was caused, at least in part, by the loss of the Hacienda de San Gabriel, along with the majority of his Mexican properties, during the Mexican Revolution.

Elena's paternal grandmother, Elizabeth Sperry Crocker, was from the United States, born in Stockton, California, near San Francisco. She came from an enterprising family, and there are still reminders of the Crocker family in that part of California, as they built the San Francisco Railway, the Pacific Railway, and the Sacramento Museum of Modern Art. Mrs. Sperry Crocker used to tell her granddaughters horrifying stories of the Mexicans she had read about in the pages of *National Geographic* magazine, portraying them as terrifying barbarians who tied bones in their hair and ate human flesh.

Elena's mother, María de los Dolores Amor, was better known as Paulette because Dolores (which translates as sorrows) did not seem to suit her amorous last name. She was the daughter of Don Pablo Amor and Doña Elena Iturbe, and was born in France in 1908. Doña Paulette met her future husband, Jean Evremont Poniatowski Sperry, in Paris. He was a descendant of the last king of Poland, Stanislaus II, and of Prince Josef Poniatowski, who was appointed marshal of France for siding with Napoleon against the Russians in the Polish struggle for independence. Doña Paulette relates that she met her husband at a ball held at the home of the Rothschild family on the Place de la Concorde. In the middle of the party the young man leaped from the floor to the top of the piano in a single bound. They were married shortly thereafter, and their two daughters were born in Paris: Hélène in 1932, and Sofia, known as Kitzia, a year later. In an autobiographical essay published in English, Elena recalls her family life in France:

My family on my mother's side (my great-grandmother, grandmother, and mother) were always traveling. They had lost their land during the Mexican Revolution, but they still had enough money to live in Biarritz, then in Paris, and later in "Fairlight," England. (I would much rather have called it "Wuthering Heights" but "Fairlight" it was, sweet and *comme il faut*.) They would travel from Karlsbad to Lausanne, from Marienbad to Vichy, to "take the waters." They would get off at a station, stay for a week, then get back on the train. They would see the switchman grow smaller and smaller, his lantern turn into a firefly. My grandmother's house was filled with portraits of Goethe and Wagner, and with books in German; she loved Germany. Mamy-Grand, who was a very young widow, was called "the Madonna of Sleeping Cars," because she took so many, so very many trains. She always dressed in black, her white milky throat and décolletage illuminating the blackness of her veils and *crêpes de Chine* . . .

The traveling companions of Elena Iturbe de Amor were three little girls in ruffles, petticoats, ribbons, and hats, their little faces lost amidst billows of embroidered cloth: Biche, Lydia, and Paula—my mother. The nanny who stands behind them in the photographs was also covered in starch and crepes. Mamy-Grand would carry her samovar with her (because my great-grandmother, Elena Idaroff, was Russian), as well as her silk sheets to put on the hotel beds. It's not that we were gypsies, although we do have some of that in our blood, it's just that we seemed not to belong.[2]

High Society

Elena is a true princess, unlike the many who pretend to be one, spending their lives wishing it were so; but she is far from becoming a future queen of Poland should the Poles decide to reinstate the monarchy. That is all for the best, because she is noticeably uncomfortable about coming from such noble stock. Moreover, it can be said in truth that she is not at all interested in royalty, and even that she finds it contemptible. They say that opposites attract,

Fairlight Castle, in England, was the home of Paulette, Elena's mother. Elena occasionally referred to it as "Wuthering Heights."

whence perhaps comes her fascination with those belonging to the lower classes in her adoptive country, so distant from her own world and her experiences as a rich little French girl growing up in Mexico. Although she is a distant relative of Benjamin Franklin on her father's side, she arguably also has plebeian blood in her veins. Her bloodline is duly recorded in the *Registro de los Trescientos* (The Register of the Three Hundred), a lovely volume bound in scarlet velvet with letters embossed in gold leaf, a veritable encyclopedia of Mexican aristocracy. The page devoted to Doña Paulette Amor is full of royal relatives, national heroes, and other figures of noble lineage. It is worth reproducing here, since the book is not easy to find; it may be discovered only among old volumes bound in calf-skin, hidden in dusty bookshelves of once-stately mansions built during Porfirio Díaz's thirty-year dictatorship but now lost in the rabble and chaos of today's Colonia Tacubaya:

> Doña Paulette Amor, Princess Poniatowska
> Husband: Prince Jean Ciolek Poniatowski
> Descendants: Helene, Sophie (Kitzia), and Jan Stanislaus—
> 19, 18, and 4 years of age
> BACKGROUND:
> Princess Paula Poniatowska occupies a high position among

Mexican aristocrats and European nobility. From 1939 to 1941 she served in the French army as an ambulance driver. She is the daughter of Don Pablo Amor, a prominent Mexican gentleman whose haciendas were the largest in the state of Morelos. This lady's mother is Doña Elena Iturbe. The houses of Amor and Iturbe have always been widely renowned in the social and economic life of Mexico.

Prince Jean Ciolek Poniatowski was awarded the Croix de Chevalier of the Legion d'Honneur and the Croix de Guerre for his participation in the Second World War. In 1930 he married Paula Amor in Paris. He has lived in Mexico since 1946, where he is involved in banking, mining and pharmaceutical ventures. He belongs to a branch of the Italian House of Torelli which proceeds in direct line from the ducal dynasty of Saxe (Rudolphe, Duke of Saxe, pp. 843–863).

Data from the *Ghotta Almanach* tell us that Count Joseph Salinguerra Torelli was killed during the siege of Asti (1615). His son, Guido Severo Salinguerra Torelli, dispossessed of his fortune by the Duke of Parma, established himself in Poland and married Sofia Poniatowska Lesczinska in 1629. On his adopting Polish nationality, the name of Torelli (Il Toro) became Ciolek. His son, Jean Ciolek Poniatowski, founded the Polish branch of the Torellis under the name of Ciolek Poniatowski. His grandson, Count Stanislaus Ciolek Poniatowski, married Constance, Princess Czartoryska, and was comrade in arms of King Charles XII of Sweden. Eight descendants were born from this marriage, among them Stanislaus-Augustus, king of Poland from 1764 to 1796, and Prince Casimiro Ciolek Poniatowski (1721–1800), the eldest brother of the family, who was married in 1751 to Apollonia Usttrycka, from whom descends the gentleman that concerns us here. In their time, the most prominent members of the family were Prince Stanislaus Ciolek Poniatowski (1754–1833), son of Casimiro. His son, Prince Josef Ciolek Poniatowski, married Countess Perrotti. His grandson, Prince André Ciolek Poniatowski, married Elizabeth Sperry Crocker, a descendant of the family of Benjamin Franklin (1706–1790), in Paris in 1894. From this marriage four sons were born, the youngest of whom is the current Prince Jean Ciolek Poniatowski. (p. 479)

The Red Princess

Elena's mother, Paula Amor de Poniatowski, never looked upon royalty with the same indifference as her daughter does. When I was helping with the Spanish translation of the letters Paula wrote in English during the Second World War to her husband, nicknamed "Bouzoum," I recall in one of them Doña Paulette mentions having taken her children to a resort near Cuernavaca, but to her total disappointment, it was filled with *horrible people*. Her daughter was not pleased with this description, for it is the poor, or "horrible people," in her mother's words, that she considers the most important and interesting. Elena is much more concerned with the conditions of the seamstresses, laundresses, servants, victims of disasters (natural and human-caused), Indians of Chiapas, and garbage collectors. This is not an assumed attitude, as I have witnessed it many times over the years. Her mother, on the contrary, was a princess with all the corresponding privileges and immunities. She even received letters from France addressed to Princess Paulette Amor de Poniatowski. I wonder what the mail carrier must have thought of this appellation. She truly enjoyed her noble rank, whereas for her daughter it is a sort of punishment, something like a scarlet letter.

However, Elena has not lost her connections with the Poniatowskis who still live in France, although they do not see each other frequently. The relative to whom she feels closest is her first cousin Marie-Anne, a painter and extraordinary designer, to whom Elena is especially devoted. When they were teenagers, Marie-Anne used to tell Kitzia and Elena that she was more of a princess than they, for she was a princess two times over, as her mother was Anne Caraman Chimay, a princess in her own right, whereas the surname Amor is not of royal blood. Besides, Marcel Proust had based his Princess Guermantes on her aunt, Countess Greffuhle. For years, the two cousins' hero was Marie-André Poniatowski, because he served in the Polish army during the Second World

War and died very young in January 1945 while in the Nether-
lands, where he commanded the second Polish armored division.
He was hit by a bullet while exiting his tank after a battle. Marie-
André was a truly handsome man and, as Elena would remind
Marie-Anne, she was the only one to appear in her grandfather's
memoirs sitting on Marie-André's lap, a fact that has become al-
most a family legend. In Paris, Elena has visited her first cousins,
Philippe, Albert, Jean, and Edmond (Babou), the last of whom she
sees most frequently because he is a regular at Careyes Beach in
Mexico, which he visits every two or three years.

Elena shares literary and intellectual pursuits with Michel Poniatowski, former minister of the interior under Giscard d'Estaing.
Their grandfather, André Poniatowski, who taught Elena to read,
also wrote two books: *From One Century to the Other* and *From One
Idea to the Next*, published by Presses de la Cité. In addition, he
handed down his love for literature to his grandchildren; Michel, a
great admirer of Talleyrand, composed five volumes about his life
and work, including *Talleyrand in the United States*, *Talleyrand in Ancient
France*, and *Talleyrand and the Consulate*, among others. Talleyrand,
along with Mirabeau and Lafayette, was a leader of the French
Revolution. Michel is a talented researcher, and some of his works
currently available in France are *The Socialist Catastrophe*, *Europe or
Death*, *Socialism French Style*, *History Is Free*, *The Future Is Not Written
Anywhere*, *A History of Russia in America*, and *Alaska*, in addition to
biographies of Henry IV and Louis XVIII, among many others.

On the maternal side, Elena is close to her Mexican cousins
Mariana and Margarita—the former the director of the Gallery of
Mexican Art and the latter of the American Bookstore—as well as
to Pablo Amor, a painter; Javier Sepúlveda, a psychiatrist; and the
other Sepúlveda cousins, who range from medical doctors and ar-
chitects to government officials such as Bernardo Sepúlveda Amor,
former secretary of foreign affairs.

A Wartime Childhood

Hélène Elizabeth Louise Amelie Paula Dolores Poniatowska Amor
was born in Paris on May 19, 1932, the first daughter of Paula

Amor Iturbe and Jean Ciolek Poniatowski. When she was seven years old, Elena's sweet childhood was suddenly interrupted when France and the United Kingdom declared war against Germany. For their safety, their mother took the girls to the relative tranquility of the south of France: first to Vouvray, then to Mougins, near Cannes, and finally to Les Bories, near Cahors. In 1939, Doña Paulette and her husband went off to war, and for three years the former worked as an ambulance driver. Elena's first memories lie in the historical context of family dissolution as the result of the crisis of war. In a personal narrative that she shared with me, the future writer recalled her elementary education, including some details about her early childhood:

> In France I went to school in a small village called Francoulaise; this was just before coming to Mexico, because I recall that we lived near Cahors. During our stay, we lived in a country house belonging to my grandfather, called Les Bories. It was a very pretty house next to a forest where there were said to be wild boars. My Poniatowski grandparents are buried in Les Bories in the manner of medieval kings, lying recumbent— *les gisants*—on two lovely tombstones in an enclosed chapel. I recall that in Les Bories I attended the community school at the village of Francoulaise. Before that I went to school in Vouvray, in the region of the Loire castles. Our neighbor was a great composer whose music I still listen to, Francis Poulenc. We visited him once, and he dedicated a small waltz to me and Kitzia.
>
> In school my sister and I were isolated from the other children a great deal because they called us "the princesses." Although I was constantly sick due to the humid climate, I used to enjoy going to school. Later, we moved to Cannes, where we lived in a very beautiful house called Speranza. There, my grandfather taught me mathematics, grammar, reading, and the history of France. I was terrified because he gave me homework—especially in arithmetic—that no one in the house, not the parlor maid nor the chef nor his assistant nor the head gardener—there were several gardeners—nor the lady who cared

for my grandmother could solve. I remember that this made me suffer greatly. At night I cried and had nightmares because I did not want to disappoint my grandfather. However, I did not fail him in spelling nor in grammar. These came easily to me, but not arithmetic nor the ability to solve problems such as how many posts would be needed to encircle a rectangular field measuring x times y. I think he gave me problems that were too difficult for my age. At that time I was about seven years old. Besides, I was shocked, because until then I had believed that "grown-ups" knew everything and all these grown-ups around me did not know the answers.

I remember that there was a magazine which impressed me greatly at that age, *La Semaine de Suzette* (Suzette's Weekly). It had stories, cultural materials for children, and articles about the sun, water, plants, and animals. One Christmas my Aunt Anne, the mother of Michel Poniatowski and of my most beloved cousin, Marie-Anne, asked what I wanted for Christmas. I told her that I would like to have *La Semaine de Suzette*, and she gave me a whole year's subscription.

Now that I look at this in hindsight, I believe that I was deeply marked by the last house that my sister and I lived in before coming to Mexico. The house was called Les Bories, and it was located near Francoulaise, a small town in the Lot region; from there we rode our bicycles to school.

The principal of the school had the curious name of Madame Cocu; that is, Mrs. Cuckold, and she treated my sister and me with great deference.

The field workers, *fermiers* as they are called in France, had two daughters, Jacqueline and Colette, who became our friends. They were two robust, strong, solid girls, and their house smelled of seeds, of sackcloth, and of earth. Probably these fermiers had other children, but I only remember Jacqueline and Colette. On some occasions I ate with them, and when they finished their heavy peasant soup, they poured some wine on the plate and sopped it up with bread until it was clean and shiny. Was this the way they washed their dishes? Years later, with my uncle André, my father's older brother, I recall that again I ate with some farmers. When I mentioned their drinking soup out of the plate, slurping it up, and expressed my surprise at their lack of manners (they put their knives in their mouths), he explained that one must always do exactly as one sees the hosts do: that this is the very essence of courtesy.

My grandfather, André Poniatowski, whom I loved dearly (I still treasure his letters), owned a flock of sheep and I liked to run among them. The sheep's wool was gray, and they hid their snouts in each other's wool. Their smell was very strong and their wool greasy; to stick my hands into their tightly curled coats gave me a feeling of belonging that I have never encountered again. It was like touching the earth. Probably the children with whom I played and ate are now well-established women, much less fragile than the princesses. We were the princesses; that was what we were called in school, and I felt only that to be one separated me from the rest of the children. My sister was also marked by all this, and she has always lived her life around the fictitious princedom. It marked me much less, and in Mexico it was erased completely, but one afternoon in Prague when I heard someone calling "Altesse" (Your Highness), I immediately turned my head, because that is what we were called as children, and I felt ashamed of myself. "Something remains," I concluded, "something remains," without thinking further about how absurd it was that in a socialist country somebody was being called "Your Highness."

The flimsiness of this supposed distinction, of being a princess, could be maintained for years, just as illusions are long maintained. It was then, among the French farmers, that I discovered the constant need to work. There was always something urgent to be done. Whenever they sat, it was around the table and upon hard chairs, which they soon abandoned. No flabbiness. At sundown, they threw themselves on their beds (which I imagined to be as hard as a sack of potatoes), only to be up before sunrise. Their life went from sunrise to sunset; their hard hands were the same from sun to sun; when they rested them upon the table those hands resembled abandoned tools to be collected later. Their hands were old shovels, rakes, brooms, plows, and clods of mud . . .

Once in a while they would cover their mouths with their hands, using them as small screens to hide their smiles or their laughter at my childish questions. They answered dryly; they did not look at each other, there was no malice among them, only some surprise at these little girls who were too curious, whose inquisitive spirit had to be forgiven. "This is what the master's children are like," they must have thought.

That is why in Mexico, in Tomatlán, just a step away from Zacatlán, when I heard Don Vicente say, "This will be a good year for apples," I felt that I had returned to a forgotten cycle, to something that had to do with my soul (I don't know what to call it—my spirit, perhaps? That small ladder that descends down to where thoughts are very painful) and which provided a sense of continuity. In Tomatlán, arm in arm with Magda, with her wrinkled hands, her nails hard as bones, her braids thinning out over the years, the pockets of her apron where she kept all the mishaps of a lifetime, I have the feeling of holding my destiny, the very source of my destiny, in my hands.

The Young Writer

In 1997 the magazine *ViceVersa* published a special edition devoted to the childhood memories of several Mexican writers, including Elena. In this brief piece recalling her first years in France, before her arrival in Mexico, Elena reveals the first steps of an insecure and timid little girl who is both obstinate and tireless, and who confesses that a sort of self-contempt has propelled her from the beginning and continues to give her impetus today. In her narrative one may glimpse a little girl for whom everything represents a great challenge, an attitude that according to her is intimately linked to a feeling of inferiority due to her petiteness, which has continued to affect her throughout her entire life; she grew up with a mother and a sister who are both much taller: her mother measured 5'4" and her sister is 5'8". Elena is only 5'1". She is terribly demanding of her small body, however, and gives it stern orders to go ahead and finish the task at hand; in this case the sketched outline of a human figure drawn with a pencil whose point is too thick for this purpose—although deep inside Elena thinks her difficulty is due to her incompetence:

A white sheet of paper, a pencil. The lines are thick because the pencil has not been sharpened properly. Nonetheless, the line widens, becoming stronger. I am six or seven years old. I already know how to write. I draw men with trousers, a belt, a hairless head, and stiff arms. I draw one, then another. Because I don't like the man I draw, I call him "Jedaure," a word that I'm not sure exists and which sounds horrible in French. I draw another figure. When one comes out right, I will give him a lovely name, John, my father's name, or André, like my grandfather.

Now I'm drawing women, with their skirts tied at their waists; they are pyramids and that is why their waists are all so tiny. Their legs are two sticks. Their faces are like a balloon. I give them hair, but since the pencil is so thick it looks like spikes. Some day they'll come out right and I will call the loveliest one Paula, like my mother, who is slim and moves with a fascinating grace; she walks on air and doesn't fall, she looks out the window, goes through it and continues stepping into space, and she even stops to think of something, lighter than the atmosphere.

I draw a lot, I try very hard, and my efforts go back to that moment of my childhood. I feel angry at myself because I am awkward, too small. I am demanding with myself. I tremble. My head gives me orders, my hand does not obey. I'm cruel.

At that precise instant the cruelty I carry inside of me arises, that which I began to apply against the six- or seven-year-old girl in France, for whom I felt the same unhealthy contempt that I would later find in a story by D. H. Lawrence: "The Prussian Officer." I remember that I asked God to take me back to wherever he had pulled me out from.

Now, at age sixty-four, I feel compassion for that desperate little girl that I was and who exasperated me so. I never got to give lovely names to the men and women, because they never came out as I wanted them to.

Even today, stooped over and wearing eyeglasses, when I am faced with a blank page of paper, I give out the same orders I did in my childhood, and something instinctive arises from my desk and rebels, something laughs at me: sarcastic and blue eyed, something that only I can recognize, it is cruelty.

Interestingly, Elena has again taken up the brush to paint unusual pictures: I remember in particular the one she painted on top of a portrait of her mother as a child, in which she transformed Paulette into an exquisite *china poblana*, covered with sequins and spangles. Young Paulette, formerly dressed in lace and crêpe de chine, appears in this well-known Mexican costume, full of ribbons and sequins. Elena still attempts to capture that elusive form, now mostly in words, for her dream is still to write a book that will be the full reflection of a life worthy of a novel.

The SS *Marqués de Comillas*

As there was no end of the war in sight, and in order to protect her daughters from the difficulties and dangers of the conflagration, Elena's mother decided to take them to Mexico, her homeland, which she had visited only once before, when she traveled to the capital during the second decade of the twentieth century, just after the Mexican Revolution, and from there went to the family's landholdings, the Hacienda de la Llave, in Querétaro. Nonetheless, her own mother lived in Mexico City whence, leaving her beloved dogs behind, she proceeded to Veracruz to meet her daughter and granddaughters when they arrived in a twin-engine plane from Havana. Elena's recollections regarding her departure from France reflect the anxiety and enchantment of a little girl transplanted "from sweet France, the land of the handkerchief-size gardens (*lieu commun*) and of tender vegetables that fit in the palm of your hand . . . [to] an enormous plain surrounded by mountains and live volcanoes traversed by buzzards."[3]

Elena and her sister, Kitzia, with their parents, circa 1941.

In an interview, Elena reflects on this key moment in her life which, at seven years of age, was to mark her destiny forever:

We traveled from France to Bilbao; from there we boarded the *Marqués de Comillas*, in which there were already many Spanish refugees. It was in this ship that we arrived in Cuba. In Havana they wanted to send us to Triscomía, and there put us in quarantine. My mother proceeded to ask them how they could possibly quarantine us, considering that she was a princess. She also defended a pregnant girl that they wanted to quarantine. We were in Havana for only a day or two, and then took a single-prop twin-engine plane home to Mexico. Our grandmother met us and took us to live with her. Her house was very impressive, as it had small turrets, like a castle. It was one of those old mansions in the Colonia Juárez, located at #6 Berlin Street, enormous and very well appointed by Grandmamma. I recall that there was a giant doll on each bed: I had never seen dolls that size. We lived with our grandmother for many years, because my mother went out a lot while Grandma always stayed home. She wanted to save all the homeless dogs that roamed in the streets, and she brought them to live in her back yard, and I believe there were almost thirty of them.

Elena with her mother and sister arriving in Mexico from Havana by twin-engine plane.

An English Education

Shortly after settling in Mexico City, Paulette enrolled her two daughters in a private school where they would be certain to learn the Queen's English, as they had spoken French since infancy and continued studying it privately in Mexico. Spanish they learned in the streets and through the mouths of the servants, as Doña Paulette recalls in her autobiography entitled *Nomeolvides* (Forget-Me-Nots):

> The colorful language of the servants very quickly became familiar to the girls. In the Windsor School, three blocks away from the house, they learned good English, and in order that they not forget their French, the university professor Bertie Sauve agreed to give them lessons four days a week. Piano at

Miss Belén Pérez Gavilan's academy on Liverpool Street, and dancing with Miss Carroll, rounded out their primary education.

In an interview, Elena provided some curious details regarding her elementary education from the perspective of a newly arrived little girl:

> First we went to a school whose name I don't recall, but we did not speak a word of Spanish. I have always said that we didn't even know that my mother was Mexican until we came to Mexico. Then we went to the Windsor School, which had an exceptional principal by the name of Edith Hart. There were very good teachers there. Half the morning was taught in English and the other half in Spanish, as established by the Secretaría de Educación Pública (Secretariat of Public Education). In English, we learned to count in pounds, shillings, and pence, because it was a British school. Every day we sang, "God save our gracious Queen . . . God save the Queen." There I completed the third through sixth grades of elementary school. Afterwards, I attended the Liceo Franco Mexicano with my sister Kitzia, but she did not like it. By that time she already had a very strong character and imposed her will on my parents. It was always so.

The Teachings of Doña Magda

One day, after Doña Paulette had settled down in a home near the still-elegant boulevard Paseo de la Reforma, a rather petite young woman showed up demonstrating a firm intention of gaining employment. At that time Paulette was taking care of her two little girls while her husband was still with the French army in Europe. This was around 1943, when Elena was eleven years old. The young woman had heard that Doña Paulette was looking for somebody to help out with the girls, and she considered herself capable of handling this job. Her name was Magdalena Castillo, and her presence in Elena's home was to have a great influence on the development of the young writer. As Magdalena recalls, Elena and her sister, Kitzia, were attracted to her from the beginning, and thanks to their entreaties, Paulette gave her a chance to prove her ability as a nanny. From that day on, Magda became an indispensable part of Elena's life, and to this day comes up from her small farm in Puebla to visit Elena and chat with her niece Isabel (Chabela), who is now Elena's housekeeper. Magdalena, with dark aviator-style glasses always perched on her nose or hanging from a thin cord that she wears around her neck, recalls in her particular down-home style how she came to Mexico City and Paulette's reaction at this little country girl who considered herself capable of taking care of her daughters.

When did I meet Elenita? I'm not too sure, because I can't quite recall how old she was at the time. But she was a little girl. I was about eighteen, and at the time I was staying with a relative on Guadiana Street. She was working for a French lady. I had hoped to get work too; I like to work. But I really didn't know how to do anything. Sure, out of sheer necessity I knew how to make tortillas and how to grind corn. I could sweep and do the laundry, but that was about it.

There was a lady with two small girls who was looking for a person to take care of them. I said, "All right, let's go see her," and so that's what we did: we went to see her. I remember that she wasn't home, but the cook said, "Wait here." So we waited.

The lady came in from wherever she had gone, and I told her that I was looking for work and maybe I could be of service. She told us to go upstairs. So then we went up there, and she asked me, "Are you the person seeking employment? No, you cannot be right for my daughters, you're too young."

"Yes, I am young," I answered, "but the trouble is that I'm not very tall, I'm just too short."

The girls, who were close by, without even knowing me, ran up to me and hugged me. They shouted, "Mami! Mami!"

I just stood there, I was embarrassed, see? When you come from a village you do not open up easily. We are all very tight-mouthed. Then the lady said: "Well, look at that! They like

you! Stay for a week. If it doesn't work out here, I'll send you
to my mother's house . . . "

Her mother had a dog shelter in her own home with around
thirty or forty dogs, and a cook that served them heaping
plates of food downstairs in the patio. You see, that lady gathered stray dogs from the streets.

Magda's job was to go everywhere with the girls, give them
their baths, oversee their meals, and take care of them and pamper
them when they didn't feel well. Truth be told, Magda has spent
her whole life with the Poniatowski family; she was nursemaid to
Elena and Kitzia, and later to Elena's children, Emmanuel, Felipe,
and Paula. Magda has many memories of Elena as she was in those
days, which help re-create the life of this young French girl recently arrived in Mexico. Magda insists that as a child Elena was
simply a little angel:

> I had to help her bathe, take her to school, go on walks with
> her, and take her to the movies, to her dancing lessons, to
> her piano lessons, and to gym classes. She was lovely, very
> obedient and kind; she was an especially compassionate per-
> son. Once a woman came to the house begging for alms. She
> needed money to bury her son. At that moment, I was about
> to take Elena to school. As we walked out the door she said,
> "Magda, please, do try to help that poor lady."
>
> I answered, "No, dear, your mother is busy, and I must not
> disturb her."
>
> Elena answered, "All right, I'll be right back; I'm going to
> get my piggy bank."
>
> She brought it out and gave all her savings to the woman.
> Even back then she was generous; that has always been her
> true nature.

Elena's mother recalls her daughter's first music and singing
lessons, which supplemented her schoolwork, and she will never
forget that when her husband returned from the war, his young
daughter could already play the piano:

Elena took piano lessons close to home. She and her sister went together. Elena's hands are small, but she did well at the piano. This must have been around 1944–45, because when my husband came back from the war he found that she could not read music very well, and being an excellent musician, he said that her teacher must not be very good. Elena was a bit discouraged by this. She also sang very well. Her voice was lovely. Elena says that once, when she was singing while driving down Mexico City's freeway, something seemed to split inside her throat. She also had other problems with her throat and even had surgery to remove her tonsils. She was not strong like her sister. I remember that ever since she was a little girl she would fall down easily and scratch up her knees.

Miss Jujú

Elena discovered her first teacher in the young Magdalena, who came from Zacatlán de las Manzanas, a small village in the mountainous area of Puebla state. As she had recently arrived from France, Elena did not speak Spanish well, and Magda taught her to pronounce the words, at least well enough that they could understand one another. Thanks to these early lessons, Elena still has a rather rustic dialect and an archaic vocabulary typical of the people who say *naiden* instead of *nadie*, and *suidad* instead of *ciudad*, and who use words such as *újule*, *pácatelas*, and other expressions learned only in the streets. According to her mother, it was due to this early contact with everyday Mexico that young Elena discovered a world of individuals who did not form part of her aristocratic environment:

Through the servants she began to recognize differences in lifestyles and to observe how the "other half" lived. It was then that she began to understand that there was a middle class, for instance, and the lower classes. It was surprising, because we did not normally have anything to do with the people who later appear in her books, nor did we concern ourselves too much with that kind of people, who are not quite middle class.

And I believe that her interest in such persons was due to a great extent to those she met and admired. She must have thought that society people were not as intelligent or as active as the others.

This early fascination with the lower classes, combined with the fact that Elena never took formal Spanish lessons, resulted in her speaking a Spanish very different from the refined Castilian of Juan Ramón Jiménez. For instance, according to Magdalena, the little girl had many problems with some characteristic sounds of the new language, and that is why her young teacher took such an interest in helping her to speak properly:

> She did not speak much Spanish. She chopped off the words, but I helped her this way: she would say "burito," and I would say "burrito." She would say, "There goes a perito," and I would say, "It's called perrito." You see, I had to help her correct the words and correct her speech. I always talked to her. However, with words, I know I'm a bit awkward; you mustn't think that I'm really very civilized.

With Magdalena, it seems that Elena was an exemplary student who did not even try to stay home with the flu, she was so eager to learn, either with her nanny or in school. She read a lot, first in French, then in English and in Spanish, but like all children, she was also mischievous, and often it was her nursemaid who bore the brunt of her capers. Magdalena recalls, "When she went to school she was very—how should I put it? She was very smart, this child was. Sometimes she would catch the flu, and her mother would say, 'Magda, today she's not leaving the house.' Elena would insist, 'No, Mami, I'm all right, I have to go.' She was not interested in staying at home. She read a great deal in French; they brought her many magazines from France."

Like all girls of her age, Elena loved to invite her friends over, play make-believe, and cause Magda problems. One day, when Doña Paulette went out to one of her many social events, Elena, Kitzia, and their little playmates got into their mother's enormous closet and tried on all her clothes: two-piece suits from Schiapa-

relli, elegant hats with feathers, and kidskin gloves that went up
to the elbow. As Magda recalls, sometimes these games became
tedious for her, as she had to put everything away before Doña
Paulette returned to find the disaster left behind by the girls:

> They also had guests over and played among themselves,
> all girls of their own age. They pretended to be princesses.
> Sometimes they tried on all their mother's clothes and made a
> mess with all those dresses. They would bathe in perfume, and
> even fill up the tub with perfume, because "that was the way
> princesses took a bath!" I was embarrassed because their mom
> had to scold me, not them. They were with their playmates,
> and I picked up as well as I could, so that when their mother
> came home she would find everything in good order. You see,
> they were the princesses, the ambassadors, and who knows
> what else!

Paulette also remembers Elena as a little girl who identified—
at least in the beginning—with her aristocratic forebears. It is interesting to note that among all of them the one who most caught
her attention as a child was King Stanislaus II, her great-great-
uncle, who was never acclaimed for his political successes but
rather for his cultural contributions, especially to painting: "Elena
said to me one day: 'I will become Queen of Poland.' Stanislaus
was not recognized as a good king, but he was a good man, especially from an artistic point of view. Thanks to him, Guardi and
Canaletto came to Poland. He was a very worthy individual."

Besides these inclinations toward nobility, natural in a child of
her age and social background, Elena seems to have been an ideal
daughter, willing to give away anything within reach in order to
help somebody who, from her point of view, was in need. Magda
thanked God for such benevolent and (very Catholic) inclinations,
even though she sometimes felt they were a bit exaggerated: "She
was not terribly mischievous. She liked to study, chat, and give
charity to certain persons she met in the street. We would go to
the best movie theaters, the Palacio Chino, the Metropolitan, and
the Vanguardias, which were top-notch. I also liked to accompany
them to Cuernavaca, to Pasteje, to Acapulco, and to Manzanillo."

Magdalena does not recall as much as one might wish about Elena's first writings, but she does remember that her little charge was always reading and writing, at least in French. According to her, the little girls read French magazines and comic strips. Their nanny only leafed through the comics, not understanding a word. On the other hand, Doña Paulette does recall the moment when her young daughter began to write, and that by the age of seven her narrative abilities were already remarkable. "I think that Elena was really gifted, and her talent was evident from the time she was very small. When she was only seven years old, the teacher at her school in France was very happy with her, because she wrote so well."

Regarding Elena's relationship with Kitzia, her younger sister, Magdalena noticed some differences in temperament between the two: Kitzia was tall and strong, and apparently rather authoritarian. Elena tried to get along well with her, although sometimes after a disagreement, she would go to Magdalena seeking comfort:

> The two sisters loved each other, but Kitzia was the stronger one. From the beginning she had more character and was bossier. Elenita was very noble. When Kitzia and Elena had a fight, I always took Elena's side. I would comfort her. Then she would say, "Magda, let's go pray for my papa, because he's away at war." We would say nothing to her sister. Leaving her downstairs, we would go all the way up to the rooftop "to be closer to the sky," she would say, and we would kneel. I prayed as best I could. Later, little by little, Elena taught me to pray and to go to mass; I used to be the one who took them to mass.

More than a nursemaid, Magdalena often adopted the role of a mother, especially when Elena was ill. As her mother had many social engagements, the responsibility of caring for her daughters fell on Magdalena. On one occasion, Magdalena gave Elena the nickname that lasted for a lifetime: "She was very ill, and Elena wanted me with her. So I went to her, and she began to speak very softly. I told her, 'Don't cry, Miss Jujú.' It was just a joke. I was the only one who ever called her that, and I did it because she was

fussy and sad. By then she wasn't so little any more . . . And that's
how the nickname came about."

Sacred Hearts

Like many children of good families, Elena finished her studies,
though limited, abroad. Paulette sent the two sisters to a boarding
school near Philadelphia, in Torresdale, where she hoped that they
would learn everything they needed to become truly "nice girls,"
so that, upon their return to Mexico, they would marry young men
of the highest social and economic positions. Although of strong
character and somewhat stubborn, Magdalena really missed her
girls, who sent her letters from the Sacred Heart School (Eden
Hall), complaining about all the things they had to do that they
had never done at home, for Magda was always there to pick up
after them, make their beds, serve them their favorite dishes, and
even wash their panties for them:

> Their mother decided to enroll them in the convent because
> they didn't know how to do anything. They could not even
> wash their own hair. They didn't know how to take a bath
> on their own. I had to bathe them, even though they were
> already too big for that. They sent me letters saying how
> much they missed me, that they were punished because they
> had not washed their underwear, that they had to make their
> own beds, and that it was too much work for them. They were
> also picky about the food. Well, actually, Elenita was more
> adaptable; the other one only wanted to eat cake. If Elena did
> not like the food, she kept quiet about it, but Kitzia would
> throw a fit.

In the last chapter of *Lilus Kikus*, entitled "The Convent," which
according to her mother is rather autobiographical, Elena confesses, through her fragile alter ego, Lilus, her feelings about the idea
of going to study in a convent. Elena herself admits that this short
story is at least semi-autobiographical:

It has a bit of this convent [Sacred Heart] in it, but much of it is made up and quite fictitious. It was my mother's decision to send us there because my first cousins also attended school there. They were the daughters of Lydia, my mother's sister, who lived in Garden City and worked in New York; she was close by and we could visit her there and later, at Christmastime, we would also go to Garden City, to Aunt Lydia's. In Eden Hall I recall that my cousins, Yolanda and Diana, looked upon me with a certain amount of resentment because after my first three months in school I won first place in English. Then I was appointed treasurer of the magazine *The Current Literary Coin* because I was very honest, they said. I also became an actress. I acted in Shakespeare's *Twelfth Night*: I recall that I said the lines, "Sweet Sir Toby, Sweet Sir Toby." I think I was the tavern keeper, which is the role of a very merry woman who serves the wine. I was happy in the convent, and so was Kitzia. I finished high school there. Then I was offered a scholarship to go to Manhattanville to college, the next step up from Eden Hall. However, after the devaluation in Mexico at the time of President Miguel Alemán, my parents insisted that even with a scholarship, just the cost of the plane ticket, a few extras, and I don't know what else were luxuries they simply could no longer afford.

Paulette clearly recalls this stage of her daughter's development and points out that in school Elena "always had very good grades, and when she went to the convent and learned English, she won the first prize. She wrote a story entitled 'On Nothing,' and it is very good." Originally written in English, it appeared in 1950 in volume 15 of *The Current Literary Coin*, and it is an extremely valuable document, for it provides a glimpse of the early writer.

"ON NOTHING"

There seems to be nothing to write on nothing, yet a whole world is centered about this little word. As strange as it may seem, nothing comprises that whole planet called earth and the creatures on it. In nothing man hides his deep emotions, his loves, his fears, his courage, his greatness. There are depth and breath and height in nothing, as can be seen in the nothings of daily life which so reveal man to mankind.

Nothing is perhaps the word most used by men. It is spoken by all, by young and old, rich and poor. I have often wondered at the reaction of little children when caught tasting prohibited jellies or ravaging the cookie jar. Their answer to the perilous question, "What have you been doing?" is invariably the same, "Oh, nothing!" The cause of that nothing is the embarrassment of the moment, the fact of having been caught concealing something. Yet why do we have to choose that poor word, "Nothing"? Another example which shows how good a hiding place nothing is, is found in the ordinary experience of giving and receiving presents. "This is for you!" says the giver, thrusting into the eager hands of the receiver a package which has been wrapped with the utmost care. "Oh, how wonderful!" answers the recipient, "I cannot wait to see what it is!" At this, the donor will plead in a humble voice, "Oh! It's nothing, really!" Here again, nothing plays a leading role. The giver, like the child, is concealing something, but this is an entirely different kind of concealment. Perhaps he wants to say that this package is only a small proof of his love! Thus mankind hides his self-consciousness behind that nothing. Another example of the popularity of nothing is: "Miss Clara McFlumsy of Madison Square," who was always complaining she had *nothing* to wear, has been a source of preoccupation to many. "Cinderella" could not go to the ball because she had no evening dress, yet with the help of her fairy godmother she won the prince's love!

Nothing is not only used to excuse oneself, but it may also be applied to a poor creature for whom mankind feels a notable contempt, "a good-for-nothing!" People usually mean to designate some kind of person whose gifts, if he has any, have been rejected by society. However, I cannot help but be attracted by this "good-for-nothing." I like the story of a monk who seemed to be a "good-for-nothing," yet in being "good-for-nothing," he was good for everything. He arrived late at Matins. He knew not the Pater Noster nor the Canticles nor the Credo. Wherever he went he saw the priests at the altars, the deacons at the gospels and the sub-deacons at the epistles. He could do none of these things and had nothing to offer to the Mother of God. In despair he had recourse to his former profession. He would render her homage with tumbling. So as long as mass endured, he jumped before her altar and leapt and turned somersaults until he fell to the ground and dropped from sheer fatigue. This "good-for-nothing" monk, this Jongleur, gave much honor to Our Lady and pleased her greatly, for she came down from the heavens, with Angels and Archangels, to watch the performance. By this I do not mean to imply that all men should become "good-for-nothings." On the contrary. Yet men should not condemn people whose worth they do not know. According to them, "good-for-nothings" do not accomplish the tasks of every-day life. There might be a reason for this lack of responsibility. Those "good-for-nothings" might have found a greater wealth, a spiritual life much more important than the materialistic things which give men a pleasant feeling of self-importance.

Man's life is nothing! Man's life is everything! Man's life is nothing because he is dust and into dust he shall return. Man's life is everything because he is spirit. There is greatness in nothingness. There are depth and breadth and height in nothing. "Deep called upon deep." Nothingness and helplessness call upon the abyss of Divine Mercy. Everything could be written about nothing, for it lies at the very core of creation.

Hélène Poniatowska
Fourth Academic Class
Published in *The Current Literary Coin*, 1950

Return to Mexico

Upon her return to Mexico from the United States, Elena still knew nothing that would be useful for her survival in the real world: at school the nuns had taught her good manners and other things that would make her an ideal debutante. In an interview, Elena reflected on this stage of her life, which was marked by an unstable domestic situation:

> The main characteristic of my parents was that they never planned anything whatsoever regarding anything. They never told us, as I suppose other privileged children are told: "You must get ahead, marry a rich man." My parents floated somewhere in the stratosphere. My father was a war hero from the Seventh Army; he was a French captain. He worked closely with the Americans because his English was as good as his French, as befitted the son of Elizabeth Sperry Crocker. I believe that after he returned from war, it still deeply affected him. He was sent on several very dangerous missions, in the course of which he was dropped by parachute into occupied areas. He returned as a war hero (the United States awarded him the Purple Heart), covered with decorations but in poor health. My brother, Jan, a beautiful child, was born at this time. When she was eighteen, my sister, Kitzia, married Pablo Aspe, who had been her boyfriend since she was eleven years old. My brother, Jan, who was a marvelous boy, was my mother's salvation. My father was a very good man, a hypersensitive, extremely creative composer, but his life revolved around the

Portrait of Elena as a young woman.

business that he dreamed of setting up but never got off the ground. These failures were very hard for him to bear.

Like my parents, I seldom make the smallest decisions. I let things fall of their own weight, even if they hit me on the head, or rather, on my soul, and squash me like an overripe fruit. For me, everything is dual natured: good and bad, ugly and pretty, at the same time. I make no moral judgments and that, of course, has brought me some problems. The first of these were with my own character. I never judge. It is easier to evade issues, to float along without taking a single precaution, while the infected pustule grows bigger day after day. This is an inherited trait. My mother floated, but that saved her from much suffering and allowed her (although it nearly killed her) to withstand the pain caused by the death of her only son, Jan, who was killed when he was twenty-one years old. It also allowed her to overcome, two or three years later, the paralysis that afflicted my sister's son Alexander, her grandson. Kitzia inherited her extraordinary maternal fortitude, and like my mother lived in a latent state of pain that she never showed, perhaps due to her upbringing, but which filled the air around her. Once the three of us, my mother, my daughter, Paula, and me, went to San Joaquín Cemetery (where my father, my grandmother, and Jan, my little brother, next to whom I shall be buried to keep him company, lie at rest). Paula was taking pictures of the family tombs; my mother stood before Jan's, and Paula said, "But smile . . . " And she answered, "How do you expect a mother to smile by the grave of her dead son?" I believe that Jan's death hastened that of my father. He survived for ten years, almost eleven, but for father, living his own life became very difficult.

I am very proud to be the daughter of Johnny and Paulette Poniatowski. I like their attitude toward life. They were never social climbers nor money grubbers or political climbers, nothing of the kind. On the contrary, they were themselves, somewhat out of this world, unreal, generous, beautiful, poetic, credulous, devoted, and profoundly respectful of others; in all honesty, they were to some extent from another planet, and I find that very moving. To think about them brings me closer to myself, to my best self, to the best inside of me, to my own death, and in death I shall go on loving them, as my younger brother, Jan, died loving them.

My mother has always been within me, and now more than ever, I keep her deep inside; she is my strength, she is always (or almost always) with me. "Maman," I call her in French, and she appears by my side; I find her in the air I breathe, in the bouquet of flowers that I receive, in the light that remains lit at night, and on the pillow upon which I lay my head before falling asleep. My children always miss her as well. Paula, my daughter, was her favorite granddaughter, and on my mother's last day in the hospital, Paula asked to be allowed into the operating room. Something they read in her eyes made them open the door for her: my mother never let go of her granddaughter's hand. She had once said about Paula: "I have never heard that grandchild of mine tell a lie." According to my mother, if one wants to know the truth, it will be as Paula Haro tells it.

Upon her return from abroad, Magda noted that her two favorite girls were now interested in boys. Nonetheless, as soon as one of them showed interest in Elena, she did not like him anymore. To decide among her various suitors, she would ask for her nanny Magda's advice:

Elena was very good-looking—she is naturally good-looking—and she had many suitors. Oh, how they fell for her! But she didn't fall for them. There was one suitor who acted very silly, and Elena would ask me, "Magda, which one do you want to be my boyfriend?" She was always asking me the same question. She didn't follow my advice, but she insisted that I answer her question. One of these young men, named Javier Carral, used to call Elena "Rat" whenever he came by to pick her up to go to a party.

Bilingual Secretary?

In the early fifties Elena was nineteen years old. She recalls that "when my father informed me that I would not be returning to the United States to continue my studies, I told him that I wanted to study medicine, but none of my courses could be approved in Mexico. Then my friends would interrogate me: 'How will you study medicine? What will you do in anatomy class where the bodies are nude?' I meekly obeyed, for I belonged to a very mundane environment, mine was that of 'nice people.'"

At that time women in Mexico—as well as in the United

Kitzia and Elena in front of the portrait of their grandmother Elizabeth, painted by Boldini.

States and Europe—had little or nothing to do with the world of business or politics, much less with journalism, a field dominated by men in nearly all its aspects. Faced with a future full of balls, cocktail parties, and fashion shows, which was the destiny await-ing all the young ladies of her social class, Elena realized that she would need to do something to change her life.

I was surprised to discover that Elena was an actress before she became a bilingual secretary or a journalist. She began to develop her acting talent while she was still in France, when she was about ten years old, and continued this pursuit after she emigrated to Mexico:

> I had acted first with the Girl Scouts in France, and later with André Moreau and the Cuit Poulet. Then, Brígida Alexander, Susana Alexander's mother, saw me in a play in a French theater group and called me because she needed a young woman in her group. I worked in a TV play with an actor called Antonio Passy. It was called *The Man Who Married a Silent Woman*, and I was the silent woman. I never said a single word. Later, Magda Donato, who was charming, gave me the role of a chambermaid in a play, but this time it was professional theater, for pay. The only thing I had to do was to come on stage carrying the breakfast tray, open the curtains, and say to the actors—Carmen Montejo and Tito Junco—who were in bed: "Your breakfast is served." Once, when our paths crossed backstage, I heard Tito Junco say, "There goes the future mother of my children." I felt so offended that I did not show up for work the next night, which was completely unprofessional, because there was no maid to take my place for that night's show.

Doña Paulette recalls that when she wanted to send her daughter to France for her debut, Elena set down her own conditions. "Elena had a strong and obstinate character. She insisted, 'I do not want to depend on anyone, and if you send me to Europe, I will go on my own, paying for the trip, and taking care of all my expenses.'"

Curiously, it was precisely her mother's connections among the *socialité* of Mexico City that enabled Elena to discover her true calling:

> At home we subscribed to *Excélsior*—Elena explains—and I read the interviews signed by "La Bambi," whose real name was Ana Cecilia Treviño. A friend from Eden Hall, María de Lourdes Correa, told me that her uncle was editor of the soci-

Elena with Antonio Passy in a still from *The Consequences of a First Marriage*, XLT TV, 1952, directed by Brígida Alexander.

ety section of *Excélsior*, and went with me to tell him that I wanted to be a journalist. To let me down gently, Eduardo Correa said, "Why don't you interview my niece? Bring it to me and we'll see how it comes out."

That same afternoon I went with my mother to a cocktail party hosted by Countess Helen Nazelli—an American woman married to an Italian nobleman—in honor of Francis White, the new U.S. ambassador to Mexico. During the party, I asked my mother, "Why don't you tell him that I'm a journalist and that I would like to interview him?" When we were introduced, the ambassador patted my head and said, "Good child, good child, let her come to my office tomorrow." The next day I went to the embassy, which at the time was opposite the Bellinghausen restaurant in the Zona Rosa. It was a very stupid interview; he gave me his picture, and I took the article and the picture to *Excélsior*.

However, Doña Paulette did not think it proper that a young lady of Elena's class should enter the world of journalists, full of rather low-class people, as she would have described them. "In my family," Elena relates, "it was said that nice people do not appear in the newspapers. So, on one hand, I felt that my parents were happy because their friends would say, 'Look at the great things your little girl does!' but on the other hand, it wasn't quite what they wanted for me."

The interview with Ambassador White was published on May 27, 1953, and was the first of 365 interviews, one for each day of the year, in an almost infinite series of dialogues that, for more than fifty years, would constitute only one facet of Elena's literary production.

Bambi and Dumbo

In an interview with me, Elena provided some details about her early experiences as a journalist in the newspaper *Excélsior*, which was to be the most decisive period of her professional life:

> "You joined *Excélsior* in 1953, not exactly as an interviewer, but rather as a social columnist, is that correct?"
>
> "Well, all women inevitably began in the Sociales section. Later, you might move up, but the first step for a woman at any newspaper was the Sociales section. When I started, I wanted to use Dumbo as my pen name, to match Bambi. Eduardo Correa objected, 'We're not going to have all Walt Disney's characters here. You will use your own name.' I wrote interviews, reviews of social events, everything that must be reported on in that section of the newspaper."

The recently deceased Ana Cecilia Treviño, La Bambi and Elena's colleague during that first year in *Excélsior*, recalled the impact she had at the newspaper from the very beginning:

> Although there were few women in the field of journalism, I do not believe that Elena faced serious obstacles. In the beginning she was not included in the Sociales section; she did not have a formal contract with the newspaper. I was in Sociales, but not due to *machismo*; it was rather that they were

trying to protect me. They had the somewhat silly idea that something bad might happen to me if I worked in a different area. It wasn't because I was a woman [that I was assigned to that section]. And I was sincerely grateful. Elena never had the limitations that the Sociales section imposed. She has the great merit that, not having studied journalism, she followed her own instincts, and I feel that that has also been very good, because she is quite original and extremely intelligent. Elena is highly inventive, and her interviews were very successful from the start.

Thanks to this sweeping success, in a year's time there was so much competition between the two young journalists that one would be forced to leave *Excélsior*, since the paper was not big enough for both.

A Bumbling Reporter

After Elena's first interview with the ambassador of the United States, Eduardo Correa commissioned her to do another one. In an interview, Elena remembers the panic she felt before her first assignment as a journalist:

> I was walking down the street and I asked myself: "What am I going to do now? I have no idea whom to interview." Then I passed in front of the Hotel del Prado, walking in the direction of San Juan de Letrán Avenue, where I was then taking typing classes in order to become an executive secretary. As I walked towards my school, I saw a sign that said: "Amalia Rodrigues Sings Portuguese Fados." Upon entering, I asked to see Mrs. Rodrigues. They asked me what for, and I explained that I was a journalist from *Excélsior*. During our successful interview, she even invited me to be her guest at the nightclub so that I could hear her sing, even though I had asked her, "What is a fado? Where is Portugal?" My questions were so stupid that they even made my readers laugh.

Reporters under contract to the Sociales section of *Excélsior* had to write feature articles and reviews of social events, so to be allowed to publish interviews was a luxury. It also meant going to the most exclusive parties, shows, and cocktail parties of the time, but her presence was de rigueur at these events anyway. During that year Elena conducted an interview a day with many distinguished figures in the Mexican and international cultural world: Cri-Cri, Andrés Henestrosa, Alí Chumacero, Cantinflas, Ana Sokolow, Juan Soriano, Gutierre and Carletto Tibón, Lola Álvarez Bravo, Max Aub, Dolores del Río, Luis Nishisawa, Carlo Coccioli, Gabriel Figueroa, Carlos Mérida, Pita Amor, Carlos Pellicer, Jean Sirol, Octavio Paz, Henry Moore, Matías Goeritz, Manuel Toussaint, Luis Barragán, and even Santa Claus himself enjoyed an amusing conversation with the young reporter.

Surprisingly, upon being asked if, since she was doing so much work for *Excélsior*, the editors offered her a formal contract, Elena answered in the negative:

Nothing. Never. All my life I have worked freelance. I have never had social security or a pension. If I had wanted to, perhaps I could have had a desk. My father gave me a portable Olivetti typewriter as a gift, because at the time I was studying shorthand and typing. I kept it for many years and decorated it with a sticker depicting a cartoon of the "Supermachos."

Misogyny has pursued me ever since I began working as a journalist, or rather, since I tried to do something that went beyond the beaten path, but I realized that my experience was no worse than that of other women, some of whom even lost their minds. There was at the time—and there continues to be—a strong determination to cut women off from any future other than that of matrimony and motherhood. How to fight against this state of things? It is easier to adapt than to struggle; inaction is easier than action, but in the end inaction, not doing anything, is the same as adapting. In the long term, to give up becomes much more dangerous than any action we take, because it destroys everything within us, all we have to offer. I had before me the example of my aunt, Pita Amor, a free spirit and creative being who finally lost her marbles because she yielded and did whatever other people demanded of her. She obeyed the law only to break it later, and she made a spectacle of herself. Her scandals made her a laughingstock for many; she lost her sense of direction, her compass, and I never saw a friendly hand stretched out to help her, perhaps because she stretched her inner self to its very limits. She transcended good and evil. At the end of her life, she was part of the decadence of the Zona Rosa, always plying the same streets—Londres, Amberes, Niza—with her walking stick, a flower on top of her head, and her thick-lensed glasses. She had much to give and by then only a shadow of her former self remained. Women who stand out run the risk of becoming caricatures of themselves. In my case, both men and women expected me to falter. I could hear them snickering behind doors and walls. I could hear them laughing, expecting a thunderous fall that would make me come to my senses and join the sheepfold, that would make me realize that I had chosen to go down the wrong path. But it's a fact that everything that is different is frightening. It frightened me, too, but others were frightened as well. They preferred to nudge each other and laugh. "Look where she is headed, the poor thing." Like Aunt Pita, into the abyss? What I mean, Michael, is that for women, especially in the fifties—I don't know if it is still so—to follow one's own vocation was to defy others, and was a daily challenge that wore you out. You had to be very strong. My mother, my sister, and I are strong women, but not that strong. In the eyes of my mother there was infinite sadness, and also in those of my sister. Nonetheless, I feel that a great deal of the time I spent on my creative work was unfortunately spent defending myself from the other Elena who asked, "What for? Who the hell cares, anyway? What are you doing with your life? Right now your life could be so peaceful, your persistence is laughable. You are sacrificing too much, you don't see your friends, go to Acapulco, or have massages the way the others do all the time. These people will never be grateful to you, you are throwing pearls at swine, it is not your scene. We will all soon be dead, and how much enjoyment will you really have gotten out of life?"

Sexual discrimination made me feel betrayed, as it usually does. I was never paid the same as a man. I was never given the same space as a man; I never received the same recognition. I never knew how to approach someone powerful. On the contrary, my feeling was "just turn on your heel and run" and I was never sure what was best for me. I would have been ashamed to do "what was best for me." Furthermore, only my staying power, and in a certain way, my lack of clear-sightedness, made me push ahead. I awoke each morning and there was no response from the heads of the newspaper. I had been taught that one must never complain—that it is very bad manners to do so. Consequently, at the time I was proud, and perhaps I still am, that I never asked anyone for anything. Perhaps it was just my arrogance. I was also taught that one must not demand payment. Journalists are very poorly paid, and I am no exception. I attribute all this to misogyny. Of course, if I had married a rich man, perhaps I would have earned the respect of others, but the mere idea of seeking out a man for his fortune seemed a thought worthy of a lackey. Perhaps more than anything else, my pride is to blame.

What? Where? When? How?

A growing zeal to discover and describe the experiences of women in Mexico's cultural milieu characterized the majority of Elena's interviews in this period. For example, Alfonso Reyes' wife, Manuelita, provided an inside view of what it was like to live with an eminent leader of Mexican and world literature. The following extract from that interview—entitled "Love Wore Curls: Doña Manuelita Reyes"—is illustrative of the daily interviews Elena did throughout 1953. In this conversation, Elena uncovers Reyes' domestic life to such a degree that Doña Manuelita even reveals some of the more intimate facets of her beloved husband. Elena begins the interview by focusing upon their home, located on Benjamin Franklin Street, and its real proprietor, Doña Manuelita:

Elena as a young
woman. (Photo by
Úrsula Bernath)

In a prodigious library, "The Alphonsine Chapel" (known
thus in Mexico and abroad), a two-story construction with a
vestibule, similar to that of the Palafoxiana Library in Puebla,
Manuelita and Don Alfonso Reyes have made their abode,
and they receive me in the area they call the Choir. Don
Alfonso extends his characteristic informal gallantry, which
is so gracious. Then Manuelita Reyes came in, with her eyes
full of mischief and her whole person revealing a strong sense
of humor. It is difficult to express, but she exudes fortitude, a
sweet and subtle fortitude.

Although not all the questions she asked are transcribed, due
to the particular style Elena used in her interviews from the beginning, from the answers it may be deduced that they were always of
the most straightforward kind: What are your husband's favorite lit-

erary works? What is your favorite country among those in which
you have lived? How did you fall in love? It is as if Elena based her
interviews on the basic questions any journalist asks: what, when,
where, why, and how. Nonetheless, elements can be discerned in
the course of this interview that illustrate the couple's matrimonial
dynamic, elements that are not the product of the reporter's questions. In Elena's portrayal of husband and wife, we may glimpse
details of their relationship, even including a mention of Alfonso's
taste for "very lovely objects," that is, the young female poets for
whom the master has corrected some elegy, quatrain, or sonnet.

In July of the same year, Elena landed an interview with María
Izquierdo, one of the most distinguished Mexican painters of the
twentieth century, the creator of images that sensitively define in
many ways the manner in which Mexican women interpret the
world around them. Born in San Juan de los Lagos, Jalisco, in 1902,
Izquierdo incorporates the fauvist, cubist, and surrealist styles in a
very personal way in her work. Their conversation, entitled "Orozco Is the Master, in the Opinion of María Izquierdo," appeared in
the Sociales section of *Excélsior* on Saturday, July 18, 1953. In this
interview, which is also a chronicle, Elena creates a religious, if not
fanatical, scene in describing the artist, so devoted to her people
and to her culture:

> María Izquierdo is perhaps the most eloquent living testimony
> of the devotion to painting; but her devotion to Mexico, to
> her career, to her work, is in the manner of those religious
> oaths, or *mandas*, which finally lead you into the sanctuary
> after you have ascended the steep rocky incline leading to it
> on bare knees. María Izquierdo, so Mexican, is not beautiful,
> she is charming.

"THEY THOUGHT I WAS A MAN"

"In 1928, I began to paint in the San Carlos Fine Arts School.
For a year I followed their curriculum and painted at home.
Then I went to Piedras Negras, in Coahuila, where I participated in a contest and won the first prize with three paintings,
among them one of a rooster. This was my first show. Upon

my return to San Carlos there was another show of the students' paintings and the director of the school, Diego Rivera, selected three pictures by M. Izquierdo, assuming that the painter was a man. Later he declared, 'María Izquierdo is the best student San Carlos could aspire to have.'"

Her professors, Rivera, Gedovius, and Toussaint, admired her. Unfortunately, this praise unleashed the anger and jealousy of the rest of the students, who chased her away with buckets full of water and literally slammed the door of San Carlos in her face. As her teachers and art critics had already declared her a full-fledged painter, María Izquierdo retired to her home to paint and has never since taken a single class.

"Femininity"

In Elena's never-ending attempt to understand and promote the role of women in the contemporary world, the "luxury" of her affiliation with *Excélsior* afforded her opportunities to approach, speak with, and learn from women whose professions might be very different from her own. That is why it is not surprising to discover during her formative years interviews with female personages as unlikely as Gertrudis Duby, a Swiss anthropologist who devoted her life to exploring the remotest jungles of Mexico, full of danger, insects, and other inconveniences. Elena was drawn to this woman who, like she, was trying to succeed in a male-dominated field, a new world. "Women in general attracted my attention," she points out, "but due to my cultural background, I was most inclined toward those who came from France."

In her interview entitled "Woman and Explorer: Tireless at 52," appearing in *Excélsior* on July 28, 1953, Elena asks Gertrudis Duby, the wife of Franz Blom and a resident of San Cristóbal de las Casas, Chiapas, about *femininity*, a term that in the mid-twentieth century was still full of domestic implications, far from the reality of this exceptional woman captivated by the flora and fauna of Mexico and so aware of the terrible problems of rampant tree felling that were leading to severe deforestation. Her aggressive

explanation and negation of masculinity was a pleasant surprise
for the young reporter:

> "More horrible things happen in Acapulco, the 'lovers' para-
> dise,' than inside my jungles. One of the dangers that does
> exist is the wild boars. When a herd of fifty to a hundred of
> these animals is guided by a brave leader who is willing to lead
> the attack, they will fall upon the expedition, and the only
> recourse left to humans is to climb into the trees full of mon-
> keys of all kinds, including *saraguatos*, also known as howler
> monkeys. This seldom occurs, as none of their leaders are
> brave, just like what frequently occurs among men . . . "

In this world there still is, Gertrudis Duby tells us, the belief
that a woman cannot be an explorer. "I can navigate rivers,
swim across them, open paths with my machete, climb up and
down mountains for ten or twelve hours, and ride on horseback for fifteen hours a day under a scorching sun, notwithstanding my fifty-two years.

"I do not believe that this makes a woman lose her femininity. In the first place, it is very difficult to analyze what femininity really is. If one understands by this concept that one
must not reveal one's age (which I have just done) it just seems
like a lot of nonsense. I don't understand why other women
do not want to reveal their age, because it always comes out
in the end."

Thanks to her continuous stream of work in the pages of *Excélsior*, Elena's interviews soon began to attract the attention of many
readers, and at the same time, she succeeded in interviewing ever
more prominent individuals, such as Mexican actress Dolores del
Río. Neither her questions nor her observations go beyond what
might be expected in the Sociales section, however. Yet the young
reporter succeeds in getting Dolores to discuss her personal val-
ues as well as the way she thinks and acts, concluding that, as
the headline reads, "Notwithstanding Luis Buñuel: Sentimentality
Counts." This concept, considered too feminine, criticized, and
relegated to the nonliterary contexts of radio soap operas or, at

best, to the popular serials sold at newsstands, is the same employed by the Chilean poet Pablo Neruda when he declares that "literature without sentimentality falls on the ice." At the same time, it is the mood that best characterizes the novels of the so-called Latin American post-boom, headed by writers such as Isabel Allende and Angeles Mastretta, and before them, Rosario Castellanos and Elena Poniatowska herself. Elena's literary work, at this time still in an emergent stage, will later explore the emotions, often accompanied by sadness and despair, of female protagonists such as Jesusa Palancares, Angelina Beloff, and Tina Modotti. The reporter's descriptions of her interviewees are also full of poetic similes:

> A hand like a small dove, two hands like two little doves. Slender, tender, small, a bit disdainful, fine hands with hard nails, sweet hands that alight gently upon things, with a certain quiver. With these hands, Dolores del Río serves tea, and for herself a large slice of chocolate cake, saying at the same time: "I hate people who have no illusions about anything . . . I am attracted to those who wish to succeed at something; I do not like 'dullards.' I am distressed by people who accept everything and care about nothing. I grow impatient with the expressions, 'What can you do?' the Mexican concept of 'tomorrow,' the 'we'll see what happens,' and the common expression 'I don't give a darn.' . . . Contrary to what Luis Buñuel might think, for me sentimentality is a value in itself."

Gossip Columnist

Notwithstanding her privileged position in the pages of *Excélsior*, which allowed her to interview so many personalities in the Mexican cultural milieu, Elena also had to take less desirable assignments, especially writing society columns covering the whole gamut of events that took place in Mexico's capital during the fifties. She never complained about these assignments, because they provided her with opportunities to become acquainted with many people in intellectual and literary circles. Even though when she returned from the United States she knew little about her mother's country (the names of Alfonso Reyes, Octavio Paz, and José Clemente Orozco were not yet familiar to her), through her social contacts, many of which she made through her mother, and thanks to her knowledge of three languages, Elena was the best choice to attend many such events. It is interesting that she did not use her Hispanicized name when signing these brief columns, preferring either her real French name, Hélène, or Anel, which is "Elena" spelled backwards, minus the *e*. According to her, the heads of the newspaper were the ones who decided that her real name could not appear so often in the same section, and that therefore she would have to invent other bylines—pseudonyms—to disguise the fact that she often published two or three articles on the same day in the same section. Nevertheless, Elena insists that she never made a conscious decision regarding what byline to use for a particular article or column. "I made no distinction. I simply knew that I could not appear five or six times in the same issue of the newspaper as Elena Poniatowska. But in general, the interviews were published under my name. The rest were what we called write-ups."

Be this as it may, by signing her society columns with the elegant names Hélène or Anel, she could compete with other, more-established Mexican society columnists, among whom were to be found such extravagant names as the "Duque de Otranto," as well as Carlos León, Rosario Sansores, and Agustín Barrios Gómez, the author of the well-known column "Ensalada Popoff" (Snob Salad).

Slaves to Fashion

Although reporting on women's fashion was an inevitable part of journalistic work for female reporters in the mid-twentieth century, when asked about this subject, Elena's answer was unconditional: "I had no interest whatsoever in such matters." She always fulfilled her assignments, however, sometimes with ironic undertones, and was able to apply her knowledge of French to interview distinguished representatives of Parisian haute couture, such as Marguerite Rostand, the designer for the Mexican department store El Palacio de Hierro. Their conversation appeared in *Excélsior* on October 19, 1953:

> Women have always had the desire to please. To achieve this purpose, primitive dress transformed gradually into attire. Like all human creations, clothes have developed over time, and the features of their evolution define each period of history and make up the essence of style.
>
> Style: an unbreakable law to which all women must submit! If there are standards for men, such as the Labor Act and the Income Tax Act, for women there is an inflexible and categorical decree: The Rule of Style. Ever unsatisfied, style advances and moves around seeking novelties. It represents the effort to provide human beauty with the setting that will distinguish it and make it stand out above insipid daily vulgarity. Madame Marguerite Rostand has given us her best talents and her good taste during the years that she has lived among us, and this is her opinion on short skirts: "For me, the spirit of style does not depend on the length of the skirt . . . I am not so much interested in whether a skirt be long or short, what is important is an elegant design and a good line. I believe more in shapes than in sizes."

Throughout her interviews, articles, and columns, Elena increasingly concentrates on scrutinizing the lives and personalities of Mexican women, although she did not normally write about the ones who buy tortillas and prepare refried beans. During her early years as a journalist, Elena was more interested in celebrity figures, many of whom were women. Although it would seem that the young interviewer was fascinated by the stars of the moment, one can always tell that, consciously or not, she attempts to discover something deeper within their characters, beyond the secret of their thin waists, their diets, and their fashion designers. Elena makes them spill the beans, so to speak, with regard to the way they see themselves and the issues that are most important to them in their professions. This is exemplified in her interview with actress María Douglas on Tuesday, November 17, 1953, entitled, "The 'Bear's' Widow: The Importance of Comedy":

> "All right, please let us continue with the questions." . . . (María knits something wide, long, and complicated, but it has no shape, it is not a sweater, a scarf, nor a hat . . . What could it be?)
>
> "Oh, it's just a piece of knitting . . . stitches that are brought together . . . we'll have to see what comes out."
>
> (María Douglas is the least curious person in the world. She does not ask in what newspaper her interview will be published, in which section, when it will appear, or anything else. It bothers many people to appear in the Sociales section.)
>
> "You don't need to show me the interview before it is published, I trust you."
>
> "Oh! Thank you . . . I wish everybody were as trusting as you."
>
> "Yes. That would be very good."
>
> María Douglas has one blue eye and one green eye with some brown in it . . . Her voice burns the airwaves, the way a dragon's would. Who can forget her in *Las Coéforas*? And despite her lovely legs, she would allow herself to be made ugly for a movie in which she was acting.
>
> "Yes, it doesn't matter if they turn me into a monkey, and I don't think it would be too difficult," says María laughing. "I believe that good Mexican actresses do not mind being portrayed as older than their real age or anything like that. But in general, the public doesn't like to see their favorite screen actress looking like a toad."

"Pípiris-Nice"

In spite of her growing success with interviews of cultural luminaries, the editors of *Excélsior* never forgot that Elenita was primarily hired to do social columns, since the readers (in particular the women readers) of Section B had to be well informed about the

activities of the "*pípiris-nice*," or jet setters of the time. So her publication of dozens of brief notices devoted to weddings, first com-
munions, and other social events of the moment is not surprising.
Although such columns are mostly concerned with matters that are
by nature banal, the reporter always found a way of personalizing
them and giving them a special flavor. The following fragment is
taken from Elena's description of the "Elegant Wedding of María
de Lourdes Correa Arratia," appearing on Thursday, November 26,
1953. The notice is of special significance, because Elena met the
bride at Eden Hall and it was "Maú" herself who introduced Elena
to her uncle, Eduardo Correa, editor of the Sociales section of *Excélsior*. Later in life, when Elena was required to attend events such
as this, she would complain bitterly and sometimes threaten not to
go at all. So when the editors of *Excélsior* would send her to describe
the nuptials of Mexican regal families in several solemn (albeit
amusing) paragraphs, she would not sign the articles with her full
name but with one of the aforementioned elegant pseudonyms:

> As children, we have all played at getting married . . . "I'm the
> bride!" and one of us is covered in white, usually a sheet, a
> towel, or whatever . . .
>
> Those less fortunate were relegated to the cortege, or to be
> bridesmaids and groomsmen . . . The groom was always some
> macho who did not like to play the part . . . The wedding
> cortege would parade all around the house, under the pianos,
> jumping on the sofas, and such were the weddings of these
> lively tots who, after parading all over the place decide that
> tag is more fun, or that after a while it's time for supper, and
> "let's play something else . . . "
>
> "After a while" is a period in which children prophesied
> a black future for the women . . . since they do not allow
> "women" to participate in their games . . . They build huts to
> play at being explorers and paint signs that read: "No women
> allowed." Then some girls read, others pray, and still others
> declare: "Actually, I don't care!"
>
> But one day, a memorable day, it is no longer a game, it's
> something else . . . She descends from the automobile, a car

resembling a nest made of blossoms, followed by her long tulle train, wearing a wispy dress that extends behind her like a wake, slight as a breath or air . . . a sort of radiation of peace. It is pure happiness. No bitterness and no doubts . . . surrounded by a world of friends, relatives, photographers. She is the queen, yes, the queen . . . and it seems very natural that the triple crown of happiness, youth, and love should shine on her forehead.

We follow from beginning to end the triumphant nuptial mass (because nuptial masses have something triumphant about them). We hear the words of the Reverend Father Vértiz, and we toast their happiness, that of María de Lourdes and Rafael who are being married under the auspices of the church of San Jacinto, under the loving gaze of our Heavenly Creator, before the rejoicing of parents, siblings, and all those who have contributed to their happiness . . . All those eyes that today gaze upon them with special interest, with special sentiment, for today is their wedding day . . . and it is theirs, it all belongs to them, with all of its blue skies and its horizon open to happiness. But a wedding is a mixture of happiness and solemnity, the solemnity of the sacrament. God gives the matrimonial union a sanctification that is mysterious and sublime!

A Sudden Awakening

Little by little Elena left behind the naive little French girl of noble stock, with good manners and better intentions, as she met such memorable characters as Santa Claus, whom she encountered one day at a department store in Mexico City. In this interview, entitled "The Child Buzzards," Elena adopts the perspective of a young girl whose parents admit that Santa Claus doesn't exist and who suddenly is submerged in the cruel human reality she had never before imagined. This interviewee greatly surprised the incipient reporter, so much so that on Christmas Eve morning 1953, a few days after the interview was published, Elena presented her first socially conscious article reflecting on how artificial and unfair

Christmas is for the majority of Mexicans. The interview appeared
in *Excélsior* on Saturday, December 19, 1953, and its introduction,
similar to a description of local customs, was calculated to awaken
the spirit of Christmas in its readers, in order to expose a celebration ruled by monetary interests, always accompanied by an
overflowing cynicism. Both attitudes were completely alien to the
general state of merriment that the season had always awakened
for Elena in the past:

> Interview with Santa Claus. We had a premonition. It will be a
> sweet and sentimental interview (one of those that Luis Buñuel
> dislikes), full of Christmas decorations, with eyes sparkling
> and full of astonishment, along with a slight feeling of anxi-
> ety. We shall do something comforting and bourgeois, such as
> reclining on a plush sofa. We shall fill pages with crystalline
> voices, laughter, and childish hopes and desires, waiting by
> candlelight, chimneys, and reindeer. We shall hang stockings
> and shoes full of hopes. We shall include sleepless children
> and strange sounds in every corner of the house. We shall
> speak of the illusions reflected on Christmas ornaments, shin-
> ing and fragile as glass bubbles, of Christmas dinner, with tur-
> key and plum pudding. It will be a relaxed interview, nothing
> difficult, compact and heavily loaded with tranquility.

Yet, upon beginning her interview with Don Félix Samper
Cabello, the young reporter realizes that something is amiss, as
this robust gentleman reminds her more of Ebenezer Scrooge than
Saint Nicholas:

> "Don Félix, Santa Claus, why do you like to play the role
> of Santa?"
> Without waiting for an answer, we write: for the love of
> children? Out of solidarity with their dreams? To contribute
> to their happiness? But, oh! What horror! Here is what Don
> Felix answers:
> "Because they pay me very well. I make more here in twenty
> days than in three long months working elsewhere."

(What a materialistic man . . . But it is our fault. The question was not well constructed.)   ·

"And do you love the children?"

"During the twenty days my job lasts, I certainly do . . . "

(Oh my, this is going from bad to worse.)

"But the hopes of the children, Don Félix! They love you."

"They love me because they think I'm going to give them something. They come to me with the first spurts of egotism, the first 'I wants.' Sometimes they remind me of little pigs . . . "

Notwithstanding the sudden shock provoked by these unexpected responses, Elena soon recovers from the initial blow and continues the conversation, only to discover, to her horror, that this Santa Claus refers to his young admirers as "child buzzards." In an attempt to give Santa a taste of his own medicine, the reporter asks the unexpected but inevitable question:

"And so, what would you ask another Santa to bring you?"

"A small house where I could die alone but warm. You know, I have traveled a great deal. I have been rich and poor, a painter and a sculptor; I'm a university professor, and I have even taught nuns, for I teach several classes in a cloister. Currently, I'm a movie actor, but they do not call me to audition for twenty thousand reasons. And now I give Italian lessons. I tried to become a tenor because I have a lovely voice, but all I achieved was to dream a little in Italian."

Near the end of the interview, Santa allows Elena to ask for a wish, and Elena makes her last attempt to rescue the happy spirit of the season with an innocent plea:

"That you tell me that Christmas is beautiful, that humanity is not stupid, that children are not little pigs, that politics in Mexico . . . "

"As Dumas the younger says, 'We are born without teeth, without hair, and without illusions. We die the same way: without teeth, without hair, and without illusions . . . ' When I die, let them dress me as Santa Claus, and around my neck they will hang the sign that you want to see: 'Christmas is beautiful, children are not little pigs, and in Mexico politics are getting better . . .'"

Christmas in Mexico

The first article illustrating Elena's newfound social awareness does justice to the title of this chapter: "University of the Street." For the young writer received an important lesson in social, political, and human dissent from the mouth of that Santa Claus, so devastating in his denunciation of human stupidity and miserliness. After reflecting on the truths revealed by this mustachioed gentleman wearing a red velvet costume and ermine trimmings, Elena sits before her typewriter trying to put her experience into words. The first thing she discovers is her concern for the so-called street urchins, whom she dubs "star children." Thanks to her improbable mentor, she suddenly recognizes the "artificial sparkle" and the "commercial laughter" of Christmas. This landmark article appeared in the pages of *Excélsior* on Thursday, December 24, 1953, and is reproduced here in full:

CHRISTMAS IN POVERTY

"I truly don't know what to buy. Actually, s/he has everything . . ."
    "Some perfume, perhaps?"
    People loaded up with packages can't think of what else to buy, while some children, shivering in the cold, look at the elegant shop windows with astonishment. Christmas is for children! Adults have completely taken it over and leave only a bit of Santa Claus and other equally superficial sparkles to the children. But how can the poor understand Santa Claus? An enormous rubicund man full of satisfaction and bursting with power. The one who strolls the streets guffawing loudly. And the children have bad dreams of that laughter all night. Rich children are comforted by their parents, who reassure them with the promise of presents. But poor children get no reas-

surance from anybody that this laughter is really to promote business, which has nothing to do with the hearts of men.

So what about the Christmas spirit? What is the Christmas spirit anyway? Is it in the Dickens of old England? Scrooge? A Dickens full of miserable, pale, exceedingly unhappy children? Or is it perhaps the month for great charitable organizations? Parties that bubble with altruistic intentions, bridge parties, Christmas parties, in which everybody dances full of philanthropy for the benefit of lepers, for the tubercular, and for mothers in some free clinic. None of the aforementioned ever see these poverty-ridden souls, but each dance step, perhaps set to the rhythm of a mambo, each waltz step, each coquettish glance, all contribute to this anonymous Christmas. And there is irony in the relationship between the rich and the poor. As much irony as in the bullfights organized for the benefit of a Franciscan church. So much for Christmas charities!

But in reality charity is a personal act, it is a relationship established strictly between two people! A hand reaches out to another, which grasps it with warm affection. Charity goes much deeper, and is much harder to bear, because it is honest, it takes on another's troubles and contributes to their remedy directly and efficiently. It also includes the confession of one's own misery, living happily in the midst of so many.

As Saint-Exupéry says, "Charity is a contribution to man's recovery of his dignity as a man . . . " And at Christmas we must return to the children the dignity that we owe them as children . . .

So how can the children understand charity from the rich! They do not understand a satisfaction that is divided in half, which leaves the taste of a rather bitter fruit but is full of self-awareness.

They do not understand the gratitude the rich demand of them—those who give always demand acknowledgment. There are old ladies who put their trust in happiness and act compassionately: they teach others to "give thanks" and if they don't, they learn to call them "ungrateful" . . . All of this is as phony as Santa Claus himself, full of thunderous happiness, and as false as those Christmas tales that are the cheap and superficial comments about a truly profound celebration.

Mexican Christmas must once more be oriented to the heart of children and taught to find a new language intelligible to them, one that will bring them comfort and assistance with dignity. No country in the world has children such as those we see in Mexico's streets. Whole children . . . Star children . . . And again Saint-Exupéry speaks to us of the "beautiful human clay." . . . What is painful about a people is not their misery or their sadness, or that they let themselves be guided by a certain way of life. What is truly painful is to see life and grace murdered in the heart of a small child. Because in every man there lives a murdered artist.

Only the spirit, when it blows upon the clay, can create men. And it is at Christmas when the best spiritual wind blows . . . And it must especially reach the children. Thousands of children who wait, thousands of children who will grow up and must do so in greatness . . .

Let us celebrate Christmas with a new spirit, thinking of the children and forgetting the young people who dance rapidly, holding each other tightly, and the men and women who live in the world as if it were their dollhouse, sumptuously decorated with make-believe Christianity.

Literary Syncretisms

By 1954, less than one year after her first interview with the U.S. ambassador to Mexico, a personal style is evident—a trademark, so to speak—in Elena's interviews. A certain hybridism between reporting and formal interviews is a recipe she has profitably used throughout her career as a writer and journalist, to the degree that both genres begin to meld into a sort of literary syncretism, engendering articles that, instead of being limited to a paragraph of short biographical notes, display her personality and take over the whole interview. An example is the "interview" with the caretaker of the Hospicio Cabañas, a former orphanage in Guadalajara, in which Elena immerses herself wholly. At the same time she recognizes her marked difference from many of the people she meets on the street. Thus, Elena forces herself to bridge the enormous distance between the world of her formative years and the harsh reality in which the majority of her countrymen live, so faithfully captured and transported to walls and chapels by the great muralist José Clemente Orozco. She wanted so badly to experience the spectacle of the Conquest of Mexico, a scene that covers the walls of the Hospicio Cabañas, now a cultural center, that Elena invents a story about her friendship with the great painter, a friendship which never existed, since Orozco died in 1949 and they never met. But her uncle, Paco Iturbe, was the painter's benefactor for some time, and to this we owe the mural paintings that adorn the great staircase of the House of Tiles, which is now Sanborn's Department Store. Orozco also painted his patron's face in his famous mural of Miguel Hidalgo at the governor's palace in Guadalajara.

Apparently, her street lessons were very useful, and like the scheming rogue Lazarillo de Tormes or the Periquillo Sarniento, Elena, perhaps resembling more the Pícara Justina, has had to learn to live by her wits. Her quick thinking came in handy when she managed to gain admittance to the Hospicio Cabañas, even though it was closed for renovation.

Elena and her acquaintances do all they can not to show what they evidently are: rich Chilangos from Mexico City who, after a few cocktails at the Golf Club, decide to see the famous murals. Although at first the gatekeeper does not allow them entry, her attitude slowly seems to soften. Isn't it true that in Mexico "no" doesn't always mean no? As they enter the Tolsá Chapel, they face a somber world, and "they fall under the siege of Orozco's aggressive art," because there you have man as the "prisoner of his terrible inventions," in the midst of his "destructive technology."

Elena advises her readers to prepare themselves before entering, because they may "leave in a violent manner, perhaps in the way that the merchants had to leave the Temple." Although only a slight gesture to her readers, Elena's reaction to and interpretation of these images allows them to glimpse some of the harsher realities in Mexico's history and even aids in the subtle evangelization of its viewers, who are mainly "nice people" whose greatest dilemma may be not knowing what to give their sweetheart for Valentine's Day, whether perfume or a tie would be best. This piece, like all of Elena's work at this stage of her development as a journalist, appeared in the *Excélsior's* Sociales section on Friday January 8, 1954:

"No, you may not come in. Not even for a moment . . . It is Sunday, and besides, everything is under repair . . . You'd better go to Orozco's 'Museum Workshop.'"

And the caretaker of the Hospicio Cabañas obstinately picks up her knitting, as if to strengthen her refusal. It would seem she has realized that we still have in our eyes the remains of a frivolous spectacle: the Guadalajara Golf Club, with its formal landscape, its golf clubs and balls, its lines of cars, its trivial discussions, its lobster in mayonnaise, and its trees that are too well manicured.

"Only for a moment . . . We are going back to Mexico City right away, and we've never seen the frescoes of the Hospicio. Besides, we were friends of Orozco's . . . " (this is a blatant lie, but one must try by every possible means).

"All right, all right . . . What was Don José Clemente like?"

"Well, he wore glasses, was missing an arm, and he was a very good friend of Justino Fernández's. He never liked to talk about painting. His wife's name is Doña Margarita."

The caretaker smiles and seems to soften a bit more. She stops knitting and looks up at our anxious eyes. (We do our best not to think about the Golf Club.)

"Besides, Orozco himself said that all of his paintings belong to the people. He would have liked to have his paintings in all the public plazas . . . "

"Now, don't tell me you're so much a part of the people. I told you already, you'd better go to the 'Museum Workshop,' which is open and in service. I say this for your own good because the current state of the building would give you a bad impression now, with the scaffolding and loose bricks and all . . . "

"For just a split second, just for a glimpse . . . "

"Well, all right, only so that you won't have wasted your time coming in vain. But just for a minute . . . "

We run in. It's true, the building is under repair. But through a confusion of scaffolding, Orozco's painting transmits his violent reproach. Poverty and misery slap us in the face. It seems that Orozco strikes out at the whole world with a whiplash.

His brushstrokes are violent, dynamic, and decisive, they are like an enormous deletion of the conceited face of our placid bourgeoisie. We suddenly understand why Orozco is a difficult and disagreeable painter for so many good people. Nobody likes to be reminded to their face of their lies and omissions. Nobody likes to know that humanity is ugly, that there are jails and hospitals, and that a river of knives runs through the world. Concrete and steel threaten us from the walls with their somber structures. As we find ourselves under siege by Orozco's aggressive art, man is held prisoner of his terrible inventions and their destructive technology. Those who visit the Hospicio Cabañas must go well prepared and set their conscience in order. Otherwise, they may find themselves leaving violently, perhaps in the same manner as the merchants from the Temple.

We left the Hospicio feeling almost like robots. But it was like robots aware that they have a conscience capable of remorse. (Without wishing to, we recall all our friends, all those we left behind seeking their little white golf ball among the green grass, the ones who choose with great care the formula of salvation among their sets of 'puts,' and after the last hole is played, all go in at peace with themselves to eat pink-and-white lobster with mayonnaise . . .)

We discover another phase in the development of the young interviewer in a conversation with Juan Rulfo, published in *Excélsior* on January 10, 1954. Besides incorporating her own observations in the form of a chronicle, she persists in her surprising questions, sometimes so simple that they leave the interviewee speechless, especially in the case of Rulfo. "Wait a moment," says Rulfo, "I'm rather slow on the uptake, and you spring your questions at me so fast . . . " In her conversation, Elena gives evidence of her budding knowledge of Mexican culture, as she manages to weave together two threads and two media—literature and painting—into one strand. She learns much from this interview, especially regarding the value of testimony, a literary form which in time she will make her own. As is generally known, Rulfo was strongly influenced by the stories told by the elders who sat smoking tobacco and weaving their tales after a long day in the fields. Before invoking ghosts from his own childhood, Rulfo confesses that his literary masters were Proust, Joyce, and other consecrated writers who, if truth be told, had little to do with the fantastic reality of the Mexican countryside.

What is the secret of Rulfo's writings? Elena discovers it in an "anonymous and concrete" collective voice whose chorus Jesusa Palancares will join almost fifteen years later when she is immortalized in the pages of *Hasta no verte Jesús mío*. A voice filled with popular wisdom.

"The Mexican Woman: The Root and Flower of Mexico"

As we have seen throughout this chapter, another note added to the symphony of words that compose Elena Poniatowska's literary and journalistic work (if one can speak of them separately) is her growing concern and zeal to explore and define the role of women in Mexico's cultural world. We have already uncovered faithful testimonies of this interest in her early interviews, many of them with extraordinary women such as Gertrudis Duby, the jungle explorer, actress Dolores del Río, painter María Izquierdo, and Manuelita Reyes, Don Alfonso's wife. On one occasion, Elenita took advantage of her daily obligation to visit and take notes of social events to attend and report on a show at the Salón de la Plástica that was made up exclusively of paintings by women. The first sentence of her review is very timely, as it responds to an urgent question regarding the place women hold in the Mexican artistic world, a persistent question in the cultural circles of the time. Are they a transitory phenomenon, another clever display? It seems that the answer is a resounding NO. Nonetheless, in the list of attendees is found the poet Pita Amor in the category of "the greatest among the graces," an appellation of dubious virtue, according to Elena's parameters. The article appeared in *Excélsior* on April 10, 1953, with the byline Hèléne, Elena's true first name:

> Intellectual or artistic women always raise the same question: is it something that will pass, just another pleasant fad? Before them, before some of them, we feel overwhelmed or diminished by the evidence of their "sensibility."
>
> But in his brief words, Andrés Iduarte made clear the meaning of this show of Mexican painters and sculptors. There are only a few works, not an overwhelming number of paintings, and the public enjoyed this unusual show with a fresh spirit. The atmosphere was cordial, and it must be pointed out that there was an absence of the *poseur* tone habitually prevalent at similar events. We point out among the words of Andrés Iduarte the following:
>
> "In this show there presides a spirit of collaboration among different artists—in both meanings of the word different—because it comes from their purpose of achieving understanding and harmony among all those who cultivate and stimulate the fine arts. Women have always been the hardiest and purest in matters of building the Mexican family. Feminine resolution and fortitude, throughout our history and in our literature, have been taught to men, and there, thanks to one such woman [Sor Juana Inés de la Cruz], who during a great century lived in the center of its poetry. Without professional feminism, without malaise of any kind, without renouncing what was essential to them, Mexican women have been the roots and flowers of their country and have often produced our best fruits. This show is a consequence of the lessons in

skill, devotion, and heroism given to us by our women painters and sculptors . . . "

He concluded with simple graciousness, recognizing the
assistance of Carmen Marín de Barreda, director of the gallery,
and Doña María Izaguirre de Ruiz Cortínez, for her support
and consideration.

THE ARTISTS

Angelina Beloff is the negation of all artifice and perhaps the
artist with the greatest awareness of her work, radically unable
to appear remarkable in any manner, either in her person or
in her painting. Gloria Calero lives and paints with the pur-
est enthusiasm, with an almost childish grace, but her work
cannot be considered "fabricated." Her *Madonna with Child* is
a surprising view of that which charms and fascinates. María
Izquierdo, almost "embarrassed" in face of the compliments
she receives. Frida Kahlo, a new Frida, prolific and wise amidst
her "ghosts." Fanny Rabel, with the poetry of an astonished
little girl in *The Friend Tree*. Cordelia Urueta, atmospheric in
her "dance." And finally, all of them showing their own colors
in this warm feast of painting. We do not wish to omit names.
We lack space and some of our words are simply left out.

THE PUBLIC

Paulette A. de Poniatowski: "All those attending have intelligent expressions, but they do not look at the paintings." Only
after half an hour could the paintings be seen: before this they
were submerged in what turned out to be a large crowd. Among
those present were Magda M. de Carvajal, wife of the secretary of the interior; Amalia de Ceniceros, wife of the secretary
of education; and Margarita Rodríguez, private secretary of
Doña María Izaguirre de Ruiz Cortines, representing the first
lady. Jorge Enciso, Pilar Arce de Bernal, Lupe Marín, Efrén
del Pozo, Dr. Aurea Procell, Angélica Arenal, José Chávez
Morado and Olga Costa, Alice Rahon, David Alfaro Siqueiros,

Mariana Frenk and the art critic Paul Westheim; Andrés and Alfa Henestrosa, Margarita Urueta de Castro Valle, Mélida de la Selva de Warren, Michelle de Nefero, Margarita Nelken (taking notes), Jorge Juan Crespo de la Serna and his wife, and Doña Rosario Sansores, Antonio Rodríguez, José Iturriaga, Dr. Francisco Marín and wife, Federico Cantú, Germán Cueto, José Moreno Villa, Helia d'Acosta, the duke of Otranto and his wife, Ursel Bernarth (photographer), María M. de Orozco Romero, and Adriana Garibay.

We consider:
The most absent-minded: Rafael Bernal
The most reticent: Juan Soriano
The greatest among the graces: Pita Amor
The most beautiful: Nadia de Haro Oliva
The best hairstyle: Lola Álvarez Bravo
The saddest: Raúl Anguiano
The most backward: Octavio Barreda
The most loyal to all: Fito Best Maugard

3 "Elenita": The Young Writer

From *Excélsior* to *Novedades*

Nearly two years after entering the world of journalism, having contributed an article, interview, or column per day to section B of *Excélsior*, Elena accepted the job offered to her by the editor-in-chief of *Novedades*, the other important Mexico City daily and *Excélsior*'s major competitor:

> I stayed at *Excélsior* for only one year, Elena recalls, because one day my mother ran into the editor-in-chief of *Novedades*, Don Alejandro Quijano. They were friends, as both had worked together for the Red Cross.
>
> Quijano told my mother: "I really like how your daughter writes! Why don't you ask her to come to work for us? How much is she making at *Excélsior*?"
>
> My mother answered that I was being paid thirty pesos per interview, and he replied that he would pay me eighty. But that was not the reason I went to work at *Novedades*. I was happy at *Excélsior*, but there was a great rivalry between Bambi (Ana Cecilia Treviño) and myself. Besides writing social columns, Bambi also knew how to lay out a newspaper, and every time she took over the Sociales section she would throw my articles out the window.
>
> Once, when I told our boss, Eduardo Correa, that I didn't think this was fair, he answered: "One day I have brown eyes crying, and the next day I have blue eyes crying. What can I possibly do about it?"

Elena with Fernando Benítez in the offices of *Novedades*, 1956 or 1957.

So I went to *Novedades*, where I'm still working to this day [i.e., 1999]. When Rodrigo del Llano, the editor-in-chief of *Excélsior*, heard that I had left, he asked to see me, saying, "How could you leave without letting me know?"

I went to work at *Novedades* every day. At that time it was customary to write the articles for the Sociales section from telephone interviews: "How were the bridesmaids dressed? Was the bride's dress designed by Dior or by Manuel Méndez?" I never did it this way because it seemed dishonest, and out of curiosity I would attend the weddings, showers, and fashion shows. In retrospect, I think that I was going kind of crazy with so much work. Mane, my eldest son, used to accompany me everywhere. My first years as a reporter were splendid training but I didn't know in the least what I wanted to do. I wanted to write a novel, but I was already riding that merry-go-round of daily activity as a journalist, and I could never find the time to sit down and do my own work.

An Astonishing Book

Nonetheless, with the publication of *Lilus Kikus* in 1954, Elena began what would in time become an enormous literary output of
more than thirty works, some of which have already become clas-
sics of twentieth-century Mexican literature. *Lilus Kikus* was Elena
Poniatowska's first true published literary work since her essay
"On Nothing," which appeared in English in *The Current Literary
Coin* magazine while she was still a student at the Convent of the
Sacred Heart. As to the protagonist's enigmatic name, Elena explains that "it was an invention, because there was a childish riddle
that went something like 'Matakikus' but I really don't remember
the rest of it."

According to her mother, in the pages of her first book Elena
included one or two of her friends and she also appears as a
character, although only indirectly: "There is a bit of autobiography toward the end of *Lilus Kikus*, but not much. *Lilus Kikus*
was an apprenticeship. She had already taken lessons in order
to improve her written Spanish, because at school she had only
studied English."

For a first book, *Lilus Kikus* sold well and got good reviews, although the Fondo de Cultura Económica printed only five hundred
copies for the first edition. In his review, Ermilo Abreu Gómez,
the foremost authority on the poetry of Mexico's great baroque
poet Sor Juana Inés de la Cruz and an eminent critic of twentieth-
century Mexican literature, declared: "This is an astonishing book. No
one writes this way in Mexico today. Elena Poniatowska, like very
few current writers, has what is called a 'feeling for language.'" In
an allusion to the precocious childhood of de la Cruz, Abreu Gómez ended his review with an implicit comparison between Elena
and the Hieronymite nun, who also surprised her superiors with a
great literary talent at a very early age: "I can hardly comprehend
how someone so young has managed to achieve such mastery in
her writing style," the author of *Juana de Asbaje* concluded.

Elena, although proud of her first attempt at literary creation,
admits that the short novel "was very successful because they
printed five hundred copies." She also recalls Emmanuel Carballo

saying that what he liked best was that her text wasn't the least bit influenced by Juan José Arreola. According to Elena, "Arreola launched the Los Presentes series and taught me to avoid the present perfect tense."

One of the first to review her book was Carlos Fuentes, author of *Los días enmascarados* (The Masked Days), also published in the Los Presentes series. The title of his review, "Elena Poniatowska, Lilus Kikus," published in dialogue form in the *Revista de la Universidad de México* in 1954, alludes to the curious—and tacit—relationship between Elena the writer and the little girl Lilus Kikus, who is both an alter ego and pseudonym:

"Listen, have you read *Lilus Kikus?*"

"Yes, sir, I wrote it."

"How come? Are you . . . ?"

"Yes, I'm Lilus Kikus. Funny, isn't it?"

"Sit down, young Lilus, let's chat . . . "

"I can't, sir. On Saturdays it's my turn to pray."

"Look, I've wanted to talk with you for a long time. The other day I was discussing your book with some people. In particular, we were wondering about its influences. You know that looking for a book's inspiration is quite a profession. There are critics who spend their lives in anguish, trying to determine the influence of Kafka and Borges on Mexican writers, and when they manage to get as far as Branch Cabell and his famous Jurgen, it would seem that Empedocles had once more jumped into the crater of Etna."

"In the convent we were taught a small verse that goes like this: Great Empedocles, that ardent soul, / leapt into Etna, and was roasted whole . . . "

"Don't interrupt me, Lilus Kikus . . . I was telling you that, in seeking its influences, we were able to find two: one, *The Young Visiters*, by Daisy Ashford . . . "

"What is that?"

"A novel written by a nine-year-old girl. Sir James Barrie encouraged Daisy to publish it when she was a woman of thirty. Some said that the piece had actually been written by

Elena at her
typewriter,
1956 or 1957.

Barrie himself. But anyway, what's important is that *The Young Visiters* reveals the same natural astonishment, that perverse ingenuousness of *Lilus Kikus*. If in Daisy Ashford's work—as Barrie declared—having breakfast in bed is raised for the first time ever to the level of a great literary and human occurrence, in Elena Poniatowska's book the terrible problem of the ownership rights over lizards comes to life."

"But the gentleman in apartment 4 . . ."

"Let me continue. The other would be *Tiko* by Consuelo Pani. Tiko is a chow chow. Don Alfonso Reyes says that Tiko 'trots among a cubist display of scenes and landscapes . . . as if he were playing with his kaleidoscope in the middle of everything, the lakes and the mountains' . . . This, of course, is in reference to the lack of a panoramic illusion of space amongst things. But isn't there a bit of the same in *Lilus Kikus?* Reality is seen sort of sideways, as if from an obelisk in the air or under the sparse foliage among the weeds. Each second that passes, the world acquires an absolute form; it is a gentleman who is 'uneasy for just having fallen asleep'; 'success by the seaside,' young Jesus among the drunkards in Canaan, the rose-colored lily of the Lamb. Fantasy wears ribbons and braids and has scraped knees. The universe of Lilus Kikus is measured by a small sprig of rosemary sewn into one's underpants.

"Do you think this is right?"

"It seems to me that the critics are blockheads. Besides, my real influences are not those, they are others."

"Which ones?"

"The witches, sir . . . "

"Oh my, Lilus Kikus is still ignorant of many things. All little girls like you speak in the plural. You must know—soon you will recognize the value of scientific proof—that in the whole world there is but one witch. Norman Matson has written a definitive book on the subject, *Fletcher's Magic.* There he proves that only one witch exists, because all the rest committed suicide in the eighteenth century. It seems that Newton made them lose all their optimism."

"And how did that happen?"

"Well, you see . . . "

Another reviewer of Elena's first book was Emmanuel Carballo, a respected critic and author of many essays on Mexican literature, whose review appeared in the pages of *México en la Cultura,* the cultural supplement of *Novedades,* on November 7, 1954. It is the first of many essays Carballo dedicated to Elena's literary work; over the years he has devoted himself to expressing his opinions, not always positive, regarding nearly all of Elena's oeuvre. For Carballo, one of the most interesting aspects of *Lilus Kikus* is precisely its literary pedigree, that the book seems to cross genres:

Lilus Kikus strongly resists being pigeonholed in the categories usually employed by literary critics. Strictly speaking, it is not a short story, nor is it a novel. Unlike a short story, it lacks a link to an anecdote; to be a novel, it would have to build up a plot, to develop its characters. The common thread that links the twelve short and lovely chapters is this little girl, apparently an ingénue, this astonished girl for whom life may be understood through hieroglyphs, signs, symbols. Lilus Kikus enlivens with her suggestive presence the minute incidents that happen to her, and offers in passing a lesson for mid-twentieth-century writers who seek exceptional topics: literature is not produced only through good intentions and transcendent problems, but rather is founded on an adequate treatment of scenes, characters, and actions. Daily events treated as they are in this book become marvels . . . *Lilus Kikus* is a book that no writer approaching literature for the first time would be embarrassed to write. It is something more than that. It is a sparkling work, with a structure that, in its own way, is perfect . . .

Although Carballo hits the mark with respect to the book's structure, it is the prophetic article published by Artemio Garfias under the ominous title "Lilus Kikus in Danger and without Salvation" that best foretells the impact that Elena's work would have upon the Mexican literary community during the second half of the twentieth century. Although the brief notice is signed only with the initials A. G., the full name of the mysterious critic appears jotted down in Elena's own hand, albeit somewhat blurred, in one of her many books of newspaper clippings. Garfias underlines the young writer's talent for observation, a talent that will serve her well throughout her literary career; her descriptions, reflections, and analysis of Mexican reality are the elements that, years later, will make her worthy of journalistic and literary fame grounded in her insatiable curiosity regarding what goes on in the streets, in the markets, in the poorest neighborhoods; the reality of a Mexico built of adobe and maguey:

Lilus Kikus, newly appeared before the world of literature, is in certain danger of becoming the great writer her book heralds or, to the contrary, if other circumstances prevail, turning into the inefficient housewife of a family whose best memories will remain sealed in the letters that she will have written to two or three intelligent friends . . . If the promise of the writer comes to pass, as soon as this child matures, our society, or certain parts of it, will achieve the glory of being happily destroyed and left with its flesh and bones exposed. Because this child sees all, what is said and what is silenced, her maturity will consist precisely, if not in telling all, in analyzing what she omits . . .

The news is bad, very bad, for our society; it is very good, on the other hand, for Mexico. It is not often that a first book in Mexico, or in any other country, carries with it the certainty that its author is a great writer.

Lilus Kikus has launched her challenge, and she has done so with an outsized audacity. Although it would be splendid for some cliques in today's Mexico, it would be a misfortune for the country if within ten or twenty years, and those to follow, these delicious initial fruits do not have, over time, any more impact than that of banal gossipy epistle.

In 1967, nearly fifteen years after the first edition of *Lilus Kikus* was published in the Los Presentes series, Juan Rulfo, the author of *Pedro Páramo*, wrote back cover copy for a corrected and expanded second edition entitled *The Stories of Lilus Kikus*, published by the University of Veracruz. As his text appears only in this limited edition, I have reproduced it here in full. Although they are the only thoughts that this reticent author has recorded about Elena Poniatowska's writing, they anoint her and welcome her into the great abode of Mexican literature:

Many years ago, perhaps twenty, perhaps a few more, there appeared a book of dreams, the tender dreams of a little girl called Lilus Kikus for whom life took shape too fast. The only way Lilus knew how to put the world in order was merely to keep still and sit on the spiral staircase of her imagination, where the most astounding things would take place, while with her eyes she gazed at the vanishing dew and a cat chasing its tail or the smile of spring.

Then, she suddenly felt that the lime trees were ill and that only by giving them injections of black coffee with sugar could their bitterness be assuaged.

But Lilus was also devilishly restless: she ran to ask a philosopher if he was the owner of the lizards that sunned themselves outside the window.

She also digressed about how to make a nest for God in her soul without committing adultery, and she even questioned her maid from Ocotlán about the size and flavor of the kisses that she gave her boyfriend.

Everything in this book is magical, and full of waves that wash in from the sea, and love akin to the light found only in the eyes of children.

The "Enfant Terrible" in Europe

After the success of *Lilus Kikus*, Elena won the French Tourism Prize, which paid for a trip to Paris, and upon her arrival she began to interview important members of the French cultural and artistic world. On Tuesday, July 17, 1956, in the same Sociales section of *Excélsior* for which she formerly wrote, a feature appeared about Elena—already a recognized member of the Mexican social and cultural world—one of the first of an endless series of interviews and profiles that continues being published to this day. In this biographical sketch, the anonymous author christens Elena an *enfant terrible* because with her knowledge of French, she delves into the innermost thoughts of her Parisian subjects. One should not forget, however, that her surname carried quite a bit of weight in postwar France, as her relatives had occupied important positions within the French government from the time of Napoleon Bonaparte, when Prince Josef Ciolek Poniatowski was named marshal of France:

This *enfant terrible*, the blonde and intelligent Helena Poniatowska, continues to live in Paris . . . Here choruses of broken hearts decry her absence . . . Helena Poniatowska has not decided to return to Mexico yet; the *enfant terrible* has devoted herself to interviewing all the notable figures in current French literary and artistic circles . . . She spoke at length with Jules Romains who, as you may recall, lived among us during the war . . . The young Poniatowska has also interviewed Jean Cocteau, who day after day manifests his incredible genius and versatility . . . Later Helena will go to Italy . . . Meanwhile, she lives with her uncle, Prince Michel Poniatowski.

Elena remembers only a portion of those figures she interviewed in this period, interviews she often obtained thanks to her grandfather's social connections:

When I was in Paris I interviewed the celebrities of the period: Jean Marais, Jean Louis Barrault, Pierre Fresnay, the husband of actress and singer Yvonne Printemps, Jules Supervielle, Françoise Sagan, and Grace Kelly, who was already married to Prince Rainier of Monaco. My grandfather, André Poniatowski, was very well known and consequently I was able to obtain many interviews thanks to him. Every day I would try to find Simone Signoret, Yves Montand, Germaine de Beaumont, Princess Bibesco, Ionesco, and Rubinstein. I worked very hard and lived in the home of my uncle André Poniatowski, my father's brother. I sent my articles to Mexico, to *Novedades*. I interviewed Abbé Pierre, a socialist priest who was one of the founders of the proletarian priests. I also interviewed a great scientist, Louis de Broglie. He was the French Einstein. He didn't have much time to waste with a girl who knew nothing about science, or anything else for that matter. However, after the interview at the Collège de France he invited me to lunch; he was very kind to me and he treated me very well. I also interviewed François Mauriac, with whom I failed horribly, because I had not bothered to read his books. Henri de Montherland refused to give me an interview because I arrived five minutes late. I did many interviews, and I worked like a madwoman. But the most important event at that time of my life was the birth of Mane. My eldest son was born in Rome on July 7, 1955. I returned to Mexico with him, wanting to write a novel, but in order to earn a living I did thousands of interviews for *Novedades*.

Drawing of Elena, the
"enfant terrible," by
Alberto Beltrán, 1956.

Mother and Writer

In 1957, Elena received a fellowship for young writers from the Centro Mexicano de Escritores (Mexican Center of Writers), founded by the American novelist Margaret Shedd. Elena recalls that because of this fellowship she was able to work with such aspiring young writers as Héctor Azar, Emma Dolujanoff, Juan García Ponce, Carmen Rosenzweig, and Emilio Uranga. "I believe I started two or three novels," she recalls, "but the critiques were terrible, devastating."

The original proposal that Elena sent to the selection committee of the Centro Mexicano de Escritores was recently published in a useful compilation entitled *Los Becarios del Centro Mexicano de Escritores (1952–1997)* (Fellows of the Mexican Center of Writers), edited by Martha Domínguez Cuevas. Elena proposed to write

a novel composed of twelve chapters written in the third person. I seek only to reflect the confusion of a young girl, her mistaken idea of life, her position within the society she is immersed in, and at no time have I considered falling into movie-like descriptions. I believe that the only way of evoking a caress is through the spirit and, finally, the only sensuality I find worthy is that which leaves us enveloped in our own soul, for it is then that the soul encloses our body like the skin of a grape compresses its pulp. More than the description of a romance, I want this novel to consist of the effects on the spirits of those participating in it.

Three-Penny Literature?

During the same productive year of 1957, one of the first interviews of Elena was published. Conducted by Lya Kostakowsky, wife of writer and art critic Luis Cardoza y Aragón, this lengthy dialogue, "The Interviewer Interviewed, or Payback Is Certain," was published in *México en la Cultura*, the cultural supplement of *Novedades*, on May 27 of that year. The interview is particularly interesting because it provides a glimpse into Elena's thoughts, projects, opinions, and tastes at a decisive moment of her life. Throughout the extensive interview, what stands out the most is her growing zeal to explore and document what happens in everyday Mexico: the misery in which many of its inhabitants live, and their everyday activities and diversions. This is precisely the world that she discovered through an improbable Santa Claus and in a short time would make her own through the publication of her chronicle of daily life in Mexico City entitled *Todo empezó el domingo* (It All Started on Sunday), in 1963:

> Mexico's most brilliant young journalist is an object of curiosity for many people, especially for our readers in the provinces. This is because in Mexico City, after all, we all know each other. In the Yucatán a gentleman assured me with utmost seriousness that Elena Poniatowska was an elderly lady who pretended to be an ingénue. In Guadalajara, another woman assured me that Elena Poniatowska was the pseudonym of an older, mustachioed writer, who had fun making his fellow citizens rant and rave. But here is Elena in person: she is petite, with light-colored and innocent eyes, a small nose, and a slightly open mouth showing some very white teeth. Blonde, vivacious. Age, 24 years (authorized information).
>
> "Elena, all Mexico wants to know who you are, and how

that terrifying young woman of journalism with French esprit and Mexican malice has managed to converse with all the celebrities in art, science, and banking. In your interviews, you make one think of those precious angels painted by Chucho Reyes, who ride a witch's broom and have innocent eyes and a keen, quick wit."

"Had I known this, I would have gone to a beauty parlor first! Does my hair look terrible?"

"No. Besides, I'm not taking any photographs of you . . . Tell me, do you consider the work of Mexican women in literature and journalism important?"

"Why don't you let me write my answer out for you? This matter sounds too formal . . . "

"No! I'm the one doing the interview."

"All right. Women hardly ever appeal to the routes of reason. But through their own intuition they may capture the very essence of things and hit the mark . . . Look, Lya, we do hit the mark and we often break the piñata of truth without even realizing it . . . I believe that it is necessary to write books about women with tenderness and a sense of humor. Something like Kathryn Mansfield. But women generally are not intelligent, they are intuitive. They are the vessel of men and of life."

"Are you satisfied with your books?"

"No. *Lilus Kikus* is a diary of my impressions in the convent where I was educated. *Melés y Teléo* was written in two months and I finished it when the first part was already at the printer's. In the beginning it was a sketch about intellectuals who became deformed as they went from gag to gag and from quotation to quotation. I believe it is a good example of automatic writing, and through it I learned that I mustn't write hurriedly, willy-nilly."

"What would you like to write?"

"Well, a good book, whatever that might be, but good. I want to have the courage one day to take whatever comes to my mind to its last possible point of perfection and not go out on the tangent of charm and ridicule."

Elena in profile,
sketch by
Alberto Beltrán,
1957.

"Who are your favorite writers?"

"Rilke, Saint-Exupéry, Mansfield. One of my favorite books is the *Diary of Marie Bakirtcheff*, who died of tuberculosis. It must be nice to die of tuberculosis surrounded by camellias!"

"And among Mexican authors?" (To this question she always answered that it was Alfonso Reyes, with his "bibliophilia.")

"To tell the truth, I have read little by him: 'Amapolita morada' (Little Purple Poppy), 'Visión de Anáhuac' (A Vision of the Anahuac), 'Homero en Cuernavaca' (Homer in Cuernavaca). But one night I heard him speak at the Fondo de Cultura Económica publishing house, the time he gave his testimony in favor of 'Los Cachorros' (a group of young writers) and delivered to them the legacy of his literary vocation. The room filled with murmurs that threatened to turn into growls or roars, and whenever I see him I want to run up and hug him, as if I were his little nanny. But I haven't read Dostoyevsky or Stendhal, or Whitman! Mamma used to give my sister and me a small green book on each birthday (no, not only that) which belonged to a collection of 'green education.' They were *The Iliad*, *The Odyssey*, and *Don Quixote*, in children's versions. There were more color illustrations than anything else, and the text was reduced to the bare minimum. I remember that the illustrations had captions such as 'Ulysses' boat breaks down . . . ' or 'Orpheus chases Eurydice . . . ' Perhaps this was a mistake, because I have never read *Don Quixote* except in the children's edition. And I may say the same for *The Iliad* and *The Odyssey* . . . But our juvenile minds remained haunted by sirens, lyres, statues that were more alive than the living, tritons, and seahorses, Ulysses and his battles, Jupiter who turned into a swan to make love to Leda and transformed himself into a white bull to rape Europa.

"With regard to Mexican authors, what happens is that I cannot separate the person from the work, and I love the isolated phrases taken from their books. Like this one by Andrés Henestrosa: 'and I am sure that she cried all the tears that she held back before me. I am sure because I feel anchored, just like a small boat in a river of tears.' But why don't you let me write all this down for you? Right now I don't remember anything."

"I don't want you to write it down, because then there would be no point. You would tell me that your favorite authors are Dostoyevsky, Whitman, and Simone de Beauvoir. By the way, what do you think of Simone's books?"

"Simone de Beauvoir seems to me the most talented woman of our day—after Simone Weil passed away, of course. I refer, naturally, to her great book on women. Nobody like her has looked so deeply into the female consciousness, their biology, and their soul. Don't you think that in Mexico some woman should write a sincere and simple book; for example, the story of a man confronted by a woman?"

"I don't know, Elena. I am not the one being interviewed. Tell me about your interviews."

"The funny thing about my interviews is that they revolve

around saying silly things or making my poor victims say them. It may be that perhaps I abuse the strategy of posing idiotic questions, but I can assure you that asking dumb questions is the best means of acquiring knowledge. Do you know what that wise man de Broglie answered when I asked him what his favorite flower was? He described the Andromeda Nebula, which goes through sidereal space like a rose with drooping petals, and he also spoke to me about the twelve infinitesimal petals that surround the magnetic rose that opens up at the center of matter. I believe that all women consider art and literature and even science as a sort of makeup that makes us more interesting, but that doesn't go deeper than the skin. I have even heard it said that spirituality is the best beauty cream in existence. But in any case, the woman is not at fault, for her true drama is that of being a woman under observation. She is scrutinized not because she is ugly or beautiful, charming or repulsive, but simply because she is a woman. My real problem, deep down, is that I feel like an actress whom people want to continue watching in her eternal roles of ingénue and of the cute young girl with extroverted tendencies. I would like to be a real writer and not get mired down in 'liluskikusism,' for example, wondering about a giraffe that was very sad because she did not know to what point she should pull her décolleté up or down . . . The only problem is that fighting against this comes very hard to me . . . I am much more interested in reading in the newspaper of April 13 (for example in *Novedades*) that a little African girl bewitched her classmates so that they all disappeared mysteriously from the classroom and were found up in the trees, sitting upon the weakest branches or hanging from small ones that normally would not hold even the weight of a bird . . . I prefer that to anything else, even to the Constitution and the Clayton-Bulwer Treaty."

"And finally, what would you have liked to do if you had not gone into literature and journalism?"

"Once my Aunt Carito told me, 'Little girl, I will let you write novels, but not live them.' And she was right. For example, I can think up thousands of answers to your question: 'I would like to have been one of those women who make strawberry tartlets for the spirit and succulent roasts for bodily hunger. I would like to plant melancholic daisies and pull their petals off under the moonlight. I would like to go to war, even as a mere soldier, under the orders of Captain Jean Poniatowski, who was awarded eight medals; finally, I would like to shepherd those clouds that look like sheep. I would like to take my first communion all over again, fall asleep and never wake up . . . ' But deep down, none of the above is true except the part about the first communion. I would like to look at life through other eyes, to see things—streets, barrios, gardens, faces—not as I see them, but as they truly are. To have my eyes show me a door and then say, 'Look at that door. It is thus, made of wood, with nails, heavy, but moreover, it has this and that which one cannot see. Of course, I can imagine thousands of things about the door. That there is a witch behind it, calling the spirits to join her, or that the singer María Victoria is behind it trying on a dress which is very difficult to get into, that a little blond boy with sad eyes is going to open it and slowly emerge, that a woman is knitting a sweater with only one sleeve that is really, really long . . . ' But, you see, I can only think up cheap little bits of literature worth only three for a penny, while those eyes could create a new world, totally magical and scintillating; not necessarily literary, but real, imbued with the poetry of real life.

"What else do you want me to tell you, Lya? I would like never to die, and I am jealous of the children not yet born who will be in good shape in the year 2000 and go to the moon, marry Martian women, and have children who will be able to live at the bottom of the sea, which they say is very healthy for small children, because the water at great depths is an exact equivalent of physiological serum. And besides, there they would have so many things to play with: seashells, submerged stars, sea horses, coral bouquets, snails, harmless crabs, and domesticated turtles. On the other hand, I feel that I have an enormous advantage over those who have already lived, and I do not understand those individuals who would have liked to spend their youth at the mellifluous court of one of the various King Louises, illuminated by enormous crystal chandeliers and accompanied by false, bewigged, and rather untidy courtesans. I would also like my children not to be men and women of letters, but to be devoted to science, astronomers or biologists, and to spend hours gazing at something through a microscope. I will always remember Louis de Broglie's face (an unpleasant man and a great interviewee whom I frequently mention) when I asked him about his favorite authors: 'Literature? But, young lady, I have no time for such things.' Simone de Beauvoir says (and if she didn't say it, I say it myself), that because writers do not live a real life, they devote themselves to creating one out of lies. This greatly impresses me. And what if literature turned out to be useless? Writers have a great tendency to feel different from the rest of the world. Women with intellectual aspirations also like to feel 'misunderstood.' But in all sincerity, I am like everyone else, even though each person may be in a certain way different, unique, and irreplaceable. I am trying to say that I am normal, and that is why I believe that I can say things that everyone can understand. Lya! How difficult and how rare it is to define oneself, to speak of oneself. Sincerity may make one insolent, and it nearly always indicates a confession in more or less bad taste. I am saying very personal things, and perhaps it is not a good idea to say them. I believe that the books which are valuable are true and sincere; that is why I do not understand much (of course not, because I have not studied them) of surrealism and the other *isms*, although I know that there is as much truth in fantasy literature as there is in realistic literature. Have you, for example, read *Josephine the Singer of the Mouse Folk?* But there are other things that concern me besides literature, and I would like them to become much more important than literature.

"Once I told my mother that I wanted to help her with the crooked old ladies (crooked due not to wickedness but illness), with the drunkards, the children that don't eat, live, or anything. But she told me, 'No, not yet. Do your own things, your journalism, and the rest of your nonsense. Do what you

Elena strapless.

have in front of you right now.' And I believe that was good
advice. We are able to do whatever we please, but at some
point in our lives we will realize that the misery of others
weighs on our shoulders, and we will have to do something
to remedy it, even to a minute degree, in order not to feel too
much guilt. I don't believe that misery is a problem that only
political parties, communism, or world organizations should
face. I believe that it is a problem of personal conscience that
each human being must solve. Men depend strictly upon one
another, directly on one another, and the immense organizations, which are absolutely necessary from the practical point
of view, stifle those who benefit from them because there is
no human or personal contact between he who gives and he
who receives, between the abstraction which is the beneficent
institution and those human beings in need. I do not believe
that it is a matter of having to take money away from the rich,
but rather of making each one feel that his or her wealth is
intolerable, to make them feel ashamed of the mere insolence

of their Cadillac before those miserable children they pass on the streets . . . But, Lya, I talk too much. What else can I tell you about myself?

"My sister, Kitzia, and I have always had more imagination than common sense. Every night we would take turns peeking under the bed because we believed that there was a thief hiding under there. We would invent ghosts; we would see faces outside the window, and elves that jumped on us at night. We believed miraculous events were about to occur which, naturally, I now know cannot happen. I have always expected everything to come from the outside: that all of life's gifts will fall into my hands, that suddenly an angel or a fairy will appear, or an archangel, or a supernatural event that will solve my problems and bring me joy. In the morning when I get up, I think, 'This is a special day, because thousands of wonderful things are going to happen. I will wear my alpaca skirt and my fancy blouse.' And I leave my house gleefully, full of curiosity, and of course, nothing out of the ordinary happens, but away I go, skipping and jumping through the streets, entering the bookstores, looking at the clothes in the shops, chatting with the salespeople, because today is a lucky day. Now, Lya, in all modesty, I don't know if I should tell you this, but it's the truth:

"My interest in journalism was probably born out of an inferiority complex. In my family everybody is tall except for my great-grandmother, who died before I was born. My parents became concerned when my younger sister began to grow taller than I did, and they gave me shots and pills, syrups, and cod-liver oil, until x-rays (of my ankles and wrists) showed that my bones had already set and that I would never become any taller. To console us, the doctor said something along the lines of 'good things come in small packages,' but that very day I decided to become somebody worthwhile. I did this exclusively for my dad, no doubt because he is the tallest in the house and is proud of it. I know that I still haven't done anything worthwhile, that I continue to be deficient at everything, but at least I love my work, I like to write, I want to learn, to read (yes, yes, Dostoyevsky, Stendhal, and Whitman) and to truly make a difference, as some women have done . . ."

A "Dyed in the Wool" Journalist

Elena was fascinated by more than the comings and goings of the most famous Mexican and international intellectuals. In order to more fully develop one of her many talents, that of essayist, she joined a group of contemporary writers led by Carlos Fuentes. Some of these writers would soon became Mexico's most brilliant literary stars, while others disappeared entirely from the literary map. In one of the first articles she dedicated to one of her colleagues, Elena introduces these writers, many of them fellows at the Centro Mexicano de Escritores. According to her, among all the writing fellows, Carlos Fuentes is the most extraordinary. In fact, her review of the sixth issue of the *Revista Mexicana de Literatura* reads almost like a profile of Fuentes and his short story "Chac Mool." Elena describes the writer with elaborate and imaginative similes that take her review beyond an academic or journalistic essay to become a work of fiction, full of images and conceits that demonstrate not only the young Fuentes' creative powers, but those of the talented reporter as well. Although Elena authored one of the stories in this issue, she does not comment upon it at all, and in keeping with her well-known modesty only mentions herself in the third person. Her review, entitled "Young Mexican Literature," appeared in *Novedades* on September 2, 1956, and constitutes her first leap into this area of journalism, until then a terrain dominated by men, with few exceptions:

> Number 6 of the *Revista Mexicana de Literatura* has just appeared, skillfully edited by two solid national literary figures, Emmanuel Carballo and Carlos Fuentes. This issue has been devoted to, that is, has filled all its pages with some youthful members of contemporary Mexican literature, writers ranging in age from twenty to thirty-five.
>
> No doubt, the most important short story in the *Revista Mexicana de Literatura* is that of Carlos Fuentes. Carlos writes gruesome

Fernando Benítez, Carlos Fuentes, Ricardo Vigón, Roberto Fernández Retamar, Severo Sarduy, and Fayad Jamis with Elena in Havana, July 30, 1959.

novels. But as often happens with him, he mistakes blood for ketchup, and the hearts of his people beat with rubber arteries, pumped from the laboratory of a wicked alchemist. Careful, wet paint! Carlos Fuentes' characters always seem to be recently painted, and if we touch them our hand gets stained with their visceral coating. Sometimes, Carlos Fuentes walks down Paseo de la Reforma with a bucket full of entrails—hearts, livers, and kidneys—that he has taken from passersby; he then takes them home and puts in the refrigerator, to employ this morbid and cubist chopped flesh little by little in his novels and stories. He collects false teeth, flaccid lips, and cheeks like a DuPont sponge, and with them he invents and combines smiles and grimaces, all of which he himself wears sometimes to play at making the most devilish imitations.

Carlos Fuentes is the only man carrying a full measure of intelligence in his head, bigger than a distillery, more complicated than a factory that makes threads and knit goods, speedier and noisier than a three-level printing press, surrounded

by a squadron of linotypes. Due to all of the above, whatever Carlos Fuentes does in life and in literature will always be
important and necessary, we would almost say indispensable,
although now he writes texts whose final purpose is *épater les
bourgeois*, that is, to dazzle the bourgeois.

The story by Emilio Carballido is close behind Carlos', not
because it is similar to it, but because both are high-quality literature. Carballido, however—despite being an excellent novelist and an even better playwright—lacks forcefulness. Jorge
López Páez comes close to being a landscape artist and trans-
ports us to Acapulco with his transitory *gringuitas* who know
how to smile and get too sunburned. The story by Carmen
Rosensweig is impressive because it reveals a writer who is
without a doubt the best and most fully developed among the
women whose texts are published in this issue: María Amparo
Dávila, Enriqueta Ochoa, and Elena Poniatowska.

Beauty and Philosophy

When obliged to fulfill the other half of her duties, that of social
columnist, beauty consultant, and reporter of the activities of the
elite, Elena (who often signed the articles with her real name Hélène, or the anagram Anel) always discovers some way to interlace
a more abstract and intellectual view of the world and its inhabitants into what seems superficial and ordinary. Such is the case
with an article that appeared in *Novedades* on December 2, 1956,
entitled "1957's Lips Will Be Bright and Smiling." Here, while
describing the new shades of lipstick, Elena emphasizes the most
appropriate colors for women existentialists, adherents of the philosopher Jean Paul Sartre who represented a metaphysical trend
among fifties youth. Nor does she set aside political criticism, as
she challenges a looming and reigning style: that of the United
States which, at least in Elena's interpretation, wishes to convert
women into mere articles for consumption. After her philosophical-
political-aesthetic harangues, she becomes a sort of promoter of
natural remedies, suggesting to her readers fruit-based cures and
capillary treatments, all in the name of feminine beauty:

The new style for 1957 is one of lightly tinted lips, smiling and natural. No more dark shades of lipstick, such as "deadly orchid" or "brilliant purple," nor are the lips white and Vaseline-covered, a style formerly in vogue among the existentialists. 1956 highlighted eye makeup, nearly killing the color of the mouth with pasty red lips in "old rose" or "chocolate rose," the famous hue used by Italian actresses. Now we are returning to a natural look. During the day, women will use bright—but not shocking—pink. For the evenings, "warm rose," or for those women who cannot give up red, a special tone that has been created with shades of orange. The United States wants to launch the Renoir style, which returns women to the stature of dolls and where eyes acquire an almost porcelain-like quality.

These articles were written, as Elena would say, for the "leisure class," that is, for the upper class, the same class to which she unavoidably belongs but whose limitations she recognizes and attempts to overcome. In another article of this kind, Elena gives advice on hair—the "crown of physical beauty"—and how to emulate the tresses of María Félix, Ira von Furstenberg, or Marina Vlady. The article, entitled "How to Care for Your Hair: What to Do to Have Hair like María Félix," appeared in the pages of *Novedades* on January 4, 1957:

> All of us know that until a short time ago María Félix had the most beautiful long hair in the world. She—who now wears a modern hairstyle, which does not detract from her beauty at all—like the young Princess Ira Furstenberg, who has a dark head of hair as lovely as herself, and the no less beautiful Marina Vlady, who also has hair that, although different from the other two, is nonetheless beautiful although completely straight . . .

"Activities of the Upper Crust"

Following a tradition established in Mexico by popular social chroniclers such as Agustín Barrios Gómez, "Ensalada Popoff" columnist, the duke of Otranto, Enrique Castillo Pesado, and Mario de la Reguera, Elena presents her readers with the "Activities of

Elena with the flu,
by Alberto Beltrán.

the Upper Crust." These are superficial descriptions of the comings and goings of the Mexican elite, whose weddings, dinners,
charity events, and other social activities were duly transcribed
by her "Hellenic" pen. Although Elena never found these assignments very interesting, as she knew the milieu all too well,
until her entrance into Mexican journalism, this area had been
dominated by men, with the exception of the Yucatecan writer
and poet Rosario Sansores, who wrote for *Novedades*, and Bambi,
whose interviews appeared in *Excélsior*. Her brief columns always
mentioned the activities at embassies (especially the French one),
lunch parties, fashion shows, charity balls, and dinners in honor
of the celebrities of the moment. The column reprinted here il-
lustrates this aspect of Elena's journalistic development. It was
published in *Novedades* on June 5, 1957, and the author, in order

to conceal her association with such events, uses the pseudonym "La Comadre":

> The romance between Quique Corcuera and Wanda Sevilla is going full steam. Mel Ferrer bought two Covarrubias (paintings) at the Antonio Souza Gallery. All went to visit the gallery with Audrey Hepburn, even more charming than she appears on the screen. Carlos Fuentes is in Mazatlán, typing away at his novel. The couple in vogue among intellectuals, Conchita and Juan García Ponce; Jaime García Terrés has just returned from Acapulco . . . Patricia Romandía and Celia Chávez are as happy as larks while studying in the foggy and labyrinthine city of London. An excellent piece of fantastic literature by Augusto Lund is soon to be published. The marquise of Mohernando, Lorena Braniff, is now very busy organizing the raffle of a set of porcelain china for Carmen and Nacho Amor. The tickets cost one hundred pesos. Octavio Barreda has breakfast every Sunday at Sanborn's, but he says that he's not going to write his memoirs after all. Countess Elena Amor de Celani is on a business trip to New York. She will be back in Mexico on Friday . . . Our choice for the most attractive and best-dressed lady of the week: Doña Adriana Ochoa de Teresa, the wife of Marcos de Teresa.
>
> And so we come to the end of today's gossip by La Comadre.

Markets and *Tianguis*

A different kind of reporting, more representative of the Elena we have all come to know, is found in an article she published on April 6, 1958, also in *Novedades*, describing the markets of Mexico City. This chronicle of the ubiquitous *tianguis*, or outdoor markets, that are set up and taken down all over the city day after day, reflects the budding social conscience of the young reporter, who now decides to explore previously unknown territory. A faithful witness to Elena's personal and professional change of direction was Carlos Fuentes, who at the time decried that poor "Poni" was

always poking around in the markets, finding out the prices of tomatoes and of those typically Mexican birds called *chichicuilotes*, or
in the slaughterhouse, watching the cattle being killed:

"Tomorrow is market day!" They gave us the land and we tilled
it to make it bear fruit. We plant and everything grows. Every
year, the earth is stripped of its harvest of fruits, every year it
is covered with more abundance, and it gives us the bounty
of life.

Mexicans eat millions of tons of beans a year and an amount
of corn that could cover the top of the snowcapped Nevado
de Toluca.

And the sugar that comes from our sugarcane.

And all of this ends up in the markets.

"Órale marchantita, Come on in, güerita! . . . Marchantita,
come on in . . . I've got it all, real cheap. I've got some great
summer squash! Come on in . . . Fresh corn on the cob. Just
look at it . . . Come on in . . . Ora . . . güerita, you can have it
all cheap . . . If you aren't going to buy, don't manhandle."

But until two years ago, this merchandise that had received
loving care from the sun, water, air, and the ever-vigilant hands
in the fields was piled up on the floor in the markets, in a filthy
and incredible disorder . . .

The buyers would shop without realizing that they were
taking home infection and death.

The entire stone floor was shiny with muck and mud . . .
rats running everywhere, so much merchandise . . .

"Make way, make way . . . *ahí va el golpe!*" The moms lost
their children: "I told you not to fall behind." And the police
couldn't keep up.

Beside the fish stand was the one selling colorful ribbons,
and just a step away, the women selling herbs to cure the heart,
the lungs, a bad temper; ignorance and dirt gamboled around,
happy in their total freedom. The market had a life of its own,
alien to that of the great city. A fleshless life. It was painful
to see the stands and the people who came seeking human
warmth. The poorest ones picked up the fruit pits abandoned

Elena as seen
through the lens
of Katy Horna,
1960s.

on the ground and girls with braided hair sharply called out:
"Limes, limes!"

These forays into the world of traditional Mexico that Elena em-
phasized in her conversation with Lya Kostakowsky would provide the material for her first literary work with a decidedly social
orientation: *Todo empezó el domingo* (It All Started on Sunday), where
Elena re-creates the activities of popular classes in the Mexican
capital on the Sabbath.

"If Aristotle had cooked . . . "

Proof of Elena's versatility as a reporter is found in the articles on
Mexican culture and history that she published side-by-side with

beauty tips, society gossip, and her incipient urban chronicles. Such daily experiences prepared Elena for her future profession as essayist and novelist. Thanks to her formative years as a jack of all trades, poking around streets and plazas, markets and *tianguis*, as a free-roaming and anonymous individual, Elena would soon become the creator of a new literary genre in Mexico, that of the novelized chronicle, a hybrid form.

Today, "a bit older and wiser," Elena continues in the same vein, for these are precisely the daily experiences that provide the themes for her writing; and her encounters with *mecapaleros* carrying loads on their backs, newspaper vendors, and shoe-shiners continue to be the raw materials for her literary work. Were it not for these unlikely encounters, her work might perhaps be similar to that of many other Mexican women writers.

Throughout the fifties, Elena learned from some of the most important and intelligent men and women of her time. She did not go to the market to check on the price of tomatoes every day; on many occasions she had the luxury of meeting and becoming friends with such figures as Alfonso Reyes, Octavio Paz, Diego Rivera, David Alfaro Siqueiros, Ignacio Chávez, Rufino Tamayo, Rosario Castellanos, and other Mexican intellectuals. These luminaries provided her with the college education she never had. In her later years this education by experience would be duly recognized by several universities that awarded her honorary doctorates—including the New School of Social Research; the Universidad de Sinaloa, the Universidad del Estado de México; Florida Atlantic University; Manhattanville College, which would have been her alma mater had financial considerations not obliged her to return to Mexico; the Universidad Autónoma de Puebla, the Universidad Autónoma Metropolitana, where her son Mane is a professor of physics; and in the autumn of 2001, the highest institution of learning in Mexico, the Universidad Nacional Autónoma de México.

What does it mean to be Mexican? This question underlies Elena's natural intellectual inclinations, not to mention her philosophy, even though many times she concerned herself with more mundane matters closely related to the streets, the markets, and the shantytowns. Yet, recall Sor Juana's dictum: "If Aristotle had cooked, he would have written much more." Following this advice, Elena finds nourishment in the mundane magic of daily life and then proceeds to re-create, analyze, and transform it into articles and books. In an article published in *Novedades* on January 19, 1958, she asks, "What does it mean to be a Mexican?" and she proceeds to enumerate all the thinkers of the time whose philosophical and historical works paved the way for Mexicans to gain self-knowledge and thus discover their identity as members of a cultural collective. Through this article, Elenita joins a Mexican school of thought inaugurated in the nineteenth century by Justo Sierra and continued by modern intellectuals such as Samuel Ramos and Octavio Paz, whose essay *The Labyrinth of Solitude* (1950) remains a classic among the studies devoted to the so-called "Mexican psyche." Besides revealing what she was reading at the time, the cultural and philosophical articles she wrote helped Elena delve deeper into a topic of great interest to her, the destiny of Mexico and the Mexicans:

> A while back, I recall having attended a discussion with Juan Soriano, Diego de Mesa, Justino Fernández, Octavio Paz, Jorge Portilla, Dr. Raoul Fournier, Jomi García Ascot and María Luisa Elio, Celia and Jaime Garcia Terrés, Carlos Fuentes, and Edmundo O'Gorman regarding Mexico and what it means to be Mexican. Juan Soriano closed the discussion by saying that he did not care to be Mexican, and moreover, that he would not mind if Mexico disappeared someday from the world map. Everyone was indignant, especially Justino Fernández, but the truth is that no other people in the Americas have devoted so many essays to themselves as Mexicans have.
>
> A Frenchman is not concerned with being French. He is naturally French. But a Mexican is greatly preoccupied with who he is. The philosopher Leopoldo Zea wrote: "Many disparate things have been said, and are still being said, about the Mexicans, all based on feelings of inferiority, resentment, insufficiency, hypocrisy, cynicism, etc." Now, if we carefully analyze these comments to see what they have in common,

we will soon realize that all of them underline a certain lack of something in the Mexican. An inferiority complex springs up before this "something" which they could or should possess, for reasons which they do not—or they do not wish to—make explicit . . .

A Mexican Melodrama

An early example of how Elena Poniatowska's journalism became the basis of her later literary production is found in a play that she wrote in 1956 at the urging of Víctor Alba, a Spanish expatriate and editor of *Panoramas*, a literary journal sponsored by *Excélsior* and all but forgotten today. The play, entitled *Melés y Teléo: apuntes para una comedia* (Ireadyou and Youreadme: Notes for a comedy), which she dedicated to her father, Prince Jean E. Poniatowski, takes up more than 150 pages of that issue, which also includes pieces by Jaime Torres Bodet and Raúl Prieto. According to Elena, the work is a "satire inspired by contemporary Mexican intellectuals, a soporific play . . . and enormously long." The title refers to a tacit agreement among intellectuals of that period—and ours— which says "if you read me, I read you" and which Elena transformed into two Greek characters, Melés, or "Youreadme," and Teléo, or "Ireadyou." Contemporary critics pointed out that this play was really Elena's creative response to a contest of wits with writer and critic José Luis Martínez. The interview with Martínez was published in *Excélsior* on December 31, 1953, and is of interest because it touched upon the subject that three years later Elena would develop as an impossible-to-stage tragicomedy. Containing fifty-eight scenes, the play, as she points out, would take two or three days to perform—a true Mexican *Mahabharata*. The provocative title of the earlier interview, "Literature Is Worthless: Teaching Is Much Better," provoked irritation within the closed literary circles to which Martínez refers:

Watson, Enrique González Casanova, Elena, and Arnaldo Orfila Reynal at Elena's home, where Siglo XXI Editores had its first home.

"Mexican literature has hit rock bottom. Men and women write for small admiring communities, and Castro Leal, the greatest critic of our literature, stopped grasping poetry after Enrique González Martínez's demise . . . "

"But everybody is reading his anthology . . . Besides, he is talented at making anthologies, at skillfully compiling the work of our best poets."

"No, he is not the only one . . . In any case he is the only one to write 'fine and subtle . . . ' every two pages. For him, all poets are either fine or subtle, or fine and subtle, or subtle and fine . . . "

"Well, could you improve upon those adjectives?"

"In the first place, I wouldn't have chosen the poems that Castro Leal selected, nor would have I omitted the poets he left out. I would not have juxtaposed Margarita Michelena and Guadalupe Amor with laundresses of verse . . . the poem 'Song to Spring' by Xavier Villaurrutia is horrible. (Xavier wrote it to win a five-thousand-peso prize and there is no reason to include it in the anthology . . .) Besides, Castro Leal claims that Don Alfonso Reyes could have been a great poet (miraculously, Don Alfonso escapes being called 'fine and subtle,' or even 'exquisite') . . . How can he possibly say that? Don Alfonso Reyes is a pillar of all our literature . . . "

"But does Mexican literature truly have a reading public?"

"There's the rub . . . It does not. Mexican literature is literature without an audience. It is not the readers' fault but the writers'. Nobody reads novels by Revueltas or Rubín because they are terminally boring. Let me tell you something. Cute literature is more widely read than serious literature . . . yes, yes, yes, I mean the literature written by frustrated ladies, short poems, etc."

"Why do people like it better?"

"Because it is sentimental, and makes you cry, dream, and laugh . . . "

"Oh my! It appears that you read *True Confessions.*"

"Not exactly."

"But what can men and women of letters become if not writers? Bank tellers?"

"No, Let them be country teachers."

"What?"

"Yes, have them teach others to read and write. Let me tell you something . . . I was an intellectual through and through, waxing poetic but full of problems. At night I would stay awake philosophizing. I wanted everything to have a transcendent meaning, and I sought an answer to everything. I used to lecture and teach philosophy and philology. In the evenings I would gather with my friends, most of them authors of short and languid poems that, deep down, were no more than private pastimes for the enjoyment of the *petit comité.* As you know, I accompanied Agustín Yáñez during his political campaign, and one day, in the small town of Mascota, I came across two young female schoolteachers. They were rural teachers. Not only did they teach, they spent their whole salaries on clothing and food for their pupils. They had an admirable idea of the human condition, and their attitude toward life was irreproachable and inspiring . . . a certain personal conviction that none of us small and vain men and women of letters could ever attain. It was then that I realized the pointlessness of current Mexican literature. Of the need for all that I could write."

"But isn't there anyone in Mexican letters who could write something different?"

"I don't believe so. Of course, there are writers (but the good ones are already universal, and they will soon be included in the *Nouvelle Revue Française*). There are poets like Octavio Paz, who is an untiring explorer, but what they write will neither improve the country nor change it nor add anything to it."

"Then what is valuable in Mexico?"

"What are valuable are those people who educate others . . . humble young women who finish their elementary education and go back to the schools to teach the younger ones . . . What is valuable is not the splendid campus of University City (utterly ridiculous when one thinks of the poverty and the lack of schools in the Mezquital Valley), but those individuals who, putting aside their personal preferences and pleasures, devote themselves to those around them, trying to fight the ignorance that envelops them and to help others improve their lot in life. They are doing something for Mexico. Something that is great and valuable and noble . . . As you can see, this interview has a fundamental defect. I am no longer an enthusiast of our literature. To be one, I would need to go back five years in my life and join my literary friends who are stuck back there and continue believing that for a nation as full of problems as ours, one must continue to pluck, in their egotistical solitude, a small and rusty lyre . . . "

Enrique González Casanova's review of *Melés y Teléo* in *México en la Cultura* on July 15, 1956, was the first to point out how José Luis Martínez's inflammatory words had influenced Elena. In his review the noted critic speculated that all the characters in the play were based on real men and women, claiming that Elena's "Hellenic" pen had portrayed the celebrated writers Juan Rulfo, Alfonso Reyes, Manuel Calvillo, Juan José Arreola, Rosario Castellanos, Olivia Zúñiga, Octavio Paz, and José Luis Martínez himself, among several others. González Casanova was also the first one to point out Elena's fairy-like qualities, comparing her to Puck, Shakespeare's character from *A Midsummer Night's Dream*:

Elena Poniatowska—the author of an infinite number of interviews, which have made her famous, and of a graceful piece that upon publication merited praise from the critics as well as the immediate acceptance of at least five hundred readers— has just presented us with a new play, *Melés y Teléo (apuntes para una comedia)*, as she herself points out in the subtitle.

This small Puck of our literature was careful to ask her publisher to warn her readers that this work does not have hidden meanings and that "the characters in it do not correspond to figures of our real world, but are more like prototypes." The work is not short, it takes up a good 150 pages in the last issue of *Panoramas* magazine, and many of these pages are in small print. It is not truly a comedy nor a misplaced novel nor a screenplay, although it does have elements of all those; it is more like a radio script.

Elenita gives her readers two sensible warnings. First: "In writing *Melés y Teléo*, I have felt that, more than a personal work, I was writing an anonymous and collective narrative whose literary copyright should be registered in the name of all Mexican writers." And second: "The events take place in contemporary Mexico and among its literary men and women. This is the reason for some exceedingly somber tints."

The work was inspired by an incident of Mexican literary life in which Elena participated, one that received angry comments that were included in this column and expressed by many others: the interview in which José Luis Martínez spoke about rural teachers and literature, about the government and the rusty lyre. The characters seem to make up the pieces of a jigsaw puzzle, all perfectly familiar but arbitrarily placed. Even though we know that they do not fit properly, it is nonetheless easy to observe where they go . . . Elenita Poniatowska, you have written something that has made us laugh a great deal and has also left some bitterness behind. Let's hope that this acrimony will not overcome you, and that you continue being

Elena with Juan Rulfo

compared to Puck or some other gracious mythical being, but certainly not to one that is all wrinkled and hunchbacked.

More than thirty years after the publication of *Melés y Teléo*, Elena confessed to the U.S. academic Cynthia Steele the motives behind its composition, and at the same time provided the keys to the true characters hidden behind fictitious names. The interview appeared in 1989 in the magazine *Hispanoamérica*:

"Not much has been said about your play, *Melés y Teléo* (1956). Tell me about the characters and the title."

"One is called the 'Terrón de Tepetate' (Mud Clod), and he is Juan Rulfo. Another is called the 'Garabito' (Doodle), and he is Juan José Arreola, because he himself used to say that physically he was only a doodle. And then there is the poet Olivia Zúñiga, a well-known writer from Jalisco. I believe that Octavio Paz is the 'Becerro de Oro' (The Golden Calf). Another one was Alfonso Reyes, and I don't recall the others. The name of the play means that if you read me (Melés), then

I will read you (Teléo). It is a spoof of intellectuals, conveyed through two characters in a fictitious Greek tragedy, Melés and Teléo, who fight like troglodytes with antediluvian clubs, hitting each other over the head with every intention of killing each other."

"Why hasn't *Melés and Teléo* ever been performed?"

"Because it is very bad, and it resembles a movie script: it has about 160 scenes, which would take two whole days to stage."

"When did you write it?"

"It was almost the first thing I did, after *Lilus Kikus*, which was published in 1954. I wrote it in 1955 or 1956, at the request of Víctor Alba. He was a Trotskyite who took part in the Spanish Civil War, and he asked me to write a play for publication in *Panoramas*. He was a charming man. I wrote dialogues and scenes, but the play doesn't have a dramatic climax or anything: it is nothing more than a masquerade. But Víctor enjoyed it . . . Intellectuals, however, said that it was a satire, and that I was both disrespectful and spiteful."

A Spinning Top

In 1959, three years after the publication of *Melés and Teléo*, Elena decided to interview the distinguished Mexican astronomer and physicist Guillermo Haro. Although she wasn't aware of it at the time, this interview was the beginning of a personal and professional relationship that would lead, some years later, to their marriage and to the birth of Felipe in 1968 and Paula in 1970. At the time, however, the interview was simply another in a long series of conversations that Elena had held with figures of the Mexican cultural world and that, as she now confesses, exacerbated her constant state of "spinning like a top." She worked continuously while caring for Mane, her firstborn, with the help of her beloved childhood nanny, Doña Magdalena Castillo. Elena's infant son always accompanied her on her interviews with artists and writers, politicians and movie stars. Forty years later, Elena reflected on the enormous significance of the birth of her first child:

For me it was absolutely fundamental to have Mane. I believe that it marked my whole life, more than is the case for many other mothers, because before his birth Mane was already my interlocutor, for I had begun a dialogue with him that continues to this day. He was inside of me. I talked to him while he was in my womb in Montemario, Italy. My relationship with Mane has been very deep and very definitive since he began to grow inside of me; he is my rudder and my anchor to this earth.

When she arrived at Mexico's National Autonomous University, supposedly prepared to interview Dr. Haro, and after having to wait for quite a while, Elena was faced by a dry, grumpy man who did not seem at all happy about being interviewed:

He addressed me disparagingly: "Look, here are some of my articles. You can incorporate your questions into them and there you will find the answers." "Besides," he said, "I bet you don't have a pencil or paper with you. None of you journalists ever carries paper or pencils." He had a terrible opinion of journalists, although at one time he himself had done interviews for *Excélsior*. Immediately, I searched and searched in my purse and, lo and behold, I had nothing; I was totally unprepared. Moreover, I was beginning to work so much that sometimes I would go around in circles, feeling like a child's spinning top. I worked excessively. "Here are all the materials; you'll have to compose your interview from them." He literally dismissed me from his office, but I didn't dislike him; on the contrary, it became a challenge to interview him. Dr. Haro was very surprised when fifteen or twenty days later I went back to Tonantzintla by bus to interview him. By then, I had my questions prepared; I had read all the materials, and I had paper and pencils with me. I did a proper interview, with good questions. He then regarded me with some curiosity, and he seemed to like me a bit better. When I was ready to go back to Mexico City, he offered to take me to the bus station because he was surprised to find out that I had come by bus. From that moment on we became friends.

The interview with one of the period's best-known Mexican men of science was published in *Novedades* on January 10, 1959, with a provocative and not very nationalistic title: "In Mexico There Are No Geniuses: Guillermo Haro." Evidently, Elena was impressed with Haro, and near the end of the interview she inserted a note that sounds more like a tribute to his great scientific talents than a conclusion:

> Although Guillermo Haro eschews compliments, Dr. Manuel Sandoval Vallarta has said that Haro's great accomplishments in the scientific field have brought him international fame. Haro is the youngest member of the Colegio Nacional, and in addition to being the director of the astrophysical observatory at Tonantzintla, he was named director of the astronomical observatory of Mexico's National University in Tacubaya. While at Tonantzintla, he discovered twelve new stars (nòvae), and in a paper published in 1950 in the *Astronomical Journal*, Haro demonstrated that the heavenly objects that Hubble and Baade, of the observatory at Mount Wilson in California, had classified as stellar cumulus are in reality brilliant nebulae of the same type as Orion. This paper immediately received worldwide recognition as a first-class contribution and placed Haro among the foremost contemporary astronomers. Later on, he also published in the *Astrophysical Journal* his great paper on stars with alpha emissions and unusual objects in the region of the Orion Nebula, and he attempts to demonstrate, through multiple observations, that stars have been formed and continue to grow by directly capturing pulverized interstellar matter. When corroborated, this will be one of the major discoveries of modern astronomy.

Family Life

Upon her return to Mexico from the Convent of the Sacred Heart boarding school in the United States, Elena went to live with her grandmother, Elena Iturbe, who lived at 430 Morena Street, in La Colonia del Valle, which was a recently developed residential district south of downtown Mexico City. Her parents lived next door, and the gardens of the two houses were connected. Consequently, Elena could see them every day, and at the same time be a companion to her maternal grandmother, who was widowed very young but married again late in life:

> My grandmother was the most important figure during my adolescence and early adulthood. She was the person who helped me the most in my life. Her second marriage was to Arthur de Lima, as her first husband, Pablo Amor, died in France when my mother was seven years old. My grandmother lived alone for many years, until at age 70 she married Archie.
>
> "Listen, Archie has courted you for nearly a century and you never give in. Why don't you marry him?" my mother used to ask.
>
> My relationship with my grandmother was essential to me. According to some people, my grandmother was eccentric because she had twenty-two dogs. I loved her very much, and she loved me just as much and I lived with her until she died.

The most memorable tenants of the house in La Colonia del Valle were the editors of a new Mexican publishing house, Siglo XXI, founded in 1966 (the same year in which Elena also helped cofound Mexico's national movie house, La Cineteca Nacional). The director of Siglo XXI was Arnaldo Orfila Reynal, who woke up one day without a job. According to Elena, his abrupt dismissal was a consequence of his having published Oscar Lewis' study of poverty in urban Mexico, *The Children of Sánchez*: "The Sociedad de Geografía y Estadística (Society of Geography and Statistics) announced that the book disparaged Mexico. Orfila was an Argentine, and Mexico can be quite xenophobic. That day I remember I phoned him to offer him the use of my house. If he wanted, I said he could install himself there and start a new publishing company."

"Heart and Soul"

In recognition of the great popularity and excellence of her journalistic work over almost ten years, in 1961 the then recently founded Ediciones ERA published a collection of her most successful interviews: *Palabras cruzadas* (Crossed Words). It would be the first of more than ten works that Elena published with this well-regarded and still very productive publishing house, now run by Neus Espresate, the daughter of one of its founders, Don Tomás Espresate.

Elena is quick to credit painter and graphic artist Vicente Rojo for choosing the interviews and designing the book cover. The anthology includes some of Elena's most memorable interviews: those with Diego Rivera; David Alfaro Siqueiros; Alejo Carpentier, the Cuban writer who invented the Latin American literary genre known as *lo real maravilloso* and who, like Elena, was a fashion reviewer before becoming a novelist and who signed his columns with the pseudonym Jacqueline; as well as José Gorostiza, the great poet from the Mexican state of Tabasco who, together with Carlos Pellicer, is the cornerstone of modern Mexican poetry. Also included are conversations with some of her most important teachers and friends: Alfonso Reyes; Juan Rulfo; Spanish film director Luis Buñuel (an exile from Franco's Spain who made some of his most celebrated movies in Mexico, including *Los olvidados* and *Viridiana*); former Mexican president Lázaro Cárdenas; Alfonso Caso; Álvaro Mutis; and the Italian scriptwriter Cesare Zavattini, director of *The Bicycle Thief*.

Following the publication of *Palabras cruzadas*, the *Diario de la Nación* published an interview with the "number one reporter in the art of interviewing":

> According to Elena Poniatowska, "We Mexican journalists can never tell the truth. Not even the writers themselves dare criticize or give the final word on matters of culture. And why not? Well, simply because the majority of them are relatively well placed, or they themselves have a 'deal' to protect somewhere or a well-placed friend. Consequently, in Mexico everything moves through influence and friendships, and as a result, one is

Elena with David Alfaro Siqueiros in the Black Palace of Lecumberri, beneath a portrait of Alfonso Reyes in 1960.

always gagged and silenced. Moreover, the newspapers themselves will always censure whatever does not suit their interests. What kind of freedom of the press is that? Freedom to flatter? During Lázaro Cárdenas' presidency, all kinds of criticism of him and his government was permitted, even cartoons and jokes. Today, however, everything must be equivalent to burning incense for the president and the noble members of his government. They are untouchable, or they buy silence through monthly stipends. I don't know everything, but what I can assure you is that our press is highly discredited. Its opinions are for sale."

"Who is or are those most guilty of discrediting our press?"

"More than anyone else, the newspaper editors are to be blamed for the corruption of our national press."

"Why?"

"The editors do not have the moral courage to fire anyone

and, in consequence, they automatically become accomplices to these individuals who are guilty of giving Mexican journalism its bad reputation."

"Don't you think that the majority of these cases are caused by financial considerations and that they originate within the newspaper itself?"

"Exactly. The low salaries of Mexican journalists have forced them to provide for themselves whatever income they need to live on. This is what leads them to sing the praises not only of government officials, but also of all the other prominent members of the establishment."

"For example . . . ?"

"For example, tell me where you can find criticism of Alfonso Reyes, Alfonso Caso, or Jaime Torres Bodet. I do not deny that they are talented writers, but I would never declare that they must be placed on pedestals as untouchables. Ha! But no, the caste of 'untouchables'—from the president of the Republic on down—has been created, strengthened, and supported by journalists, writers, and critics who only know how to praise them in their commentaries or interviews."

"Speaking of interviews, which type do you think is best suited to the daily press?"

"Well, there are several important features, but at the heart of them all is the shaping of the personal contact between the journalist and the interviewee. If the topic is politics, the interview should be summarized as an important piece of news; if it is cultural in nature, it should resemble a written portrait in which the life and work of the person are accurately portrayed. If, finally, the interview simply touches upon a news item, it becomes simple, straightforward reporting."

"What interests you more: the person or the news item?"

"The person does, provided that in the course of the interview, he or she comes off well."

"What kind of person?"

"I prefer to interview men, for the majority of them—except for painters—do not adopt 'poses.' For me, the most sincere individuals are those who passionately advocate a position, be it political, scientific, or artistic, because then the interview really holds a high degree of human interest."

"How should a newspaper interview be done?"

"In keeping with modern journalism, it should be quick and concise."

"What can make an interview lose its value?"

"The detestable and antiquated system of 'passing,' of giving a 'pass' or 'free ticket.' I am referring, of course, to the daily interview. This is very common in interviews by Fernando Revueltas and Scherer García."

"Suppose you were the publisher of a daily newspaper, what direction would your publication take?"

"Principally one of an absolute and honorable independence of criticism. I would walk an unwavering line of journalistic duty and ethics. I would demand that my newspaper do as the French and British dailies *L'Observateur* and *Spectator*, as well as many others, do: openly point out to the government leaders their mistakes through healthy and constructive criticism. Likewise, I would try to direct the information toward more concrete fields, those that are less vacuous and pointless, to avoid printing ever more pages of nonsense."

"Would you have a section devoted to social events, as newspapers have always had?"

"Absolutely not. I would try to lead my newspaper in a different direction from that of dim-witted vanity and the obsequious flattery and praise of insatiable feminine narcissism. I believe that women's organizations, like newspapers, should lead the social columns down paths that are less vain and superficial—those we have today are even downright silly and stupid."

In January 1962, the well-known journalist María Luisa "China" Mendoza also published a profile that contained an interview of sorts with Elena, her new colleague at the magazine *La Mujer de Hoy* (Today's Woman). The most significant part of their conversation

concerns how this well-established reporter describes and analyzes the work and unique personality of her younger colleague:

> Completely at ease, like a cruel little girl who never loses her
> smile, she can delve into the heart and soul of her subjects in
> order to extract their deepest truths, and they never stop lov-
> ing her, so gracefully does she proceed, with an elegant sense
> of humor that is the product of true intelligence.
>
> She generally dresses in gray, doesn't smoke, and wears no
> jewels except for three simple strands of pearls around her
> neck. Petite as Elena is, she wears the appropriate attire for the
> occasion, and she is always perfectly groomed. Once we went
> to Aguascalientes together and all her dresses were white. She
> looked sensational, and during the five days of our stay, an
> "audacious reporter" incessantly shadowed us, trying to corner
> us. We would even hide under the table and there was that
> pest, inviting her to dance with him.
>
> As a truly professional journalist, Elena has created a style
> that many around her imitate with mediocre results. Who
> knows where she gets that very personal style of sprinkling
> her chronicles, interviews, or columns with the names of per-
> sonages that make them unique.
>
> Elena's journalism is inspired by memories, coincidences,
> and similarities. She woos the subjects of her interviews and
> leads them on until—totally unaware of what is happening—
> they become trapped in the heart of the matter at hand. She
> questions them with such innocence that they end up reveal-
> ing what is truly important.
>
> She is a woman who clearly belongs to the period of transi-
> tion that young people are living through today. Despite hav-
> ing a profusion of noble titles to her name, she puts them aside
> and goes into the fields, the factories, the schools, gaining rec-
> ognition as one of today's best journalists. Of journalism she
> declares that "it is the art of saying things that are important,"
> but she does so without solemn attitudes or somber tones.
>
> "The point is to joke without overdoing it . . . Yes, some-

times I overdo it and it becomes grotesque . . . I believe that if someone asks you, as a friend, not to publish something, you must not do so, without committing the sin of unprofessional conduct. In the course of my career I have faced only two serious complaints. Shall I tell you about one of them? Well, there was a little German girl named Cristina von Tannstein, daughter of the ambassador, who told me that Germans were 'dull, boring, and gray'; of course I published that, and I think her parents sent her off to a concentration camp . . . "

"Will you continue your career in journalism?"

"I would like to abandon it and devote myself to studying; either that, or do journalism more seriously and write essays. I want to learn to think, to draw conclusions, to make deductions. I would like to leave Mexico City and go to Jalapa or Morelia, to study there and to devote myself to reading, but for that you need courage and you must give up many things . . . "

"Did you inherit your writer's vocation?"

"My grandfather wrote his memoirs *From One Century to the Other*, and he dedicated it as follows: 'For my children and grandchildren, who do not seem to know very well where they are going, so that they will at least know where they come from . . . ' His name was André Poniatowski."

Life on Sundays

On November 24, 1957, Elena published the first of a series of articles about the activities of the Mexican people on Sundays, material which six years later would make up her third book, *Todo empezó el domingo* (It All Started on Sunday), published by El Fondo de Cultura Económica and illustrated by the engraver Alberto Beltrán, who was a graduate of the Taller de Gráfica Popular, an art institute with leftist political leanings. According to Elena, "Alberto Beltrán said he wanted to make sketches for the articles I wrote. He then proposed that we go out and see what poor people do on Sundays. I did not know the city and he guided me and my son, Mane, who often accompanied us, in exploring it."

Elena recalls that her social awareness was born in the late fifties, with the publication of this book and her first visits to the so-called Palacio Negro (Black Palace) of Lecumberri, Mexico City's infamous penitentiary (now converted into Mexico's National Archives), to interview the railroad strikers who led a social movement that was to inspire the student movement of 1968 ten years later. She visited the Palacio Negro in the company of Spanish filmmaker Luis Buñuel, another of her former interviewees who liked to visit the jail's cellblock "J" because that was where they put the homosexuals, transvestites, and others jailed for "sexual perversion." At one point, I asked Elena when she had discovered "Deep Mexico," as it was called by author Guillermo Bonfil Batalla, and her answer was quite revealing.

A young man wrote me from the Lecumberri jail inviting me to see a play he had written. I felt great sympathy for him and went to see *El Cochambres* (The Sooty One). In jail, I also met railroad men on strike and obtained many stories of their lives. This was marvelous for me, because prisoners are always willing to talk and will seek out anybody who is willing to lend an attentive ear. Prior to that, I had already become interested in social issues, but this interest was intensified in Lecumberri. I began to go there at least two or three times a week. Mane, who was five years old in 1959, accompanied me to watch the activities of the poorest people. That is how *Todo empezó el domingo* came to be.

At the time I was a young woman who had seen lovely homes with beautiful people and in beautiful surroundings. I was familiar with the VIPs, the Mexican nobility, the haciendas, the French expatriate community, but through my work as a journalist, I also discovered the slums and poverty; I saw much satisfaction but also much misery. I then realized that the dark side of the picture was more representative and more demanding than that which was depicted inside the satin covers of *Vogue* or *House and Garden*, which had been my natural habitat, and that was where my inclinations led me. I never was able to foresee the extent of the resentment this would

With
Argentinean
novelist Julio
Cortázar.

awaken. At receptions and dinner parties at embassies, they asked my mother what her connection was to the communist who wrote in the newspapers: "What is your relationship to this pro-Castro lady?" and this made her suffer. When she got home she would look at me disapprovingly.

Elena would rather submerge herself in the poorest slums than go to balls and fashion shows given for charity. Her visiting the jail at age twenty-five was looked upon as an affront to society: "Isn't your daughter quite morose?" "Isn't she very depressed?" "Why does she write about street urchins when there are so many nicer things to write about?"

As mentioned, her mission began a few years after she joined *Excélsior*, when Jesús Sánchez García sent her a letter from the Lecumberri jail inviting her to the play *El Cochambres*. She was soon joined by Alberto Beltrán, a leftist of a working-class background, a distinguished member of the Taller de Gráfica Popular, a militant in the Partido Popular, and the founder of the Mexican paper *El Día*, to which Elena contributed interviews, chronicles, and in-depth articles. Elena and Alberto eventually produced a book, *Todo empezó el domingo*, which would lead Elena closer to social problems, to minorities, to those who had been abandoned, to homeless children and, finally, to lend her full support to the Movimiento

Estudiantil (Student Movement) of 1968, a political position Beltrán did not share, as can be seen from his illustrations published in *El Día*.

Elena's parents were rather reticent and never wanted to be in the limelight. Of course, there were exceptions on the maternal side of the family, such as Guadalupe Amor, but Pita was willing (consciously or unconsciously) to accept all the consequences of her attitude.

Elena soon sought refuge on life's margins, among those who were marginalized in health, education, and opportunities. She has kept a low profile, and her whole life has been marked by the services she has rendered to others. She has no secretary, no chauffeur, none of the attributes of power, no one at her service. The triple day's work schedule was made just for her. Her neighbors in Chimalistac are astonished to see her walking down the street in sweatpants. People stop her in the market; they recognize her on the subway and in other public places. Used to jumping to it, Elena Poniatowska, in contrast to her celebrated aunt, Guadalupe Amor, appears not to have the least idea of her own importance.

Mexican Vignettes

One of the first and most complete reviews devoted to *Todo empezó el domingo* was written by María Elena Espinosa de Puga for *Novedades* magazine, the same supplement where the articles by Elena and Alberto which led to the book had been appearing since 1957:

> Here, in this "Sunday Magazine," a new series by Elena Poniatowska and Alberto Beltrán appeared for the first time six years ago (on November 24, 1957). "Chapultepec" was the first of sixty-three articles that would create, through Elenita's incisively gracious writing style and Alberto's drawings, a prodigious synthesis where humor sometimes attains the profile of a social diatribe on the ways in which Mexicans habitually enjoy their leisure on the seventh day of the week.
>
> Those Sunday features were enriched with many others that the authors composed about other parts of Mexico and

that, although they do not describe Sunday diversions, depict scenes with interesting social and traditional content: the balconies, the rooftops, children being let out of school, carriage drivers in Mérida, Yucatán, news vendors.

Todo empezó el domingo, magnificently published by El Fondo de Cultura Económica, allows us to enjoy once more a sojourn through the animated, throbbing vignettes (text and engravings) of today's Mexico, struggling amusingly between modernism and tradition. We have witnessed these images and situations; their conversations are familiar to us, because all Mexicans have gone, at least on Sunday and even if only once, to those places where all of Mexico has congregated for so many years.

In her review, the journalist re-creates scenes of the many trips Elena, Alberto, and often Mane, made to several parts of Mexico City, always in the old car Elena owned at the time:

Every Sunday morning at nine o'clock, Alberto Beltrán would arrive, with his Depression-era shoes and his shirt buttoned up to his neck, to pick up Elena and Mane. They left the house in an old Hillman that would break down all over the place, whose tires tended to go flat, but which safely took them off to and brought them back from all their expeditions.

"Our first trip was to Chapultepec Park," says Elena, "and I was rather scared, trailing Alberto until he very nicely insinuated that I should go my own way, listen to the people, observe them, and let him work on his own. That was how I began to sit among the groups of people resting on the grass, to play with their children, and join in their conversations:

"'What kind of milk does your baby drink?'

"That would be the beginning, soon they would forget me and I would listen to their conversations and watch them, pretending not to be overly interested . . .

"Meanwhile, Alberto made his sketches, always standing while drawing. He is very timid at heart and doesn't like people to watch him as he draws. And besides, the type of articles we did required that people act naturally, in their everyday manner, so he also tried to go unnoticed . . . "

The two artists, changing their observation posts, worked all Sunday. They would eat in markets and share their observations at the end of the day, on the way home in the heroic Hillman through crowded and dusty roads. That is the reason why, perhaps without meaning to, each left traces of his or her personality in the other's work . . .

But in the book, one reads not only of the customs that illustrate ancient traditions, but also of those born more recently, such as the political meetings where they saw "worn men's faces, their hair combed back with Vaseline, showing off a golden tooth when they smiled, and offering at each corner the stuff of their own political aspirations." And the militia, marching with wooden guns . . .

Perhaps so that we understand that if there are poor people, it is because there are rich people, elegant areas are described only as the framework without which the existence of poor slums could not possibly be explained . . .

And thus, Mérida, the city of "balconies that take flight," speaks to us through the pencil of two artists, both of whom, although they use it differently, possess the same language: that of truth and poetry.

Emotions without Sentimentality

I was surprised to discover an article referring to *Todo empezó el domingo* in "Exhibitions," a column devoted, as the title indicates, to the most important art shows of the Mexican capital, authored by the distinguished art historian Margarita Nelken. Upon leafing through Elena's book, however, the reason Nelken included it in her series of descriptions regarding the Mexican artistic world becomes clear. At that time art was rife with aesthetic populism, an ideological holdover of the Mexican Revolution that was depicted on the walls of public buildings throughout the city; the majority of it was the work of "the three" Mexican muralists: Diego Rivera, José Clemente Orozco, and David Alfaro Siqueiros. Nelken admires the manner in which the work of the two artists, Poniatowska and Beltrán, merges to such a degree that one cannot be explained without the other. The article appeared in *Excélsior*, on Wednesday, June 24, 1963:

> Often and over the course of many years, we have regretted our lack of appreciation for books that elsewhere have stimulated a wide range of artistic illustration, providing an ample scope of activities for artists who are totally or partially devoted to this aspect of artistic production . . .
>
> Thus, the appearance of a book such as *Todo empezó el domingo* seems so important to us and gives us the right to comment upon it as if it were an art exhibition in itself. Basically, it is an exhibition of Alberto Beltrán's illustrations.
>
> But the illustrations form an indivisible whole with the texts that he illustrates. And it is impossible to comment on the former without speaking of the latter, which are its immediate source. It has already been noted that in *Todo empezó el domingo* it is impossible to separate Beltran's illustrations from Elena Poniatowska's texts with which they form an indissoluble body.
>
> Which came first, the texts or the drawings? We, at least, are unable to answer this question. So we assume that they were born in unison, the impressionist eye of the visual artist together with the psychological penetration of the writer offering us a kaleidoscope of popular vignettes frozen, synthesized, and re-created with a singularly fine perception of their emotional impact.
>
> Because in its composition this work of art is deliberately marked with emotion without sentimentality—deeply and well appraised—we would say it rings true. It is as distant from the demagoguery of the artificial "populism," from the folklore that has been so much in vogue (and fortunately is now going out of style), as it is from the icy examination of a objective sociological study. It is something like the opposite of persuasive tenderness, the reverse of Oscar Lewis' *Anthropology of Poverty*, in whose entirely negative portrayals some

have thought they recognized the faithful image of a people. Here, we find the fraternal communion of drawing and literature with their models, bringing to light whatever gloominess is within them without coloring reality rosy, yet with all their human qualities.

A Human Bond

In what seems to be a direct answer to Nelken's provocative words, María Luisa "China" Mendoza published in her column "La O por lo Redondo" a paragraph in which, instead of recriminating Oscar Lewis and his polemical study of contemporary Mexicans (*The Anthropology of Poverty* and *The Children of Sánchez*), she presents the three (Poniatowska, Beltrán, and Lewis) as a sort of inseparable trio whose journalistic, graphic, and anthropological work invites fellow Mexicans to recognize something they sometimes find hard to accept: their socioeconomic problems, as portrayed through the visual and literary descriptions of the lives of their more deprived citizens. In fact, Elena came to know Lewis and his work because, as she recalls,

> Lewis asked me to revise and edit the manuscript of *Pedro Martínez*. Through working closely with him, I saw that he had a university team of Americans and Mexicans doing the fieldwork. His wife, Ruth Lewis, also helped him. They would count how many chairs there were in people's living quarters; how many bathrooms, if any, and how they were used; what time the people got up, when they went to bed, etc. They made layouts that Oscar Lewis used, while Ruth Lewis questioned the women. In the slums, Oscar Lewis was perceived as a physician and they entrusted their secrets to him.

Talent and Grace

With Elena's sudden plunge into waters until then unknown to her, some critics began to question how a young French princess had the audacity to involve herself with the life and struggles of

Mexico's lower classes. Remember, however, that Elena was essentially brought up by her nanny Magdalena, so she did receive a populist education, in many ways unconsciously, at the hands of someone similar to those she would later observe so enthusiastically in the parks, marketplaces, and streets of Mexico. One of the first journalists to recognize this was Elvira Vargas, who includes a reference to *Todo empezó el domingo* in her column "Multicosas," in a piece entitled "Estampas vivas: tres autores y dos libros" (Living Vignettes: Three Authors and Two Books) in which she reviews the most recent work by Mexican author Abel Quezada and the duo formed by Elena Poniatowska and Alberto Beltrán:

> Notwithstanding her blue-blooded origins and titles of nobility, Elena—and it is important to mention this—is as Mexican as anyone. Down here, we forget nobility and repudiate discrimination. What counts is talent and what those who possess it do for Mexican culture, for the sake of the country and for its good name. And Elena has just compiled it in one precious volume recently published by El Fondo de Cultura Económica. It is a series of articles that—even were they not entitled *Todo empezó el domingo*—would still be living vignettes of Mexico today . . . In all those vignettes, the majority inspired by our capital city, Elena's agile pen (with grace and talent both in form and style, and basically well-thought-out intentions) undoubtedly gives testimony to the manner in which, on Sundays and holidays, the members of a community blow off steam with a relaxed and placid happiness that they all enjoy to the maximum, letting their existence flow, as the great majority of them know they can forget their routine responsibilities . . .

An Illustrated Biography

Forty years after its publication, one of the most important aspects of Elena's book, still ignored by most contemporary critics, is the place *Todo empezó el domingo* occupies in the history of Mexico's national literature. It is well known that the earliest writings devoted to the recently discovered American continent were born through an infinity of letters, chronicles, commentaries, and other epistolary and historiographic documents written throughout the colonial period, the most important example of which is the novelistic history written by Spanish foot soldier Bernal Díaz del Castillo, entitled *The True History of the Conquest of New Spain*. In his zeal for remuneration for the services he rendered to King Phillip II, Bernal compiles for him a text full of minute details that range from the names of all the horses belonging to the conquistadors to an astounding list of the delicacies prepared for Montezuma, from which the Mexican emperor might select only one dish for his personal enjoyment. This tradition of the descriptive epic never quite disappeared throughout the history of Mexican literature, and it reappears with different motifs and various nuances even today. In his weekly column published in *Excélsior* in June 1963 and entitled "Fables of Abel, Elenita and Alberto," correspondent Luis Guillermo Plaza mentions quite superficially the kinship between Elena's book and others of previous periods, such as the well-known *Life in Mexico*, by Fanny Calderón de la Barca, written in the early nineteenth century:

> In *Todo empezó el domingo*, Elena Poniatowska and Alberto Beltrán, "arm in arm" like in a musical, have wandered all over Mexico City, its surroundings, and some places in the provinces. Observing everything, listening, feeling they artistically legitimize the life of Mexicans through her texts and his drawings . . .
>
> And with equal ease they discover the customs, places, persons, and characters—some already gone but continuing to live in memory here [in the book]—that form an animated but nonetheless melancholy biography of many things Mexican. The drawings are suitably gray, depressing, and distressing. A French writer recently questioned by a correspondent from *The New Yorker* about why he lives in Mexico answered: "Because if Christ were alive today, he would live in this coun-

try." The Middle Ages permeate Poniatowska and Beltran's entire book.

A Spanish friend of ours, during his short stay, used to say that Mexico is a country for which one feels nostalgia even before one leaves it. *Todo empezó el domingo* is full of this kind of nostalgia. Even as we read it, peruse it, some of its subjects are already disappearing, but they nonetheless remain recorded here.

Thus, due to its value of preservation (we are certain that after many years we will need to return to *Todo empezó el domingo* the way we now return to *Life in Mexico* by Mme. Calderón de la Barca), how could we not forgive Elenita's delightful expressions? "They graduated into the next grade, and as they had promised the Virgin, they went on their knees to give thanks to her. Nobody had explained to them that one 'is promoted to the next grade' because one studies one's lessons . . . "

An Art Book

Perhaps the most extraordinary feature of Elena's book was identified by the Guatemalan poet and essayist Luis Cardoza y Aragón, in a lecture given on Radio Universidad on July 6, 1963. Cardoza y Aragón points out that it is precisely the harmonious collaboration between two artists, so seldom achieved in a work of this kind, that gives the book its singular originality, because the melody created by the hybrid graphic and literary reading of the work presents the reader with a total experience in which the images speak through the text and vice versa. In this sense, Poniatowska and Beltrán's book remains simultaneously faithful to a narrative tradition already well established in Mexico while opening a new path in the development of the arts in the mid-twentieth century. Nor is it, as the author reminds us, an expensive and inaccessible book, but rather an inexpensive edition that will provide Mexicans with a hitherto infrequent experience: that of enjoying a book as both literature and art. This phenomenon takes us back to the prehispanic period, when glyphs were accompanied by drawings—often within the same ideographic representation—in order to interpret and simultaneously give depth to their meaning.

Cardoza y Aragón points out that the duo's work is worthy of being treated as an art book because that is exactly what it is. In *Todo empezó el domingo* he discovers

> a perfect relation, a magnificent balance. We could use the term, sometimes so greatly overused, of integration. We could say "lyrics by Elena Poniatowska and music by Alberto Beltrán." The drawings come alive in the atmosphere provided by the brilliant author's texts; they are part of the texts, yet they live independently because they are the drawings of a great artist. Beltrán, with his textual illustrations of *Todo empezó el domingo* creates not ruptures but connections, and the text and the drawings, or the drawings and the text, sustain each other reciprocally but could also stand by themselves because they have more than enough quality to do so. But our point is to evaluate not the relative merits of the text and drawings separately, but rather their functional connection as an art book . . .
>
> And I believe that this book will grow in meaning over time. It is a family album of the Mexican people, of contemporary Mexican society—something like *Mexicans Depicted by Themselves*. But how distant the book is from such a name! Distant through its vitality, through the penetrating vision that does not stop at the surface but rather goes deep into its subjects and provides us with living images, full of warmth and action, with a reality whose presence imparts joy and the spiritual lightness of a dance by Elena Poniatowska and Alberto Beltrán; drawn by both, written by both, it is a great book . . .

Unsolved Mysteries

In 1998, thirty-five years after its original edition, Editorial Océano republished *Todo empezó el domingo* in a shorter and much less attractive edition. The book provoked a renewed interest from critics, who praised the reappearance of a volume that had been out of print for decades and belonged to the great Mexican tradition of the urban chronicle; the same *admiratio urbana* present in the texts of conquerors and poets such as Hernán Cortés and Bernardo de Balbuena, and later Salvador Novo with his *New Mexican Grandeur*. Nonetheless, the polemical comments of Alberto Beltrán—Elena's erstwhile faithful companion and collaborator—regarding the literary paternity of the book came as a surprise to many.

On March 13, 1998, journalist Oscar Enrique Ornelas published in the newspaper *El Financiero* a conversation with Beltrán entitled "Elena Poniatowska Knew Nothing about Mexico: Alberto Beltrán." In the course of the interview, Beltrán revealed a certain duplicity on the part of the editors of Océano that resulted in the mysterious disappearance of the original book manuscript:

> It is seldom known what lies behind a book. This is the case with *Todo empezó el domingo*, with text by Elena Poniatowska and drawings by Alberto Beltrán . . .
>
> It was in the late fifties . . . Alberto Beltrán García (Mexico, 1923), a veteran cartoonist and member of the Taller de Gráfica Popular, was doing illustrations for the daily *Novedades*. "Because the newspaper had an illustrated Sunday supplement," Beltrán recalls, "it occurred to me to make street sketches of the scenes of people's Sunday activities. I showed them to the person responsible for the supplement, Raúl Puga—the brother of a cartoonist for *Excélsior*, Jorge Puga—and since he was a man who, not being a stuffy journalist, liked new ideas, he considered my idea of sketching what people did on Sunday worth publishing."
>
> However, Beltrán continues, "Puga suggested that the drawings be accompanied by text: I had thought of simply having captions for the pictures"—the artist explains. "My idea came from graphic supplements published in other countries. But if Puga had a different proposal, well, I thought we might as well try it."
>
> Beltrán had illustrated the interviews that young Elena Poniatowska used to publish in *México en la Cultura*, the cultural supplement of *Novedades* at that time. Puga's proposal was to reverse the roles: she would write the text to accompany Beltrán's drawings.

At first the illustrator balked. "Elena knows nothing about Mexico," he told Puga. "That's right"—he responded in a conciliatory tone—"but remember that she has a very accessible way of describing things. There are so many people in journalism that do nothing important, why don't we give Elena a try?"

Poniatowska "knew nothing about the country," Beltrán insists. "She was French by birth and was educated in a Catholic school in the United States. Her mother went to Paris and married a Polish aristocrat who had fallen on hard times. I was acquainted with him. Elena knew about Mexico only from what her family talked about, and it was always related to high society: owners of haciendas, pulquerías, and tenements. My drawings related to reality, so I asked Elena simply to recount what she saw, without attempting to provide any interpretation."

Poniatowska did not always accompany Beltrán. According to him, several of the texts that appear in the book were written by him, particularly those referring to places outside Mexico City. Such is the case when he speaks about Pancho Villa's house in Chihuahua (p. 193), where Beltrán's imprint may be observed.

"Today, Elena refuses to recognize it, but if one goes through the back issues of *Novedades*, the ones I wrote are distinguishable from hers," the artist remarked.

"Could you identify them precisely now?"

"I don't recall them all. But when this edition was being prepared, Rogelio Carvajal Dávila, from Océano, promised me that the appropriate credit would be given. Besides, he told me that for the new book, they would consider the original texts taken from Novedades, as El Fondo de Cultura Económica had published only a selection rather than the full series. But neither of these two things came to pass: Elena Poniatowska's byline appears on all the texts, and the book continues to be only a sample of that work."

"What do you attribute this to?"

"I believe that it was Elena who refused."

Beltrán also remembers that there had been another attempt

to bring out an edition of *Todo empezó el domingo* with Grijalbo, but Poniatowska's publishers refused because, he declares, they were rival companies. Moreover, he adds, the original manuscripts held by El Fondo de Cultura Económica were "mysteriously" lost.

In the course of other interviews, particularly those done at the time of the original publication of *Todo empezó el domingo*, and in statements Elena herself made, it is clear that she never denied Beltrán his due credit. On the contrary, in the Fondo de Cultura Económica first edition, as well as in Océano's, she wanted her name to appear after Beltrán's, as both had collaborated equally in the book, and it would not be complete without both literary and graphic components.

5 Unknown Mexico

The Black Palace of Lecumberri

Next to her maternal grandmother, her mother, and her nanny, Magdalena, the woman who had the greatest impact upon Elena's personal, professional, and spiritual development was undoubtedly Josefina Bórquez, novelized in print as Jesusa in *Hasta no verte Jesús mío*. The writer discovered Josefina one day when she heard her shouting at the top of her lungs from the roof of the building where she worked as a laundress. Only a year before, Elena had published *Todo empezó el domingo*, an ethnographic adventure that, she insists, had led her down a path that was quite different from the road she had appeared destined to follow. By the end of the fifties, however, she had discovered the dark side of Mexico: the so-called Black Palace of Lecumberri, now Mexico's National Archives, where she went to interview political prisoners, especially railroad workers jailed in 1959 during the strike led by Demetrio Vallejo that paralyzed the country.

I can imagine Elena, petite, well dressed, with her small stenographer's notebook under one arm, walking down the old streets of San Lázaro toward the jail, full of emotion as she imagined the stories that the prisoners would share with her. It was then that she heard Josefina's booming voice for the first time. In her book *Luz y luna, las lunitas* (Light and Moon, the Little Moons)—a collection of essays containing photographs by Graciela Iturbide, Rosa Nissán, Paula Haro, and Héctor García (her photographer for many years)—is a chronicle aptly entitled "Life and Death of Jesusa," from which the quotations in this chapter are taken. In it

A pregnant Elena with the "red priest," Sergio Méndez Arceo, archbishop of Cuernavaca, in front of the Black Palace of Lecumberri.

Elena pays homage to her "Mexican Virgil," who revealed to her the mysteries of the Mexico City urban underworld produced, at least in part, by the Mexican Revolution. It, according to Jesusa, never gave anything to anybody except the revolutionary political bosses who took the place of those aristocratic Mexican families who escaped to France during the twilight of Porfirio Díaz's long-lived presidency, known as the Porfiriato.

In silent testimony to her *querencia* (fondness), to use Josefina's term for their relationship, vestiges of their devotion are sprinkled here and there throughout Elena's home in the form of popular images of the Santo Niño de Atocha, Jesusa's—that is to say, Josefina's—patron saint, later adopted by her improbable disciple, Elena. In the eulogy Elena originally prepared in 1978, the year of Josefina's death, she relates how, little by little, she enters Josefina's world, and she provides information that helps us understand this unusual friendship that, five years after she met Jesu/Jose for the first time, would come to fruition in a prodigious novel: *Hasta no verte Jesús mío (Here's to You, Jesusa!)*, originally published in Spanish in 1969:

> I met Josefina/Jesusa in 1964. She lived near the streets of Morazán and Ferrocarril Cintura, in a poor section of Mexico City whose main attraction was the penitentiary inappropriately called the Black Palace of Lecumberri . . . Jesusa lived near the penitentiary in a one-story tenement that consisted of a central corridor with rooms along it. One could hear the continuous humming of a sewing machine . . . or were there several running at the same time? The building had a damp, rotten smell. When I arrived, the gatekeeper would shout from the door: "Jose, come hold the dog!"
>
> "I'm coming," and there came Jesu/Jose. "I'm coming," with a scowl wrinkling her forehead, her head bent low, "I'm coming, I'm coming," and the neighbors would peep out . . . "Come in, come in, but quickly, hurry, get into my room." (*Luz y luna, las lunitas*, 59–60)

Every Wednesday

The first few times that Elena visited Jesusa in her home, her hostess was not the least bit welcoming; on the contrary, she was rather scornful of her curious visitor:

> "What's with you? What do you want from me?"
> "I want to talk with you."
> "With me? Look, I work. If I don't work, I don't eat. I don't have time to sit around chatting." (38)

But Jesusa did converse with Elena, although reluctantly, warning her that the only free time she had in her life was Wednesdays from four to six. So Elena began to live from one Wednesday to the next, but between Wednesdays, her admiration and affection for Jesusa kept growing. Jesusa never ceased greeting her with a sullen attitude and scornful demeanor, not willing to harbor affection for the spoiled little Mexican girl who, to Jesusa, was the

symbol of absolute uselessness and a constant reminder of the social injustice manifest in her abject poverty. Every Wednesday, as
Jesusa looked out the door of her dismal room, she would receive
her new friend with the same indifferent greeting: "Ah, so it's you
again." And so, week after week, Elena would enter a world of
overflowing toilets and no running water, dirty pieces of paper
scattered on the floor and a smell of urine that pervaded every
corner of the tenement's inner courtyard. Like a dungeon, Jesusa's
room was always dark, while gas leaking from the burner made
their eyes water. The courtyard, although narrow and dirty, never
lacked a mass of children playing soccer, their stomachs swollen
from malnutrition bearing witness to their miserable lives, entertained only by a crushed tin can they used as a ball and by the
ever-present rats that, hidden among the piles of trash, darted
back and forth looking for scraps of food.

After spending several weeks with Jesusa, Elena had the nerve,
because with Jesusa one needed nerve, to ask her about her life:
her squalid present and adventurous past, her dreams and her disappointments born with the advent of Porfirio Díaz and then her
participation in a revolution intended to overthrow him but that
did not live up to its noble promise. Jesusa pretended not to find
this weekly waste of her time interesting at all, but little by little
she began to give in to her young disciple's entreaties, always under the condition that Elena, who knew nothing about manual
labor, much less about tending chickens, help her with her many
chores, which never seemed to fit into the two hours that Jesusa
had available. In fact, the first time that Elena asked Jesusa to tell
her about her life and her absolute indignation with the rest of
humanity, the answer was a curt "I have no time." She pointed to
her interminable chores, as she always had something pressing:
tending to her five hens (her most valuable possessions), feeding
her dog, her cat, and two miserable sparrows, and, in addition,
washing those filthy overalls that she used to take in to earn a bit
of extra money.

"Do you see this? Are you going to help me with all this?"
"Yes," I answered.

"All right, then, put the overalls to soak in gasoline."

Then I learned what overalls really are. I grabbed a filthy, cardboard-like object, with enormous grease stains, and put it in a beat-up metal basin. The overalls were so stiff that the liquid couldn't penetrate them and they became an island sticking up in the middle of the water, hard as a rock. Jesusa ordered: "While they soak, take out the hens and let them sun on the sidewalk." I did so, but the hens began to peck on the cement, seeking something improbable, and to cackle all over the place, jumping off the sidewalk and scattering in the street. I got scared and ran back: "They are going to get run over by a car!"

"Don't you even know how to sun chickens? Didn't you see the little piece of string?"

They were all supposed to be tied to the string by one leg. She had all her chickens inside in a second, and began to scold me again:

"What were you thinking of, just taking them out like that?"

Feeling distressed, I asked, "What else can I help you with?"

"Well, what about the overalls?"

When I asked where the sink was, Jesusa pointed to a small corrugated washboard, no bigger than eight or ten inches wide and twenty inches long: "What do you mean the sink? Around here you scrub on top of that!"

Leaning under her bed she pulled out a washbasin and looked at me scornfully: it was impossible for me to scrub anything. The uniform was so stiff that it was even hard to hold on to. Jesusa exclaimed, "It's easy to see that you're one of those useless ninnies! Not worth a darn!" (38–39)

A Novel and a Gift

Elena began to visit Jesusa once a week, often taking with her an ancient tape recorder that somebody had lent her for her interviews at the jail—a dark-blue coffin, as Elena put it, that according to Jesusa, used all the electricity in her small room. As Elena didn't know how to use the contraption properly, sometimes it didn't record and she had to repeat the same questions she had asked the time before. Jesusa's reaction was always one of annoyed disgust that gradually became intermingled with an almost imperceptible affection:

> "Hey, didn't I tell you that last week?"
>
> "Yes, but it didn't get recorded."
>
> "So . . . doesn't that big creature work properly?"
>
> "Sometimes I don't know whether it's working or not."
>
> "Well then, don't bring it any more!"
>
> "The thing is that I don't write very fast, and we would waste a lot of time."
>
> "There it is. We'd better quit. We're not getting anything out of this, you or me!" (40)

After the debacle with the tape recorder, Elena went back to her usual steno pad, while Jesusa, who couldn't read or write, made fun of Elena's handwriting—nothing but scrawls, she said—which began to fill the pages of her notebook. Without audio tapes, Elena was obliged to reconstruct each night everything that Jesusa had told her. She was always afraid that suddenly Jesusa would lose patience with her attentive disciple, especially because of certain transgressions that Jesusa would immediately censure. For example, it seemed to be inappropriate that Elena would greet the neighbors, and to show her disapproval, once when Elena asked about some little girls who had peeked in the doorway, she sputtered: "Don't call them 'little girls,' call them whores, yes, little whores, that's all they are." (40)

In the course of all these interviews, which normally lasted from two to three precious hours, Jesusa initiated her young pupil into the true ancestral Mexico, full of suffering, hunger, ugliness, and misery. To this day, Elena invokes Jesu/Jose when she recalls the lessons conferred upon that nice little Franco-Mexican girl who didn't even know what overalls were, much less how they should be washed. But little by little, amidst scolding and scoffing, Elena extracted from Jesusa a personal odyssey. In this formidable Mexi-

can woman, Elena discovered an inner force, an attitude of astonishment toward life that coincided with her own bewilderment:

> Led by Jesusa, I came into contact with poverty, the real kind,
> the kind where water is gathered in buckets and carried care-
> fully so as not to spill any on the way, the kind where washing
> is done on small corrugated pieces of wood or tin because
> there is no sink, where electricity is obtained by attaching
> wires to the main lines, where hens lay eggs without shells
> "only the bare guts" because the lack of sunshine does not per-
> mit the shells to calcify . . .
>
> In that small room nearly always enclosed in semi-darkness,
> in the midst of the squalling of the children in the other rooms,
> slamming doors, lingering voices, and the radio playing at full
> blast, on Wednesday afternoons, at the time the sun sets and
> the blue sky changes to red, a new life appeared, that of Jesusa
> Palancares, that of the past, which she now relived as she nar-
> rated it. Through a tiny slit in the door, we would lie in wait
> of the sky, of its colors, blue then orange, and finally black. A
> slit of sky which never before had I sought so eagerly, half-
> closing my eyes so they would allow me to look fully through
> that tiny opening.
>
> Through the slit we would enter another life, the one inside
> of us. Through it we would also climb to the Kingdom of
> Heaven without our cumbersome human wrapping. (42)

Little by little, trust was born between the two women, a
feeling Jesusa called la querencia, a personal bond that was never
mentioned out loud but sometimes became palpable in the somber
room Jesusa inhabited with her hens and her memories. According
to Elena, her debt to Jesusa is enormous because

> Never did any human being do so much for another as Jesusa
> did for me. And she is going to die, as is her wish; that is why
> every Wednesday my heart races thinking that she might no
> longer be there. "Some day when you come, you won't find
> me here any more; you'll only bump into the air." And I calm

down when I see her sitting there, scrunched up in a small chair, or on her bed, with her two legs hanging over the sides, covered with thick, droopy cotton stockings, listening to her soap opera on the radio; greeting me grouchily with her hands crooked from too much laundry, yellow and brown spots on her face, her hair in untidy braids, a sweater held together with a large safety pin, and then I ask God to let me be the one to bear her to her final resting place. (44)

"I Do Belong"

The impact these interviews with her mentor Jesusa had on Elena was so strong and so deep that it altered her personal if not her genetic condition. Through Jesusa, Elena felt for the first time that something belonged to her: that her Mexican life took on, day by day, a special meaning, plotting a difficult but true road for her to follow, a road that was mapped out on the deformed and spotted hands of her soul mate. Moved and happy, Elena would go home in the evening to transcribe the scrawls that documented her interviews with Jesusa, but when she tried to share the essence of these extraordinary experiences with her family, her efforts did not get the reaction she would have wished:

I would get home and tell them: "You know? Something is being born inside of me, something new that formerly did not exist," but I got no response. I wanted to tell them: "I feel stronger all the time, I'm growing; now, finally, I will be a woman." What did blossom, or perhaps what had been there for years, was the reality of being a Mexican, of becoming a Mexican, of feeling that Mexico was inside of me, and that it was the same as Jesusa's and that if we only opened the slit, it would all come out. I was no longer the eight-year-old girl who came in a boat full of refugees, the *Marqués de Comillas*, the child of eternally absent parents, daughter of transatlantic liners, daughter of trains, but that Mexico was inside. It was a huge creature (as Jesusa used to call the tape recorder), a strong animal, strong and exuberant, that grew until it occupied the whole place. To discover it was like suddenly having the truth between your hands, like a lamp that gives out strong light and throws it in a circle on the ground . . . My grandparents and my great-grandparents had a saying which they believed to be poetic: "I don't belong." Perhaps it was their manner of distinguishing themselves from the rabble, not being like the others. One night, before falling asleep, after identifying with Jesusa at length and mentally reviewing all her images, one by one, I could finally tell myself in a low voice: "I do belong." (4)

"To Take Advantage"

One of the critical questions regarding *Hasta no verte Jesús mío*—an extraordinary testimonial, product of hours and hours of dialogue with the woman who would become its protagonist—is encapsulated in the question: Who does the book belong to? To Elena Poniatowska or to Josefina Bórquez? At one point in the long essay-elegy dedicated to Jesusa, Elena confesses that, like Oscar Lewis, the author of *The Children of Sánchez*, which caused such a scandal upon its publication in Mexico, she didn't improve the conditions in which Jesusa lived:

> Neither the doctor of anthropology Oscar Lewis nor I lived the lives of the others . . . For Oscar Lewis, the Sánchezes became splendid protagonists of the so-called anthropology of poverty. For me, Jesusa was a true character, the best of all. Jesusa was right: I profited from her, I took advantage of her, just like Lewis profited from the Sánchez family . . . The Sánchezes' life didn't change at all: it did not improve nor did it become worse. Lewis and I made money on our books about Mexicans who live in tenements. Lewis continued with his antiseptic life as an American anthropologist, surrounded by his disinfectants and purified water, and neither my life today nor my past existence has anything to do with that of Jesusa. I continued to be, more than anything else, a woman in front of a typewriter. (51)

In literary terms, Elena underlines the picaresque quality of her book, which reinaugurates a literary subgenre that had been absent from Mexico since the time of Joaquín Fernández de Lizardi, the "Mexican thinker" whose *Periquillo Sarniento* (1814) describes the adventures of his antihero of the same name. This picaresque novel, written as a subtle criticism of the most highly esteemed political and social institutions of New Spain at the dawn of independence, is also considered the first modern Mexican novel. A century and a half later, *Hasta no verte Jesús mío* came to represent a true milestone of twentieth-century Mexican narrative, and as such, has had many imitators, among which the most extraordinary is undoubtedly *Adonis García*, a neo-picaresque novel by Luis Zapata. His book, published ten years later, in 1979, relates the adventures, dreams, and disappointments of a young male prostitute of Mexico City, who, like a new Lazarillo de Tormes, goes from master to master, always attempting to improve his lot in life within the strict hierarchy of his society and times.

In her "Life and Death of Jesusa," Elena reconstructs the process of writing the novel and the manner in which it was finally composed. Each meeting with Jesusa was a long interview that Elena would transcribe that day, until she had accumulated nearly a thousand typewritten pages. Notwithstanding the amount of information she gathered, Elena confesses that in her novel she was unable to reveal the essence of Jesusa, to render the profound nature of her protagonist. Accumulating adventures, going from one anecdote to another, Elena just let herself be carried along by Jesusa's fascinating life as a vagabond, which encompassed a political revolution, loves, hatred, quarrels, disillusionment, and a newfound religious zeal that was born in her through the miraculous healer Roque Rojas and his histrionic spiritualism. Jesusa's vital and spiritual experiences are firmly engraved in the first phrase of the novel: "This is the third time I have returned to earth, but I had never suffered so much as in this reincarnation, because in the previous one I was a queen."

Elena with her
ever-present
notebook.
(Photo by
Héctor García)

"Writing Is Hell"

Margarita García Flores, a Mexican journalist, was the first to interview Elena after the publication of *Hasta no verte Jesús mío,* and their conversation sheds light on the meeting between Elena and Jesusa. The first part of the interview was published in *La Revista de la UNAM,* in October 1969:

> "How did you write this novel? Did you follow Oscar Lewis' method?"
>
> "Yes, you could say a bit of Oscar Lewis' methods if you like, although I couldn't really become 'the *gringo* with the tape recorder,' as they called him. I took many notes, which I would reconstruct immediately, as soon as I got home . . ."

"Do you feel great empathy for Jesusa?"

"Yes, I love her enormously. She is among the people who have taught me the most lessons in life. I admire her; I would like to have her moral fiber, her courage, her capacity for indignation, and her pride."

"How is that empathy reflected in the novel? Do you treat her with a lot of affection or very objectively?"

"You see, the material in the novel has been manipulated over and over. I had more than a thousand pages [of notes] because I couldn't get the book to come together, so I hid my inability by asking Jesusa things that I had already asked her. And then the same question once more! Afterwards, I would read her the answers to see if I was right, because, if you will, this novel is an immense and grueling interview. But she would tell me that it was not accurate, that I had not put it down as she had told it. I believe that it happens to all of us. If we are asked to relate something that happened to us three consecutive times, we can never repeat it in exactly the same way. The time comes when we make something up without meaning to. Each time she told me something, Jesusa would make slight changes depending on her state of mind at the moment. That is why I later opted not to read what she said back to her . . . There are some topics that she never wanted to discuss, at least not in answer to my direct questions. Later, they would come out, but I never forced her to tell me things that she did not want to. We never took up intimate subjects; she always said whatever she wanted to say, and never more than what she wanted to say . . . When I began the novel, I had but one intention, which was to listen to her, never to direct her or to push her . . . She talks a lot about the 'Spiritual Work,' and here I had to cut out large paragraphs, pages and pages. I invented many dialogues to lighten up the text; I added images and built chapters. That is why it became a novel instead of an anthropological study."

"Do you give more importance to dialogue or to monologue?"

"I don't know, I never thought about whether there is more

dialogue than monologue. I tried to make the book as read-
able as possible, to keep it from becoming heavy as a brick."

"Is the language you use the way she speaks?"

"Yes, although language was also a problem, because when I
met her she spoke very correctly and never used bad words . . .
When I came back from Europe, our relationship became very
affectionate. Then she began to speak to me in her own language, which is very crude and which I had never suspected
that she used. I remember that the first time she cursed in front
of me was when I was arguing that people are very good and
that everybody loves one another. She got angry and said:
'Don't be a stupid fuck! Nobody is good. Nobody loves one
another. You are the only ass . . . !' I'm not really sure that I
like this version of *Hasta no verte Jesús mío*; I'm really a bit afraid
of it."

"Why are you afraid of it?"

"Because I have never written a novel, because I know that
writing is hell, and because now that I have left journalism
behind, I realize that I used to do things in a rush, carelessly
but fast, without really thinking about them, in a jumbled way,
and that this approach showed up in the final result."

"Is Jesusa full of poetry? People always say that your books
are poetic: what do you think?"

"Guillermo says that now they will think that I am the most
foul-mouthed writer in Latin America. Actually, I would like
Jesusa to be a poetic and spiritual being, because otherwise my
book would have more in common with *The Children of Sánchez*,
which discusses underpants and provides all kinds of rather
unpleasant facts related to gynecology and whatnot. Jesusa
also uses a language that we might call crude, but never vulgar,
and when she refers to herself, she never loses her modesty.
She is never indecent."

"And you, a princess who always wears white gloves, how
did you manage to adopt expletives with so much enthusiasm?"

"I wear white gloves the way waiters do, putting them on
when it's time to serve the tables. Let me tell you that my

grandmother really traumatized me, because every time I was ready to leave the house, she would call from the top of the staircase: 'Do you have your white gloves with you?' They were short gloves like Minnie Mouse wears, with a tiny button. I believe that the bad words were already inside of me. That is why it was so easy for me to assimilate them. You may notice that Jesusa's language becomes much less vital without swear words. To me, expletives out of context are disagreeable, for they seem artificial. But the way Jesusa used them they were so well integrated, so authentic, that they hardly stand out. At least to me, none of them seems forced. On the contrary, I eliminated some 'damns' just in order not to provide more incentives to those who are always looking to be scandalized."

"But why do you say that Jesusa is such a rebel if you transcribe her as saying, 'Well, it's a shame but it was our lot to live like this, etc.'?"

"Jesusa, like all of us, knows that she must die and that no one can rebel against that. She believes in reincarnation. Right now she is on her third reincarnation, but she claims that she doesn't know what the hell she did in the others, but that she must have been very evil, since in this reincarnation God sent her to purge her sins as a leper."

"Do you believe in reincarnation?"

"In Jesusa's, totally. I wish beings like her would reincarnate all the time."

"Do you believe that some people would think of Jesusa as a clinical case?"

"Well, that's up to them . . . I wish there were many clinical cases like hers, don't you?"

A Prose That Astounds

On February 4, 1970, Ermilo Abreu Gómez, a fixture of Mexican literature and the scholar whose historical research helped reestablish Sor Juana Inés de la Cruz's well-earned fame in international letters, published a review of *Hasta no verte Jesús mío* that was so full

of praise it served to canonize Elena Poniatowska's first novel and
situate it as one of the most important Mexican books of all time.
Time would prove Don Ermilo right, in that according to many
literary critics, it is her most transcendent work of fiction. The
review appeared in the weekly magazine *Siempre!* (no. 116) during
its heyday, when Fernando Benítez was its publisher, José Emilio
Pacheco its editor-in-chief, and exiled Spanish artist Vicente Rojo
its artistic director:

> I will say it without further ado: Elena Poniatowska's latest
> book, *Hasta no verte Jesús mío*, is quite simply a masterpiece. As
> such, it is not to be read only once, because it is bursting with
> so much spiritual material that it is worthy of being read over
> and over again . . . at the end we realize that the whole story
> is pure poetry of the best kind, of the kind doled out by the
> hand of God with order and good measure; poetry which is
> delivered without enigmas or obscurity, like that of the poets
> who cultivate the art of hermeneutics, as do Góngora, Valéry,
> and Mallarmé, even though Juan Ramón Jiménez and the
> unforgettable León Felipe, men of excellent judgment, don't
> agree. The novel's protagonist, who plays such an important
> role within it, leads us via both straightforward and mysteri-
> ous paths to other zones where life acquires another dimen-
> sion, where reality avails itself of different roots in order to
> explain itself . . . Because we should know up front that several
> dimensions and several realities exist in the cosmos that we
> cannot explain or experience because we are intent upon mea-
> suring them with yardsticks, which are useless for determining
> either the length or the width of the stars. And as the prophets
> before us said, we observe the heavens from the "bad side"
> of the celestial tapestry, and that is the reason it deceives us
> with its disorderly appearance. We forget that the good side
> is the other one, where God used his threads and needles.
> Well, Elena Poniatowska has an enlightened and clear-sighted
> soul that serves her well for looking at the correct side of the
> world's tapestry. And from her vision came this book, a thou-
> sand times admirable, a thousand times astounding. Its char-

Elena Poniatowska's
ex libris, created by
Alberto Beltrán.

acters—so harshly real and so brutally otherworldly—have
meandered through the various levels of creation, and we are
able to enjoy the aromas from the garden with which she has
regaled us . . .

Elena Poniatowska has created, while amusing herself, one
of the few masterpieces of modern Mexican literature. For
my most demanding taste, this work will become part of the
repertoire of the best books written in Spanish, of the most
highly regarded books of all times, ancient or modern.

A Light Dusting Over

Following the critical standard established by Don Ermilo, who traces the lineage of *Hasta no verte Jesús mío* back to the medieval *Count Lucanor*, Gerardo de la Torre points to the enormous literary value of the work, connecting it to the Spanish picaresque novel and, more important, to the early testimonial novel, two formal and thematic traits that constitute the basis for any critical approach to this work. In his review, the critic also mentions the question inevitably raised by a book of this nature. Who is the author: Elena or Jesusa? His review, entitled "Hasta no leerte Jesús mío" (Until We Read Again, Jesus) appeared in *La Revista Mexicana de Cultura*:

> I had barely finished reading *Hasta no verte Jesús mío* when I recalled that many years back somebody accused Malraux of being incapable of getting inside the skin of an imbecile. Malraux's response: "There are enough imbeciles in this life without having to put them into novels as well." It did not interest me, but I thought that if the accuser were living, he could not make such a complaint against Elena Poniatowska, because in *Hasta no verte Jesús mío* the author not only got inside the skin of an ignorant, superstitious, miserable, and arrogant woman, but she identified so deeply with her that she disappeared, erasing herself, and in her place, Jesusa Palancares spoke out, fluent and sincere, to relate to us an entertaining and tragic story, ferocious and full of emotion. At the same time, as if before a Stendhalian mirror, she reflected all the landscapes and situations she passed through, and they in turn reflected through her, leading us to her very original opinions—hers, not Elena Poniatowska's—regarding society, development, backwardness, and progress. In any case, it might be thought that the author simply collected and transcribed the woman's language—in fact she is quite a unique and multifaceted character—and after giving it a light dusting over, typed it out, put it in a folder, and delivered it to her publisher.
>
> Up to this point everything seems very simple. I envisioned Elena Poniatowska procuring documents, making care-

ful notes, and hunting down popular characters with a tape recorder in hand: think Oscar Lewis and *The Children of Sánchez*, reports, interviews, para-journalism (a term coined by Dwight MacDonald). But no, in *Hasta no verte Jesús mío* I found neither interview nor reporting, nobody's children, only the minute and backbreaking work of the writer, poetic work, and re-envisioning, re-creation, re-elaboration of events, documents, sentences, psychological facts, landscapes, images.

Elena Poniatowska thinking about Jesusa, creating a character with a life of her own. Yes, with a life of her own, but at the same time a character forged with elements taken from various peasants: this Petronila and that Evodia, from this Hermenegilda, and that Refugio. In no way or manner is she Petronila, Refugio, Hermenegilda, or Evodia. But she is all of them and many more . . . Pride and generosity in a woman related to rogues like Lazarillo, Periquillo, Estebanillo, and other similar lowlifes, as well as Buscón and Guzmán de Alfarache. A woman who, alone, as best as she can, defends herself in a world of scoundrels and misfits, and in a long novelistic tour through the twenty-nine chapters of *Hasta no verte Jesús mío* gives us an image of the suffering, the cruelty, the filth, the hunger, and the terror that abound in large cities, making up an underworld into which one may sink without ever reaching the bottom. In *Hasta no verte Jesús mío* are recounted—or better, set down or reflected—prisons, battles, funerals, deaths, whorehouses, hospitals for prostitutes, children dying of hunger, drunken women, covetous creatures, husbands who leave their wives half-dead, wives who betray their husbands, abortions, exploitation, and floating over all of this like a challenge, the pervading stench of misery . . .

At the end I was left with a triumphant Jesusa Palancares, leading her memory among mementos as if through a world full of ghosts, for what else are the secondary characters of *Hasta no verte Jesús mío* but cartoons, faint drawings used as the frame for the tormented, powerful, and vital presence of Jesusa Palancares, an orphan with no father or mother, the widow of

With her "Mexican Virgil," Josefina Bórquez. (Photo by Héctor García)

captain Pedro Aguilar, mother of no one and of all who so desire.

The Joy of Reading

The most assiduous of all Elena's critics, one who has dedicated himself to commenting on her opus from *Lilus Kikus* (1954) until now, is Emmanuel Carballo, who published his review of Elena's novel in *Excélsior*, on Monday, December 22, 1969, under the title "Testimony or Novel: A Disappointed Revolutionary." His brief analysis begins by citing the novel as an example of testimonial literature but ultimately identifies it with the literary subgenre of the anthropological novel. Among the first Latin American exponents of this literary form was the Cuban novelist Miguel Barnet, with his *Biography of a Runaway Slave*. This work is also the product of exhaustive interviews, in his case with an elderly Afro-Cuban man whose life encompassed Cuba's entire modern history from the abolition of slavery and the War of Independence to the Cuban Revolution of 1959. By the fifties, in the English-speaking world, American author Truman Capote had already published *In Cold Blood*, the novelistic reconstruction of an unthinkably brutal but fascinating crime, a work he labeled a "nonfiction novel." This literary subgenre reappeared in many forms throughout Latin American literature of the so-called post-boom of the seventies and eighties, producing testimonials such as *Mi nombre es Rigoberta Menchú, y así nació mi conciencia* by the anthropologist Elizabeth Burgos Debray and her informant, a Maya-Quiché woman victimized by the most brutal physical and psychological oppression. According to Carballo, the essential characteristic of Elena Poniatowska's short fiction, particularly evident in *Lilus Kikus*, is confirmed and enriched in *Hasta no verte Jesús mío*:

> To some, this book may seem to be anthropological testimony, to others, a realistic novel raised to the exaggeration of pointillist naturalism. The former and the latter positions are both valid. This book, whose origin lies in the author's previously mentioned short stories, also touches upon—in accordance with its structure and aims—the terrain conquered by works such as *Juan Pérez Jolote* by Ricardo Pozas, and *Anthropology of Poverty, The Children of Sánchez*, and *Pedro Martínez* by Oscar Lewis, as well as the studies of an elderly slave and of a cabaret singer by the Cuban Miguel Barnet and, especially, even though Elena Poniatowska is probably not familiar with it, *Manuela la mexicana* (Manuela the Mexican) by Aída García Alonso. On the other hand, and with some attendant goodwill, it may be considered a novel that, without lacking in imagination, scrupulously seeks to document the reality (or at least make the reader believe so) in which little Jesusa, the heroine of this book, has lived since she was a child. Testimony or novel, a dilemma that I don't care to elucidate for the time being, *Hasta no verte Jesús mío* is the work of Mexican fiction of those published in 1969 that has interested me the most as a reader, and perhaps also as a critic.

This book by Elena Poniatowska deserves more than one

article; it demands an essay on its abundant excellences, which I promise to write as soon as possible. For the time being, I only wish to communicate most superficially the joy of reading an admirable book and the pain of fully accepting the denunciation it contains.

A Great Fanfare

So much praise was heaped upon *Hasta no verte Jesús mío* that in April 1970, *La Vida Literaria*, the periodical edited by author and critic Wilberto Cantón, devoted an entire issue "to one of the books which has recently sparked the most interest and caught the most attention: *Hasta no verte Jesús mío*." It included articles by Francisco Monterde, Carmen Galindo, Miguel Donoso Pareja, and Miguel Capistrán, and Elena opens the issue with an introductory essay. At the end of this tribute there is an appendix, "Critical Comments on the Novel *Hasta no verte Jesús mío*," containing a selection of commentary essential for any investigator or reader interested in documenting the remarkable commotion provoked by this novel written by a thirty-seven-year-old journalist. In the veritable chorus of critical acclaim are to be found the voices of some of Mexico's most important contemporary authors: Rosario Castellanos, María Elvira Bermúdez, Rubén Salazar Mallén, Julieta Campos, Emilio Uranga, María Luisa "China" Mendoza, and Beatriz Espejo. However, it was Castellanos, the author of *Poesía no eres tú* (Poetry You Are Not), who best sums up, in very few words, Elena's efforts and talent:

> Elena Poniatowska needs no introduction. The public knows her because they have read her intelligent and subtle interviews, always interesting and revealing. Nor is it necessary to praise her. When she assumes courage as a vocation and loyalty as a norm of conduct; when she chooses the noble cause and disdains other advantages and all opportunism, she does it not as a heroic act but as a spontaneous response, as if no other were possible. When she comes to fruition as a person and as a writer, this achievement seems almost a natural consequence to all of us who contemplate her. She has

done everything necessary on her part, she possesses all the required gifts, and she has employed them wisely. So, why shouldn't it be so? Simply because life is not logical, except in some cases. And this is one such case; therefore, there is nothing left to do but rejoice. I am not going to speak of my friendship with Elena, which is a private matter. With you, our reader, I have a complicit relationship, since I too am a reader. And in this case, an extraordinary book when judged from any possible vantage point, *Hasta no verte Jesús mío*, has just been published by Elena Poniatowska.

Not surprisingly, the most interesting article of all those in this special edition of *La Vida Literaria* was written by Elena herself, at the request of Wilberto Cantón. In it, Elena attempts to express what is ineffable and to explain through everyday examples her peculiar relationship with Jesusa:

> With regard to *Hasta no verte Jesús mío*, in a certain sense it is a book that was given to me and that, in turn, was given a life of its own. But it is also a book that required a lot of work. Reality is an excuse, a starting point. Jesusa exists, it is true, and she is made of flesh and blood, a living being. But she did not speak (except once in while) as she does in the book, nor is she what the book is. It is not a literal transcription in which Jesusa poured her life and deeds into my ears as if into a funnel. Her life is something else. And being something else, it is also mine. For the rest of us, Jesusa is a poor old woman who endlessly repeats strange, often tedious things, who watches soap operas, feeds her pets (a cat with a broken spine, doves, and malnourished canaries). She lives in a tenement and never turns off the radio. Complaining and complaining, Jesusa is similar to a lot of other elderly people: to those who walk along the sidewalk, keeping close to the wall, and whom we instinctively avoid because they get in our way, and we are always in a hurry. There where Mexico becomes dumpy and flat, there where the houses become smaller, diminished until they are barely higher than the ground they are set upon, lives Jesusa. No doubt that is where she will die. The only thing

she wants is to be left alone to die in peace, that they do not take her radio or TV away, and that nobody meddle with her. When I have brought a friend or even my children over to meet her, she is polite, but she wants them to leave quickly. The next time I go over she complains, "Why did you bring them?"

We can give value and meaning to reality, we may add something to the physical world that directly or indirectly does not belong there, perhaps in response to the way the universe around us affects our senses. But how many times does reality also end up being superior to our perception of it, to our assessment, to the invention it motivates! Jesusa, who walked so much through life, has begun to walk alone in a book. Her destiny is linked to mine, and in a certain way, so is her death.

6 1968: The Year of Tlatelolco

Dark Shadows

In the midst of her interviews with Josefina Bórquez, and like a nightmare, a baneful shadow obscured Elena's enjoyment of her editorial success and political awakening, for on October 2, 1968, Elena had to face a human tragedy of unimaginable dimensions, one that in the beginning she could not—or would not—accept. This was the tragic death and pointless imprisonment of hundreds of Mexican students that occurred at six o'clock in the evening at the legendary Plaza de las Tres Culturas (Plaza of the Three Cultures). On this site four centuries earlier the Franciscan friar Pedro de Gante had founded the Imperial Colegio de Indios (Imperial College for the Indians) with the Christian purpose of teaching his neophytes the secrets of Western artistic perspective and the mysteries of the Holy Trinity. Now it lives forever in the collective memory of all Mexicans, especially those who experienced firsthand what was later called "La Noche de Tlatelolco" (The Night of Tlatelolco). Nine weeks of student strikes had culminated in the military's invasion of Mexico's National Autonomous University (UNAM). Ten days before the opening ceremony of the Olympic Games in Mexico City, approximately 15,000 students from different universities took to the streets of the Mexican capital to protest the army's recent occupation of the university campus. Many of them carried red carnations as a symbol of protest. By nightfall, at least 5,000 students and workers, many accompanied by their families, had congregated outside an apartment complex in the Plaza de las Tres Culturas in the northern suburb of Tlatelolco, for what was intended to be another peaceful rally. Among their chants was "México—Libertad—México—Libertad" (Mexico—Liberty—Mexico—Liberty). Rally organizers attempted to call off the protest when they noticed increased military presence in the area, but it was too late. The violence that occurred that evening stunned the country. By the time the shooting stopped, hundreds of people lay dead or wounded, while army and special police forces captured the surviving protesters and dragged them away.

Elena was at that time a thirty-six-year-old woman married to the astrophysicist Guillermo Haro and new mother to Felipe, who had been born on June 4 of that year. More than thirty years after the events of that unforgettable afternoon, Elena, still shocked, recalls the immediate sense of denial mixed with outrage that the news of these senseless acts provoked in her:

> I heard about the massacre at nine o'clock that night, when María Alicia Martínez Medrano and her friend Mercedes Olivera came to my house. María Alicia had worked with me and she is very dear to me. I thought they were crazy. They told me that there was blood on the walls of the buildings, that the elevators were perforated with machine-gun bullets, that the glass windows of the shops were shattered, that tanks were in the plaza, that there was blood on the staircases of the buildings, that they could hear people shouting, moaning, and crying.

Elena, who at that time was nursing her small son, decided to go see for herself. Thus began the compilation of her most polemical testimonial book and, at the same time, her most celebrated chronicle: *La noche de Tlatelolco: testimonios de historia oral* (The Night of Tlatelolco: Oral History Testimonies, later translated into English as *Massacre in Mexico*), first published in 1971 and with more than 600,000 copies sold to date:

> At seven o'clock in the morning I went to Tlatelolco. There was no running water, and women were lined up around a hydrant. There was no electricity, and the soldiers were also lined up in front of the phone booths. Among the pre-

Hispanic ruins, next to the building that houses the Secretariat of Foreign Relations, I saw the shoes of those who had managed to escape. I returned home extremely indignant, as were Guillermo and my eldest son, Mane.

Then I began to gather testimonies. I typed up everything that María Alicia told me, as well as everything I had heard from Mercedes Olivera. I interviewed Margarita Velasco, who had been separated from her son that night but found him the next morning. The next day I went to find the Italian journalist Oriana Fallaci, who was at the French Hospital because she also had been shot. I found her in a wheelchair, very upset, but with no major wounds: two days later she left the hospital and flew to Acapulco. She placed a long-distance call to the Italian Parliament, requesting that the Italian delegation boycott the Olympic Games as an act of protest against the government of Mexico. She said that she had been a war correspondent in Vietnam and that at least there a siren sounded a warning before the bombing or shooting began, so that people could take refuge; Mexico was the only country where she had ever seen soldiers shooting point-blank at civilians. Besides, they were inside a plaza, trapped, unable to escape. I took my interview to *Novedades*, but they turned it down because there were orders not to publish a single word about the incident.

From that moment on I was very concerned and went to Military Camp No. 1, to see what had happened to the students. The soldiers would not let me in. Every day in the newspaper there was an advertisement placed by the parents of Raúl Alvarez Garín which read: "21 Days Later and We Still Do Not Know Where Our Son Raúl Is." I went to the Lecumberri jail on Sundays and sometimes on weekdays to interview the student leaders. Sometimes Guillermo would accompany me, as he had a friend who had been jailed, the scientist Eli de Gortari, as had another friend of his from many years back, José Revueltas. We would leave Felipe with my husband's sister-in-law, Yolanda Haro. Mane was older. On Sundays he would participate in mandatory military service.

An Accomplice by Impotence?

Tlatelolco had a strong impact on Elena's life. Having discovered the secrets—sometimes folkloric and charming, sometimes squalid and heartbreaking—of the lives of the poorest Mexicans through the adventures of Jesusa Palancares and of the characters of *Todo empezó el domingo*, the writer was demoralized by the enormous weight of these events. So much so that afterward neither she nor anything in her life was the same. In an interview with Margarita García Flores published in *La Revista de la UNAM* in October 1969, the year in which Elena became a Mexican citizen, she evokes her experiences and describes how an irrevocable spiritual change occurred within her:

> "Are you thinking about a new novel?"
>
> "Yes, but writing is becoming harder all the time."
>
> "Why? Because of the children and the housework?"
>
> "No, because I am older. I believe that all of us got older, older after Tlatelolco. You know, every time I hear that song called 'Those Were the Days,' I feel like crying. By the way, José Emilio Pacheco wrote a poem about that song in his book (*No me preguntes cómo pasa el tiempo;* Don't ask me how time passes). (What a lovely book!) We thought they were days of pure laughter and believed that they would never end, that we would bet and never lose. I could tell you that those happy days no longer matter to me, but they do, especially because we will not know how to bring them back. Who can bring the dead back to life?"
>
> "The outcome of the student movement and the fact that so many were jailed and others exiled has affected you that much?"
>
> "Yes, and it affected you as well, and Guillermo and Mane, too, and my mother, as well as everyone else. I feel that we do nothing, that nobody moves. I feel like an accomplice by impotence. In 1968 we lived through an ignominious event: Tlatelolco. And we remained on the sidelines, rooted to the ground, useless beside our dead. If in the United States there is such capacity to protest and the very participants in the slaughter

at My Lai have the courage to condemn and denounce themselves, where is our indignation, our rebelliousness?"

The "Night of Tlatelolco"

From the devastating testimony of numerous individuals: parents of the dead and of those who had disappeared, leaders of high school and university unions, intellectuals, poets, and others whose only connection was that of being to a greater or lesser degree involved in the terrible event unleashed that night in Tlatelolco, Elena created a chorus of appalled voices which, combined with the official news coming from within the government bureaucracy, gave birth to a decisive book.

One of those who died that year was her only brother, Jan, whose death was the result of different circumstances. Elena explains that

"*La noche de Tlatelolco* was published after the death of Jan, who died in a car accident on December 8, 1968. When I wrote my dedication: 'To Jan and to all those who died in 1968,' I created a misunderstanding because many thought that my reason for writing the book was Jan's death, which occurred in the same year. Jan was part of the student movement, and once he told me that he had gone to the National Palace to paint graffiti on the walls, and that he had participated in some of the marches, but he did not die on October 2, 1968, but later, on December 8, in Calpulalpan, when a truck with burlap instead of glass on the windows ran into the automobile he was driving.

"I was not very involved in the movement," says Elena, "because my son Felipe was born on June 4 of that year, and I was nursing him. I went to perhaps three marches, and maybe two assemblies where I met Luis González de Alba and Marcelino Perelló, Tita (Roberta Avendaño), Nacha, and Gilberto Guevara Niebla. I followed the news about the movement but could not go to the university every day. My husband, Guillermo, could and he accompanied Javier Barros Sierra in the march he called as rector of the UNAM."

Elena's
brother, Jan.

Political Disdain

La noche de Tlatelolco is an account of the bloody actions of the Mexican government. Given the political situation and the relative re-
cency of the events, the book did not receive any publicity when
it was first published, and the only review printed was written by
José Emilio Pacheco, one of Mexico's leading poets. Nonetheless,
the book became known by word of mouth among professors and
university students anxious to find testimonies and an explanation
of the events that occurred that evening in Tlatelolco:

Nothing was ever published except José Emilio's article. The book sold many copies because it was rumored that it would be pulled from circulation, that agents of the Federal Security Agency had entered the bookstores to buy up the copies. Some readers would purchase ten or twenty copies at a time. Ediciones ERA had already received a letter saying that a bomb would be planted on the premises if the book was published. Don Tomás Espresate replied that he had been in the Spanish Civil War and that he understood perfectly the meaning of war. The book came out, many legends were spread about it, and all those rumors only benefited the book.

In a demonstration of absolute cynicism, the upper echelons of the Mexican government decided that the most efficient way to reduce the book's impact was to canonize it by conferring on its author the coveted Xavier Villaurrutia Prize:

"One day, Francisco Zendejas called," Elena remarks, "to inform me that I had won the Xavier Villaurrutia literary prize. Fausto Zapata, President Echeverría's private secretary, told me that he was pleased that I had won it. I declined it in a letter to *Excélsior* where I asked, 'Who will award prizes to the dead?' It is not a book of celebration. It is a work of condemnation.

"The government had already acquired the habit of taking on everything in order to minimize the importance of everything. I then wrote another letter to the newspaper *Excélsior*, which was published, but part of it was censored. Zendejas called me the next day to tell me that I had not been given the award for *La noche de Tlatelolco* but for *Hasta no verte Jesús mío*. Years later, I ran into the critic Alicia Zendejas, who was Francisco's wife, and she told me that they considered me a Villaurrutia laureate. It is very easy to say that I am a Villaurrutia laureate, but the truth is that I never received the award itself."

The Mazatlán Prize

In the same year, 1971, Elena accepted the Mazatlán Prize for *Here's to You, Jesusa*. This award added to Elena's happiness over the birth of her daughter, Paula, on April 11, 1970. A triumphant article in *Novedades*—the same daily that had refused to publish her eyewitness accounts of the Tlatelolco massacre—announced to its readers on February 17, 1971, that "our colleague" had received the prize for the "best Mexican literary work of 1970, awarded by the state of Sinaloa and consisting of 25,000 pesos." The article makes no reference whatsoever to *La noche de Tlatelolco*, only pointing out that "the other work presented by a Mexican author was the novel *Cumpleaños* (Birthday), by the writer Carlos Fuentes, but *Hasta no verte Jesús mío* won unanimously . . . Upon being notified of the award, Elena herself exclaimed happily: 'This is a wonderful surprise! I did not expect this prize; I have never even won a consolation prize in the lottery! Besides, I have never been to Mazatlán and have always wanted to go! What generosity on the part of the jury, especially Don Ermilo Abreu Gómez, who has devoted so much affection to my book *Hasta no verte Jesús mío!*'"

A Tlatelolco Memoir

An article on Tlatelolco by José Emilio Pacheco, who was very familiar with the manuscript of the book because he helped Elena to edit it, appeared in *La Cultura en México*, *Siempre's* cultural section, on March 31, 1971, under the title "Memories '68: Tlatelolco, October 2." Recall that at the time Pacheco was editor-in-chief of *La Cultura en México*, while the magazine itself was published by Fernando Benítez; the supplement included articles by Carlos Monsiváis and Vicente Rojo, who also illustrated it:

> With an enormous capacity for creative organization, Elena Poniatowska presents in a fluid and dynamic compilation hundreds of multifaceted testimonies. The voices of participants and spectators, texts of pamphlets, signs, and posters, as well as documents, poems, and songs, form a dramatic ensemble in a volume that transcends the words on the page and re-

Guillermo and Elena with Felipe. (Photo by Emmanuel Haro)

creates for the reader the events that occurred in Mexico's most decisive year since the presidency of Lázaro Cárdenas.

Massacre in Mexico sustains its muralistic or symphonic effectiveness through montage, a cinematic technique through which literature has been greatly enriched. (Let's not forget that its creators understood that the montage is a means of providing us with increased awareness.) In this way, and by utilizing all the advantages that tape recordings can provide; their immediacy and their capacity—beyond that of the printed word—to transmit the unique timbre of each human voice,

Elena Poniatowska has erased the distance between those who read the book and the events it recounts. In its pages are to be found, first and foremost, the sounds and the flavors of those days in which the term "politics" stopped being a bad word and a foreign realm, to become common language and part of everyone's lives; and then came the rumbling, the horror of the killing which oppresses our personal and collective existence with its intolerable weight . . .

No other account has expressed the atrocious enormity of the crime in all its dimensions as well as this manifold description by the survivors does. Blood fills the scene: "There was a lot of blood stepped on, a lot of blood smeared on the walls . . . I could feel its stickiness on my hands." And just as indelible as the visual and tactile sensations are the auditory memories: "The cries, the wailing of those in pain, the tears, the pleas, and the continuous and ear-splitting sounds of the weapons, which turned the Plaza de las Tres Culturas into a Dantesque inferno . . ."

Who—singular or plural—unleashed the hell of Tlatelolco? Elena Poniatowska's book is also the book of those jailed and of the mothers who lost their children in one of the worst slaughters ever witnessed in a history as sad and violent as ours. This is an opportunity to demand a public investigation of the crime from the government, and the punishment of those responsible. Until this happens, until the attorney general's office changes its "hands off" attitude and the jails are emptied of political prisoners, any talk of true democracy in Mexico will be only a fiction.

A Sad Anniversary

On October 1, 1971, one day before the third anniversary of the Tlatelolco massacre, correspondent Elsa Arana Freire published a lengthy interview with Elena in the magazine 7 *Días* (7 Days), entitled "Elena Poniatowska and the Tlatelolco Massacre." This interview helps clarify some aspects of Elena's participation in the student movement and of the preparation of her book:

7 Días: Weren't you present at the Plaza de Tlatelolco that night?

Elena: No, no. I was at home with my children. At that time I was doing very little journalism. My friends came to tell me what allegedly had happened, and to me it seemed that they were quite hysterical (I am speaking in retrospect). Faced with their tears and their stories I thought, "It is impossible that what they are telling me really happened." In the following days, very little, almost nothing, came out in the newspapers, except for brief notices. Nothing too terrible. I kept repeating to myself, "It's not possible, they are telling me things that are only products of their imagination, because these things don't happen in Mexico . . . "

7 Días: And when did you act upon your doubts?

Elena: It became a sort of obsession. The room became filled with words, images, and blood. With regard to all the blood, I asked myself: "What is all this? I must investigate." The testimonies I include in the book were gathered in the months afterwards: October, November, and December 1968. I kept all the transcripts. There were more than one hundred . . . The next year, I began to go to Lecumberri, to interview the jailed students.

7 Días: Were you allowed into the prison with no difficulty?

Elena: Yes, because I went on Sundays, and that was the day when women, in particular, came to visit. I spoke with the young people, and it is curious that they did not refer to Tlatelolco, because it was too hard for them. They spoke to me instead of the student movement before the massacre. Based on what they told me, my first concept for the book changed. I had thought of making it only an account of the night of Tlatelolco. But later I told myself that that night could not be explained if one were unaware of the student movement that led up to the night of Tlatelolco. No one would be able to understand its dimensions if the movement were not included. Why the people spontaneously went to the marches . . . The result was a book that was divided into two parts: the first,

"Taking Back the Streets," has the testimonies of the incarcerated boys and others outside, whose names I changed so they would not be harmed or end up in Lecumberri. And the second part, the night of the massacre itself, is the most dramatic, in it are testimonies from journalists and from eyewitnesses. That is the way I put the book together, like a collage . . .

7 Días: What was the main drawback to doing it this way?

Elena: Well, most of the people answered the same way: "We arrived at 5:30 in the afternoon, a green flare was thrown from a helicopter, and then the army came in. They corralled all the people with a 'pincers movement,' so nobody could escape. Some people were able to run out through the back building . . . " Everybody repeated the same experience and I told myself: "If I repeat one hundred times *at 5:30 in the afternoon* . . . etc., the effect will be lost." Now, for instance, several witnesses concurred in saying that they saw a soldier stick his bayonet into a boy's back. I decided to choose the most striking or the most significant part of each testimony. That is why I say that my book is a sort of collage or montage, or what Americans would call *editing.* All are oral histories. People speaking. From the account of a journalist—José Antonio del Campo, of the newspaper *El Día*—who spoke to me for two hours, the equivalent of twenty pages of testimony, I chose only one phrase: "They are corpses, sir . . . " This was spoken to him by a corporal, and it seemed to me more eloquent than forty pages describing the horrors.

7 Días: Was this the first time you used this technique?

Elena: Yes, and it came from the book itself, from seeing so many pages full of repetition. The first part is very important for those who were not a part of the movement or ignored its existence or were not interested in it. My mother, for example, tells me that she doesn't know the meaning of the acronyms I cite, of the abbreviations of schools and polytechnic institutes . . . She is right. I should have explained them. I did not notice because I was so involved in the matter, and so were the editors, that the error slipped by. But in the second part, the one about the events of that night, the narrative is constructed in such a way as to create a tension that begins and ends as a tragedy. The part about Tlatelolco is much better than the first part. However, the student movement itself was also scattered and confused . . .

7 Días: Did you have any difficulty in publishing your book?

Elena: No, none. Or, well, yes, small difficulties; for example, I was given an award which was impossible for me to receive or collect. I do not believe that it is in retaliation for the subject of the book, or maybe it is, although indirectly. But these are not serious matters. What is important is that a book (and this is a phenomenon that doesn't occur frequently in Mexico or in Latin America) which does not receive a single line of publicity, which is not advertised, sells out its third edition in a single month . . .

7 Días: If you started writing the book in 1968, why did it not appear until 1970?

Elena: It went to the printer a week before President Gustavo Díaz Ordaz left the presidency. All books of this type, such as *Días de guardar* (Holy Days), by Monsiváis, another by Luis González de Alba, *Los días y los años* (The Days and the Years), and mine, all on the same subject, went into print once Luis Echeverría was president.

7 Días: What responsibility do you think our current president [has for the massacre]? He was then secretary of the interior, was he not?

Elena: I would not speak of responsibility but of guilt. I express feelings of indignation over an event such as death. But I cannot say who is responsible for what, because I don't have enough evidence to point to the one who is responsible. President Díaz Ordaz publicly admitted his responsibility in 1969.

7 Días: Have you ever been a political activist?

Elena: No, never. I do not belong to any party.

7 Días: And your ideology?

Elena: I'm of Polish descent. What is the ideology of the Poles? They are people who would throw themselves against tanks on horseback. It is a rather Quixotic, literary, idealist ideology but not a concrete or active one . . .

7 Días: Have the testimonies been modified?

Elena: Many of them have, because they were long and repetitive. Some were even bizarre. People, when relating the events, did not have an accurate idea of the time or the hour or of distances. For instance, some would say that at 5:45 they were on the rooftop of the Chihuahua building, on the tenth floor, and that at 5:48 they reached the bottom floor. No one can go down ten floors in three minutes, unless they jump out the windows. They also relate events that have never been verified, such as that in Tlatelolco the bodies were cremated, that there were bodies in the trash bins. This I do not believe . . . The Tlatelolco massacre was completely out of proportion . . . It was absurd. It is absurdity itself. Besides, it is still not known what really happened. People continue to ask themselves about the why and how . . . In the book it isn't clear either. It will never be clear.

Five Years After

In 1975, Helen Lane translated *La noche de Tlatelolco* into English for Viking Press, and at the publisher's request Octavio Paz wrote a foreword for the book. As is well known, Octavio Paz, who was then the Mexican ambassador to India, resigned his post immediately after learning of the violent events at the Plaza de las Tres Culturas, an action that briefly aligned him with the Mexican left wing. His foreword, entitled "A cinco años de Tlatelolco: entre el entusiasmo y la cólera" (Five Years after Tlatelolco: Between Enthusiasm and Wrath), was serialized in the newspaper *Excélsior* beginning on October 1, 1973, one day before the fifth anniversary of the events at the Plaza de las Tres Culturas:

> Elena Poniatowska's book *Massacre in Mexico* is not an interpretation of these events. Far surpassing a theory or a hypothesis, it is an extraordinary piece of reporting or, as she calls it, a "collage" of "voices bearing historical witness." A historical

chronicle—but one that shows us history before it has congealed and before the spoken word has become a written text. For the chronicler of an era, knowing how to listen is even more important than knowing how to write. Or better: the art of writing implies previous mastery of the art of listening. A subtle and difficult art, for it requires not only sharp ears but also great moral sensitivity: recognizing, accepting the existence of others. There are two breeds of writers: the poet, who hearkens to an inner voice, his own; and the novelist, the journalist, and the historian, who hearken to many voices in the world round about them, the voices of others. Elena Poniatowska first made a name for herself as one of Mexico's finest journalists, and shortly thereafter she was widely hailed as the author of starkly dramatic short stories and highly original novels, worlds governed by an offbeat brand of humor and fantasy in which the boundaries separating ordinary everyday reality from the eerie and unexpected become fuzzy and blurred. In both her writings as a journalist and her works of fiction, her language is closer to oral tradition than to classic literary Spanish. In *Massacre in Mexico* she uses her admirable ability to listen and to reproduce what others have to say to serve the cause of history. Her book is a historical account and at the same time, a most imaginative linguistic tour de force.

Massacre in Mexico is a passionate testimony, but not a biased one. It is a passionate book because cold objectivity in the face of injustice is a form of complicity. The passion that suffuses all her pages, from first to last, is a passion for justice, the same burning ideal that inspired the students' demonstrations and protests. Like the student movement itself, *Massacre in Mexico* upholds no particular thesis and puts forward no hard and fast ideological line; on the contrary, it is a book whose underlying rhythm, at times luminous and lyrical and at others somber and tragic, is the rhythm of life itself. The mood at the beginning is one of joyous enthusiasm and euphoria: on taking to the streets, the students discover the meaning of collective action, direct democracy, and fraternity. Armed with these weapons alone, they fight repression and in a very

Vicente Rojo, Elena Poniatowska, Nelly Keogerzan, Tito Monterroso, and Hugo Gutiérrez Vega (back row); Carlos Monsiváis, Carlos Payán, Alba Rojo, and Barbara Jacobs (front row).

short time win the support and the loyalties of the people. Up until this point, Elena Poniatowska's account is the story of the civic awakening of an entire generation of young people. This story of buoyant collective fervor soon takes on darker overtones, however: the wave of hope and generous idealism represented by these youngsters breaks against the wall of sheer power, and the government unleashes its murderous forces of violence; the story ends in a bloodbath. The students were seeking a public dialogue with those in power, and these powers responded with the sort of violence that silences every last voice raised in protest. Why? What were the reasons behind this massacre? Mexicans have been asking themselves this question since October 1968. Only when it is answered will the country recover its confidence in its leaders and in its institutions. And only then will it recover its self-confidence. (VII–VIII)

Following Two Paths

Throughout the decade following the tragic events of Tlatelolco, Elena's literary production follows two literary and ideological paths that culminated in the eighties with the publication of *Fuerte es el silencio* (1980) (Silence Is Strong) and *Nada, nadie: las voces del temblor* (1988) (*Nothing, Nobody: The Voices of the Mexico City Earthquake*, 1995), the latter a collective chronicle of the human catastrophe produced by the earthquake that shook the Mexican capital in the early morning of September 19, 1985. *Tinísima*, published in 1992, an epic biographical novel about the Italian photographer and communist militant Tina Modotti is her masterwork in the genre of merging fiction and nonfiction, and it earned her the Mazatlán Prize for the second time. These two artistic and ideological inclinations: one that documents human and natural disasters and denounces the official indifference that nearly always accompanies them, and another that celebrates the lives and work of women like Tina, are clearly reflected in Elena's literary production of the seventies.

While honing her narrative skills, Elena never abandoned journalism, and in conjunction with fellow reporters, she participated in the founding of Mexico City's alternative daily, *La Jornada*, which was born as a challenge to the government censorship suffered by other newspapers, especially *Excélsior*, where she had begun her career but which had gradually become a government mouthpiece. Elena was closely associated as well with the weekly political magazine *Proceso*, founded in 1976 by Julio Scherer García, a former editor of *Excélsior*. In 1987 Elena won the Manuel Buendía Prize along with another left-wing columnist, Miguel Ángel Granados Chapa.

A poignant example of Elena's undeniable solidarity with other women is to be found in *Querido Diego, te abraza Quiela*, published in 1976 and translated into English as *Dear Diego* in 1986. This novella is composed of a series of fictional letters that are at the same time heartrending and affectionate, addressed to the legendary painter Diego Rivera, who never replies to their author, the Russian painter Angelina Beloff. At the same time, this short work of fiction reflects Elena's own personal suffering at that time, for her marriage to the Mexican astrophysicist Guillermo Haro did not provide the love and support that she yearned for:

> Carmen Gaitán of Editorial Océano asked me to write a fore-word for the two novels by Lupe Marín: *La única* (The One and Only), and *Un día patrio* (A Patriotic Day). To learn more about Marín, I read the English biography of Diego Rivera by Bertram Wolfe: *The Fabulous Life of Diego Rivera*. There I discov-ered Angelina Beloff, Rivera's first wife and the mother of his only son, who died in Paris of meningitis. Instead of writing the foreword, I began to write letters that I thought Angelina Beloff would have written to Diego Rivera. It surprised me that years later she had come all the way to Mexico to find him. Beloff went to Bellas Artes looking for him, and he passed right by her without even recognizing her. In reality, I think I was writing to Guillermo, disguising myself as Angelina Bel-off, because he was completely absorbed by his astronomy, and I felt very alone.

The Feminine Condition

On July 12, 1978, Carlos Monsiváis, a faithful friend and guardian angel of Elena's since 1968, and a major player in Mexican culture of the twentieth century, published a review of his colleague's lat-est book in the pages of *Siempre!* (At the time "Monsi," as Elena affectionately calls him, was the editor of the newspaper's *La Cul-tura en México* supplement.) The review, entitled "En el estudio todo ha quedado igual" (In the Studio, Everything Remains the Same), evokes the first sentence of Elena's book and is in reality much more than a simple review of *Querido Diego*. In it he offers a critical assessment of Elena's literary opus as well as her intellectual trajectory, from the publication of *Lilus Kikus* in 1954 to that time:

> In *Lilus Kikus* (1954), her first book, Elena Poniatowska intro-duces a character from which she will later radically disengage herself: the young girl surrounded by the metaphors of inno-cence and contemplation, as amusing and joyous as a child's

With
Guillermo
at María
Luisa "China"
Mendoza's
wedding
in Atlixco,
1960s.

swing, a shop window, or a voyage to the center of a mirror. The ceaseless and outstanding work of the interviewer (of which we have only one compilation: *Palabras cruzadas*, 1961) slowly dismantles her "professional innocence" and transforms her into an excellent transmitter and re-creator of experiences and attitudes. Her allegorical sparkle gives way to a profound literary and testimonial need that is born in *Hasta no verte Jesús mío* (1969) and *La noche de Tlatelolco* (1971). The latter, no doubt one of the great Mexican political books of this century, is a choral montage which registers—with a strictly partisan viewpoint—the achievements of the student movement and the massacre of October 2: the epic which flows along until it becomes a tragedy . . .

For all its brevity, *Querido Diego* draws on a double process: the legendary feminine condition in its moment of absolute surrender and the artist in love with the genius. What is exceptional in *Querido Diego* is its justification of the heart-rending and exceptional abandonment of Quiela, a tragic figure because her frenzied monologue lacks an interlocutor; a pathetic creature, because she even gives up her vocation in order to hide her true objective, sentimental blackmail: "Stay with me, because I ask nothing of you, not even that you remain with me," is her genuine message. Quiela feverishly uses her epistles to exorcize loneliness and conjure her beloved, re-creating the shared experience, informing us of Paris, of the émigrés and the poor and unknown artists, and describing in detail an atrocious life devoid of all affection, friendship, or even acknowledgment.

The voice of those ostensibly vanquished: the mothers of those students who simply disappeared, the beast of burden known as Jesusa Palancares in *Hasta no verte Jesús mío*, the anachronistic creature who, when writing to Diego, expresses femininity as the sum of all defeats. But in these narratives of struggle and suffering, Elena Poniatowska finds an optimal vehicle to widen the space of understanding of lives and dramatic personal experiences. By illuminating the identities and the mindsets of victims, she comes close to them and strips them of their ineffable remote and distant character. She does not offer up the old spectacle of abstraction in service to indefinable victims, but rather very specific situations of concrete human beings under ideological pressures being crushed by very specific political forces. Quiela is not about inexplicable compulsion but about the art student who knew the heights of her profession through Diego and her greatest heartbreak with the death of her son. The loving obstinacy of her letters translates into an urgency for vital compensation for others, for how many women in the twenties were wary of that irrevocable dictum: the greatest reward for suffering is passionate love?

Gaby Brimmer

In 1979, Elena published a book about the life of a young woman with cerebral palsy whom she became acquainted with through a student in the literary workshop she headed in Mexico City. "That workshop," recalls Elena,

> which at first met in a private elementary school, was started by Felipe Pardiñas, formerly a Jesuit priest. He gave conferences that in his time became legendary. This workshop had been led by Rosario Castellanos, and when Echeverría named her ambassador to Israel, I was called in to take her place. It turned out to be a workshop for society ladies, and after the first session I thought to myself: "I'm not coming back. What am I doing here?" But I stayed for twenty-five years. Successful writers such as Silvia Molina, Rosa Nissán, Adriana Navarro, Marie Pierre Colle, Sandy Ramos, Guadalupe Loaeza, Fidela Cabrera, Beatriz Graf, and Adela Salinas were members of this workshop, and all have published books: it was very productive. Alicia Trueba won first prize in the Jorge Luis Borges competition in Argentina and traveled all the way to Buenos Aires to receive it. The professors were also very good: Hugo Hiriart, Edmundo Valadés, Juan Villoro, Álvaro Mutis, Daniel Sada, Raúl Ortiz, Tatiana Espinasa, José Agustín, Gonzalo Celorio, Rosa Beltrán, Vicente Quirarte, and many others.
>
> One of my students told me that Gabriela Brimmer wanted to meet me. I went to see her, and there met a young girl with cerebral palsy. She could not communicate verbally, and she had spasms that almost threw her out of her wheelchair. She had an alphabet at the foot of her chair, and with her left foot she would point to what she wanted to say. She was admirable because she had completed her university degree and also had an extraordinary nurse, Florencia, truly exceptional. She got her out of bed, dressed her, etc. Her mother's name was Sari,

Elena receiving the National Journalism Prize from President José López Portillo; with her are Victor Flores Olea, Jesús Reyes Heroles, and her daughter Paula, 1978.

and when she walked me to the door, she said, "We'll see if you ever come back, because they all come once, but they never return." She was right; I did not return. In December, Sari called me. I went to see Gaby and interviewed her; I also interviewed Florencia (the nurse) and Sari, and then I wrote the book. In the book I also included Gaby's poetry, which I had edited. I credited Gaby as the author, because I thought that I should highlight her enormous talent and relegate myself to the sidelines, but actually, I was the one who wrote the book. I gave Gaby all the rough drafts of the book, I left everything with her; it was a kind of penance. The book came out and was very successful. Eight thousand copies were sold in twenty days.

Shortly after the book came out, Luis Mandoki decided that he wanted to make a movie out of it, and I put him in contact with Gaby, but Mandoki cut me out entirely. Gaby no longer wanted a godmother. Sometimes she rebelled against her mother, she rebelled against Florencia, and she began to rebel against me: At the time, I thought that this was very healthy. In the movie I never got any credit whatsoever. Mandoki called it *Gaby Brimmer: A True Story as Told to Luis Mandoki.* Mandoki heard about Gaby through me. When the movie came out, Gaby came to see me in a station wagon specially adapted for her. She entered the house as Felipe was coming out of his bedroom, and when he saw her he said, "Gaby, what else are you coming to get out of my mother this time?" Then Gaby wrote with her foot: "Felipe, you are unfair." He said: "No, I'm not unfair, you are an ingrate and I only want to defend my mother, so now I'm going to take you back to your car." He turned her wheelchair around, took her away, and with a small crane, Gaby, still sitting in her wheelchair, was lifted into her station wagon. After that day I never saw her again. I felt great devotion and admiration for her, but she shoved me aside, and Luis Mandoki is the most dishonest and deceitful man I have ever met. I do not consider *Gaby Brimmer* a book worthy of being called literature; it is more like something out of *Reader's Digest.* The situation was very painful for me and affected me profoundly because my nephew Alejandro, my sister Kitzia's son, had had a terrible accident in Eldorado, in northern Mexico, that left him a paraplegic. That was one of the motivations that led me to write the book. In retrospect I now understand that, in reality, I wrote the book for Alex.

Self-Reflection

In spite of the fact that she had provided what became the script for the movie *Gaby Brimmer: A True Story,* Elena would have to wait two decades to see one of her works made into a movie: *De noche vienes, Esmeralda* (You Come by Night, Esmeralda), based on a story originally published in 1979. The dedication of the book is significant: "Throughout its pages, the author, without hiding her limitations, wishes to pay homage to love, to solitude, to children, to trees, and to those who have gone before us; to the stones on the road, and especially to the patience and goodwill of the typogra-

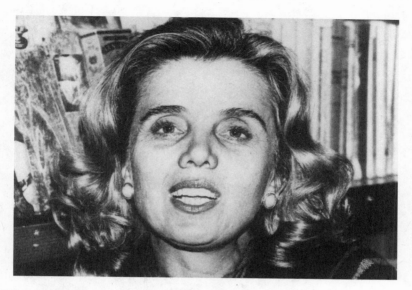

Portrait of Elena, 1979. (Photo by Rogelio Cuellar)

phers, formatters, correctors, printers, and binders who made this book possible . . . " For Tununa Mercado, whose review appeared in the magazine *Claudia* in April 1980, this succinct dedication constitutes

> a very modest but complete synthesis of Elena Poniatowska's imaginary universe or, in broader terms, of the intellectual model that her work has ended up representing on the Mexican cultural scene. What does this model consist of? In the first place, a proposal that is not formulated but emerges from the work itself: to touch, with words, different spaces of awareness; that is, to sensitize the readers regarding some matters that perhaps can only be referred to with "big names" but that in Elena Poniatowska's books do not allow any vociferation or solemnity: justice; respect for human dignity; recognition of others in their extreme solitude; the revelation of beauty in what is small; the discovery of humanity's mediocre comings and goings; the subtle dismembering of the stinginess,

The "Angel of the City." (Caricature by Naranjo)

dreams, follies, and tedium of the bourgeoisie; and so on infinitely. In the second place, she does so with all the resources and tools that writers have within their grasp to make their words worthy, in several genres and in various styles: journalism, narrative, testimonials, poetry, exposé, etc.

De noche vienes, whose cover illustration is an engraving by Gustave Doré of Little Red Riding Hood and the wolf, at the moment when she uncovers her grandmother's face and begins to doubt her identity, contains a selection of new stories as well as some originally included in *Lilus Kikus*. In his review published on December 8, 1981, in *Sábado*, the cultural supplement of the daily newspaper *Unomásuno*, Gonzalo Celorio warns readers that

> This book contains some texts from *Lilus Kikus*, but certainly, the childish spirit that enlivened the latter through her language and her theme does not predominate, as it does in those smiling stories with which Elena inaugurated her narrative talent. Through its language and subject matter, however, there persists the same curiosity, the same surprised look of Little Red Riding Hood who discovers, under her grandmother's nightcap, the open jaws of the beast.
>
> This curiosity infuses Elena Poniatowska's entire work. By their office and vocation, all storytellers are curious—let us say that they are professionally inquisitive. But Elena's curiosity goes beyond the text itself: it flows not only into literature, but also into serious commitment. As a precocious child who wants to know everything and has nothing holding back her inquisitive urge, Elenita questions, asks, meddles—like any old busybody—in people's personal lives and ends by becoming involved—in solidarity—with individuals who by the force of their own voices are more like flesh and blood humans than purely literary characters.

Celorio ends his evaluation of the writer and her work with some fragments of her forthcoming book, a collection of essays, or chronicles as she calls them, entitled *Fuerte es el silencio*, the work with which Elena will open the decade of the eighties, which is the subject of the next chapter.

7   Disaster's Widow

Defining Moments

After 1968, Mexico was changed forever, and Elena's experiences during the seventies—the era of the war in Vietnam, the international struggle for women's rights, and the Cold War—are reflected in the literary work she produced over that decade. During the eighties, she would document, interpret, and denounce human rights injustices in Mexico through two key books: *Fuerte es el silencio* (1980), a collection of essays dedicated to those who had suffered the most because they had been forsaken by all, and *Nada, nadie: las voces del temblor* (1988), her most important work of the period and a product of her growing indignation at the Mexican political system, which was sparked by the government's abysmal response to a natural disaster of epic proportions. According to the author, *Fuerte es el silencio* was the logical follow-up to *La noche de Tlatelolco* (in fact, the book contains what many consider to be the final chapter of *La noche de Tlatelolco*), as it gave a voice to a growing number of Mexicans who lacked basic services, such as electricity, water, and plumbing, and who were overwhelmed with desperation. According to Elena

> *Fuerte es el silencio* is a chronicle of the homeless. My interest in both those who sell chewing gum on the streets—those angels of the city—and the Rubén Jaramillo settlement of squatters led me to visit the jailed leaders—comrades of Florencio Medrano—of some of the land takeovers that occurred in the state of Morelos. Initially, the Colonia Villa de las Flores belonged to the son of Rivera Crespo, a former governor of

Morelos, who had subdivided it, planning to make it a luxurious residential suburb. That was exactly where the homeless decided to settle, just like in the best Italian neorealist films. Mine is the story of this occupation, and naturally, it brought down upon me the hatred of all the landed gentry in Cuernavaca, a weekend resort town located near Mexico City. Carlos Monsiváis declared that this was one of the best chronicles written about Mexico, and that comment gave me enormous pleasure. The final chapter is centered on missing political activists, as well as urban guerrillas.

I was alarmed to discover that, until a short time ago, Elena received threatening telephone calls, which were surely from some official of the corrupt government that she has attempted to expose for more than thirty years. I discovered this situation one day when I stopped by to visit Elena and found her in a small room located in the back part of the house. When I asked her about the sudden change of venue, she explained that a series of offensive calls at night had been preventing her from sleeping soundly. For Elena, this situation is not new. After the publication of *La noche de Tlatelolco*, she not only received threatening telephone calls but was under surveillance by federal agents who were parked day and night in front of her house in Coyoacán:

> They threatened me, they parked cars outside my house, with agents who watched who went in and out. I am enormously absentminded, and sometimes I would even offer them coffee. Once I traveled to the United Nations in New York with Rosario Ibarra de Piedra, when she was going there to draw attention to Mexico's missing political activists. I remember that quite a large number of photographers had set up in the long airport corridor, and as they took shot after shot of Rosario and me I was preening like a peacock; finally I said, "Look how popular we are, Rosario! Everybody's taking our picture!" "Ay, Elenita," she answered, "don't be so naive. They belong to the Federal Security Agency, and they are photographing us for their records."

During this period in her life, Elena learned not only about police harassment but also about doing time in prison. She was jailed once with her friend and photographer Héctor García and again while she was doing research for "The Rubén Jaramillo Settlement," a key chapter in *Fuerte es el silencio*. According to Elena, she was jailed in an improvised cell for more than twelve hours:

> At the Rubén Jaramillo settlement, I was held in a cell made of corrugated tin that was located in front of a field where there were boys playing soccer. For the first time in my life I was to gaze out between the prison bars and I learned about soccer. That night they let me out.
>
> Another time, I was put inside a paddy wagon in Mexico City when Héctor García threw his camera to me because one of the Federal Security agents wanted to destroy the film. Another agent scratched me so hard on the chest and hands that he destroyed a pearl ring I was wearing. We were later freed for lack of evidence. Two days later, the chief of police called me to offer a sincere apology.

The Fruits of Her Labor

On Friday, January 9, 1981, Isabel Fraire, a Mexican poet, winner of the Xavier Villaurrutia Prize, and translator of the Russian poet Mayakowski, published a review of *Fuerte es el silencio* in her column "Al margen," which ran in the Mexico City daily *Unomásuno*. Examining Elena's literary development from the perspective of a poet and a woman, she argues that a gradual refinement of Elena's creative expression is clearly evident in *Fuerte es el silencio*:

> Elena Poniatowska first became famous back in the sixties with her interviews in which, behind the mask of an ingénue or silly young girl, she would ask such brutally inopportune questions that they violently and immediately did away with the facade of importance and dignity worn by the great personalities being interviewed, who would suddenly be reduced to worms writhing under her magnifying glass.

Elena in
disguise.
(Photo by
Héctor
García)

Now, with *Fuerte es el silencio*, Elena Poniatowska has once
more succeeded in writing a book with the same immediacy
and vitality, the same historical significance, and exceptionally
high literary quality (even if it isn't obvious except to those
who share the writer's profession). She has written several
books and many essays in between, including *Hasta no verte Jesús
mío*, a biography based on taped interviews but structured like
a novel; *Querido Diego, te abraza Quiela*, a brief feminist prayer
for a dead victim of machismo and the passive acceptance of
a romantic ideal (which I found somewhat repugnant, because
both the victim and the executioner were abhorrent to me);
and *Gaby Brimmer*, a bestseller and an ode to individual efforts
in the face of almost insurmountable obstacles.

Fuerte es el silencio gathers what its author calls the "chronicles" (of Mexico City, of the '68 Massacre, of those activists
who are still missing, and of the Rubén Jaramillo settlement)

and represents the culmination of the expertise she acquired while writing all of these books. We no longer really know if it is a novel, an interview, or a chronicle. We do not know if the characters whose photographs we see are real or figments of the imagination, and whether that imagination belongs to us, to Elena Poniatowska, or to the subjects she interviews. We only know for sure that Elena Poniatowska is providing us with a truth that does not remain on the surface, that she pierces one layer after another until she has provided us with a complex, multidimensional landscape that is real and alive yet at the same time imaginary. There is no life except in the imagination because there is no truth except in the imagination, because statistics are not the truth, they only confirm the truth, and because truth can only be found in a field other than the mere accumulation of data.

The pull that Elena Poniatowska's prose and dialogues have is itself worthy of a separate comment. Elena Poniatowska's prose continuously approaches that of García Márquez or of the first poems by Montes de Oca. It is a current that moves forward irresistibly, torrentially, without pause . . . although sometimes the dialogues have that detailed slowing down, that interruption of time, which is so seductive in Japanese prints. Such is true of the one that opens the last section of the book and tells the history of the Rubén Jaramillo settlement.

And the description of the characters would be the envy of any novelist. Not only does Elena create profiles of Rosario Ibarra de Piedra and "El Güero" Medrano that are at the same time epic and intimate, but she also creates an innumerable gallery of faces and names—all clearly defined—that make up an imposing mural in perpetual movement, a worthy rival of the postrevolutionary muralism of the twenties. If we feel in her gaze a certain uncertainty, a certain vacillation that is absent in the eyes of her characters, it is because Elena Poniatowska maintains her role as the observer of an unfinished process which, as such, is confused and incomplete. She does not have, nor does she pretend to have, the blind faith of those who change the course of history, much less the peaceful security of those who describe from a fixed point of view a finished process. Hers is an open gaze, determined to take in as much as possible and to translate it ever more artistically, ever more hypnotically into words.

Kleenexeros, Chewing Gum Vendors, and *Mecapaleros*

It was, however, her close friend and colleague Carlos Monsiváis who gave the paramount tribute to Elena when he declared that her exploration of Mexico's political and social history—and of the Mexicans themselves—after Tlatelolco was a masterful undertaking. In his essay, Mexico City's popular chronicler categorically stated the enormous importance of Elena's journalistic and literary work, which had been somewhat prone to criticism until then because of the author's privileged and pedigreed childhood and adolescence. Monsiváis had been christened "the Octavio Paz of the Poor" because of the circumstances of his own life and the topics he chose to write about, so his assessment of Elena's literary work has been decisive in influencing public perception of it. This essay "El silencio de los marginados es la sordera de los marginadores" (The Silence of the Marginalized Is the Deafness of the Oppressors) was published in Mexico's important left-wing political weekly *Proceso* on January 17, 1981:

> Ten years after [Tlatelolco] the chronicles of *Fuerte es el silencio* attest to the literary and political development of Elena Poniatowska and of several major and "hidden" phenomena. Once again, the topic is another story: the fermentation of the "spirit of '68," the fate of radical dissidence, the commonalities and differences among those who have never had a voice and who take the risk to speak out, if only to break the silence of centuries. There is one reiterated idea: that the silence of the marginalized is the deafness of the oppressors, and there are three central narratives: the young people radicalized by 1968, the pariahs who organized in order to survive, and those who suffer under ongoing repression. Her work is a political condemnation and an argument in favor of human rights that identi-

fies both the progress achieved in that area and the regression of the last decade. It represents a moment of maturity in the narrative genre, as well as in the writer, while outlining the limits and causes of a civil society . . . If anything intensifies the chronicle now, it is the possibility it offers of capturing a popular yet maligned, negated, slandered epic and a stimulating series of marginal exploits that share a common denominator: the will not to give up. How can one not consider "epic" the effort which constructs a shantytown out of total destitution? Something of the indomitable will documented by Bret Harte or Jack London in their recollections of the nineteenth-century United States is gathered by Elena Poniatowska in her chronicle of the Rubén Jaramillo settlement, one of the best works of contemporary Mexican literature. It is an admirable re-creation of the "gold fever" of carpenters, masons, laborers, the unemployed, street vendors, and small-time swindlers, who decide—lickety-split—to acquire a plot of land to which they can become attached, to validate themselves while living in a melancholy ensemble of tin and cardboard, of sticks and pieces of plastic, and to recover both individually and collectively in their 200-square-meter dominions . . .

An unrestrained style—lyrical, full of analogies, and enlivened by details—captures this new foundation of Aztlán, the intertwining of dispossession with the feeling of property, of utopia, and of realpolitik. It captures the involvement of the students, the misgivings of the squatters, the intensity of the meetings they hold, the suspicions, the slander, and the language, which is half Rulfo ("To me, this has the flavor of misfortune") and half traditional naturalism ("You will never leave us stranded, Güero, because you're as fucked over as we are . . . "). In three chronicles, Elena Poniatowska examines a component of the left wing of the seventies, its slow and bitter learning about democracy, the struggle for human rights, and the resurgence that was intensified in 1968. Most uncommonly, her book does not reduce defeat simply to the language of assimilation and dispersion. It also encourages a critical climate that enriches and modifies organizations and groups, including the Communist Party, the Revolutionary Workers Party, the Mexican Workers Party, the Critical Point, unions in the universities . . .

And why does the well-known writer Elena Poniatowska describe the efforts of and affirm her solidarity with a succession of Gorkian mothers? In such cases, the impulse to reveal what is mutilated, proscribed, and silenced intervenes. But to get to the bottom of matters, the chronicler cannot exempt herself; she must also play her own character, the famous journalist who lives with contradictory feelings, the owner of an enormous house who confesses the viewpoint of her class in order to rise above it: "Will we be friends?" the young ex-guerrilla asks her, and Elena Poniatowska, the interviewer, responds, "I cannot, Benjamin, I'm bourgeois." This acceptance destroys any possible folklorism and sets the tone of this new style of chronicle, which combines literary creation, anthropology, history, sociology, and politics, and which, through a bundle of emotions and information, offers a landscape that surprises and daunts us. We truly ignored all of this, and to learn little by little is to hold back knowledge . . .

Fuerte es el silencio by Elena Poniatowska is, for the same reason, both a literary achievement and a political fact. We are also what we fail to hear, what we refuse to see, that which elicits from us only a slight twitch of our good conscience. We are still Mexicans, as in the pre-Hispanic poem, and it is still to be seen if that fact regulates the exercising or the nonexistence of basic rights.

Hope and Nostalgia

In 1961, Elena published a collection of the interviews she had conducted with the most distinguished writers, politicians, and artists of the time, entitled *Palabras cruzadas*. More than twenty years later, in 1982, she published *Domingo siete*,[1] a collection of interviews with the Mexican candidates for that year's presidential election. The latter book reflects Elena's activity in the political arena, an interest that would culminate in 1994 with her

The "Red Princess."
(Caricature by
Naranjo)

absolute allegiance to the Zapatista movement. *Domingo siete* denounces Mexico's lack of democracy and expresses hope for political plurality in the country through the creation of a literary space where readers may listen to a chorus of voices and attitudes regarding each candidate's most important goals.

Through the publication of *Domingo siete*, Elena hoped finally to eliminate the presidential *dedazo* and the custom of *el tapado* from Mexican politics.[2] Notwithstanding these efforts toward democratization, Mexico would have to wait two more decades, until 2000, before the PRI (Institutional Revolutionary Party) gave up its power to the PAN (National Action Party).

Another publication from 1982—one closer to Elena's heart—was *El último guajolote* (The Last Turkey), a long essay published by Mexico's Secretariat of Public Education. While contemplating her adventures of the seventies, Elena nostalgically evokes a Mexico City once surrounded by saltwater and freshwater lakes and populated by its native wildlife, which has all but disappeared. The *chichicuilote* birds, ducks, *axolotls* (salamanders), and whitefish, as well as their respective vendors, once created a chorus of distinctive—and nearly musical—cries that transport one back to a past that has been crushed by progress but is still visible through Elena's text and the accompanying photos by Charles B. Waite.

The Forces of Nature

On September 19, 1985, five years after the publication of *Fuerte es el silencio*, a powerful earthquake devastated Mexico's capital, leaving thousands dead, missing, or injured. Its exact toll remains unknown to this day. The government's response was slow and disorganized, and chaos reigned over Mexico City in the days after the disaster. Nearly twenty years after Mexico had endured the Tlatelolco massacre, a natural disaster of incalculable proportions demonstrated the irresponsibility of well-known construction companies, many of whom had received government contracts to erect public buildings such as the destroyed General Hospital, and cut costs by using shoddy materials and unsafe building methods.

It was not until four hours after the quake that Elena discovered the enormous magnitude of the catastrophe. In an interview, she reflects on the events of those months and reveals that, at least in the beginning, it never occurred to her to devote a book to the earthquake. Her immediate reaction was much more instinctive: "The first thing that I began doing was what other citizens were doing: boiling water and taking clothes and medicine to the local authorities."

The destructive force was tragically brought to her attention later that day when her friend, writer Miguel Capistrán, called because he had lost several family members in the disaster. Elena and her daughter, Paula, immediately went to see Miguel at the funeral home. When they got to the Colonia Roma, mother and daughter realized the devastating magnitude of the earthquake:

On September 19, I had planned to go to Veracruz with Miguel Capistrán, where I was to give a conference. I had also been told that Felipe and Paula could go with us. Everything was cancelled when Miguel gave me the awful news: the building where his family lived had collapsed, and there was a wake for

them at a funeral home on Avenue Álvaro Obregón. Paula and
I walked through the neighborhood to Álvaro Obregón and
the spectacle was terrible. Paula kept saying, "No, Mama, no
more; I don't want to walk down there, I want to go home."
After the tragedy we began to gather clothes and medicine,
boil water, look for containers to put all the boiled water in,
and take it to the places where disaster had struck. Then we
tried to get pickaxes and shovels, but found that all the hard-
ware stores were sold out.

Like her previous urban chronicles, *La noche de Tlatelolco* and
Fuerte es el silencio, Nada, nadie: las voces del temblor is the product of
Elena's own experiences and those of many other Mexicans. As
such, it occupies an important place among her testimonial work,
a genre that, in many ways, she invented in Mexico. *Nada, nadie*
is a chronicle of a cataclysm and a denunciation of the Mexican
government's inability to create a political system capable of caring for the poor, who lived in some of the hardest-hit neighborhoods of Mexico City, including Roma, Juárez, Centro Histórico,
and Doctores.

Anonymous Heroes

"Before participating in the disaster relief brigades," Elena explains,

> you needed to get tetanus shots at the UNAM, and I recall
> writer Sara Sefchovich shouting at the other workers, "Take
> good care of her!" Antonio Lazcano went to the stadium
> with Claudia Ovando, and I was assigned to a building in the
> Colonia Juárez. On Orizaba Street, I saw a couple who had
> lost their family: they looked like two frozen teardrops, two
> pillars of salt. It was a horrible sight. They were paralyzed,
> standing in the middle of the street. We formed a chain of
> volunteers, and would pass buckets full of debris to throw on
> a pile. There was no heavy equipment. Some punk kids, with
> their hair glued straight up, leather bracelets on their wrists,
> and various earrings in their ears, were part of the chain. One
> of them helped me all the time. When it was my turn to carry

the bucket full of heavy stuff, he would tell me, "Come on, Grandma, let me take that."

I recall the difficulty of finding a place where nobody would see me go to the bathroom during the long twelve-hour stints. I felt particularly moved by the so-called *chavos banda*.[3] When I asked them, "What's your name?" they would respond: "Oh, what does it matter?" They were truly anonymous heroes. Now I can go fearlessly into all the poorest areas, because I learned in 1985 that the chavos banda members are actually great people.

Professional Duty

One day Julio Scherer García, publisher of *Proceso* magazine, phoned me, saying, "I don't understand what you are doing among the ruins when you should be doing a reporter's job." Monsiváis also insisted, "Write, and don't go looking for blankets to give out." "But I'm a woman," I answered. "Others can do that, what you must do is write," he replied. I have always found it easy to get close to people, and I began to interview the people I met after the earthquake. I believe that the fact that I am quite small makes it easy for me to fit in everywhere. I spoke with the people, and they told me about their misfortunes. I went out on the streets every day for three months. Daniel Molina, Raúl Álvarez Garín, and Javier González, who went around with their pickaxes and shovels, established a center to collect information about the effects of the earthquake in the Colonia Condesa, and Monsiváis and I went several times to gather testimonies. Marta Lamas was asked to be treasurer of the seamstresses' union, as many of its members were dead or unaccounted for, and Neus Espresate, Cocó Cea, and others agreed to work with them as well. A great and strong friendship was born between Evangelina Corona and me, which has lasted to this day.

I would go around to the places affected by the catastrophe until three or four in the afternoon, and then at five o'clock I would start writing at home. I would deliver my article at 8:30 or 9:00 pm. Often I was running late, and they would call me from *La Jornada* to assure me that there was still time: "Elenita, we've saved a page for you." Thus, I wrote an enormous number of articles, which were later used in *Nada nadie*. Later, others also participated, because I told the students at the Thursday writing workshop, "We are not going to talk about literature today. If you want to go out on the streets with me, write chronicles, and see how the Mexicans really live, the workshop will continue. If not, we will shut it down." There were ladies [in the workshop] who had never even been to the poorer sections of the city.

As a result of her articles, Elena faced a never-ending chorus of urgent cries for help:

I encountered many physical and spiritual needs. I called Manuel Camacho Solís once because I needed a wheelchair for a woman who had been trapped under a wall. "You will have your wheelchair tomorrow," he replied. And sure enough, the next day I got the chair. I would also go out and buy mattresses, blankets, whatever was needed. I believe that with all that, I began to lose my sense of direction, simply because it went on for too long. In December, I fell into a terrible depression. Carlos Payán offered me the last page of *La Jornada* on Sundays to write about anything else, whatever I wanted, but I felt so bad that I never wanted to write again in my whole life. Why should I? In the end, we would all die crushed by some heavy object!

I do not think the book is very good; it just fell from my hands of its own accord. Monsiváis' is infinitely better. I left Mexico and went to teach a three-month course at the University of California, Irvine, and while there my spirits continued to be low—and I mean really low! I would only get a lift of sorts on my bicycle.

Change of Heart

In the article "La odisea de *Nada, nadie*" (The Odyssey of *Nothing, Nobody*), which was published in *La Jornada* on October 1, 1988, Alicia Trueba, who ran the "El Grupo" literary workshop, which

"Widow of
Disaster."
(Caricature by
Magú)

now bears Elena Poniatowska's name, reflected on the experiences
she and the members of her workshop shared during this time of
great hardship for all Mexicans:

> I [Alicia] was part of a writing group that Elena has led for
> many years. When the earthquake struck, she asked us for
> help, help which we knew she did not need. Her intention,
> being the good teacher that she is, was to awaken her students'
> interest. The group's response was immediate and unanimous,
> as all of us had been confronted with the disaster.
>
> We organized ourselves in order to obtain as much infor-
> mation as possible. Everything published was first carefully
> read, corrected, summarized, ordered, and filed. Hundreds
> of references were written up, the folders grew, bloated with
> data; the news invaded our space, our days, and our lives.
>
> The group lived submerged in the earthquake. Marisol
> Martín del Campo is only one example. She was intelligent
> and capable, and she changed her daily routine to devote her-
> self entirely to conducting interviews, to obtaining the most
> accurate and precise information, without being impeded by

defiance, much less by schedules or red tape. All the other group members had the same drive. Sandy Ramos interrupted her trip abroad and returned in distress over the news printed in European dailies, where Mexico occupied the headlines for more than three consecutive days. She joined our efforts and worked nonstop for twelve to sixteen hours a day. We helped the injured, we visited shelters and hospitals, and we followed all possible clues regarding the missing, going so far as to note inaccurate information given by the various daily newspapers.

Those were days of limitless activity through which, little by little and without realizing it ourselves, we were experiencing a change of heart. The earthquake modified our manners of acting, thinking, and assessing facts and people because, among many other things, we discovered that we shared humankind's miseries . . .

Day after day, Elena came to learn about our work, and the circles under her eyes became ever bigger and darker. Seeing her so small, so fragile, we wondered, "How? How can she stand it?" Everyone knocked at her door to tell her about their pain, injustices, deaths; she faced this turmoil day after day and shaped it until she had converted it all into chronicles, and then into the book as we now know it, without permitting anything to be forgotten nor allowing anyone to feel like an outsider, and she even succeeded in making it all—in the midst of so much misery—what she herself is, a breath of fresh, clear air.

Weaver of Memories

Upon the publication of *Nada, nadie*, Antonio Lazcano Araujo published in *La Jornada* an emotional review of the book that he dedicated to "the memory of Rosita Capistrán, who died in the earthquake." The article was published in the newspaper's literary section on October 1, 1988:

With the singular mastery that allows her to record the most varied of voices, Elena gathered their words and their collective memories with infinite respect, thus becoming the weaver of our memories, first in a series of extraordinary articles published in *Proceso* and in the newspaper *La Jornada*, and later in *Nada, nadie*, the book where she has gathered all the voices of the earthquake.

Because it recounts the tragic days following September 19, 1985, this book is a terrifying volume. A masterpiece among chronicles, its profoundly painful tone reflects with precision the magnitude of the worst tragedy suffered by Mexico City, our "belly button of the moon," our poor resplendent moon, so often cradled by catastrophes. Despite the suffering on every page, pain and hopelessness have been carefully meted out, transforming the tragedy's testimonies into an epic with an astounding plurality of voices, a monument to the solidarity of both ordinary men and everyday women who never knew they were heroes and heroines. They had to swallow their grief beside the ruins, but they found within themselves an unsuspected strength and performed feats of enormous generosity which we now recognize as heroic but which at the time were merely the acts of individual and collective survival.

Nada, nadie is not only a painful narrative of a collective tragedy of enormous proportions, but also the faithful register of the greatest impact a community has ever made on its governing classes in Mexico's history. In the days following the earthquake, the shameful spectacle of administrative corruption, the total vacuum of authority, and the certainty that the destructive forces of Nature had been multiplied by official irresponsibility (as in Tlatelolco), indifference to human exploitation (as in the case of the seamstresses), and negligence (as in hospitals and schools that collapsed) rapidly transformed what were no more than mere accounts of collective and individual survival into political denunciation and actions that rose to the realms of government. It was then that protests began to be heard, directed less toward the president or the mayor as at a paternalistic system whose ineffectiveness became evident from its false sense of self-sufficiency, the lack of understanding by police and soldiers, the ridiculous solemnity of the bureaucratic commissions from the moment of their conception, and the regularity with which all kinds of authorities, officials, and hierarchies demonstrated their ineptitude.

Nada, nadie is a book that can only be read while holding back tears . . . The voices that spring up as we read are those of the multitude that for several days made heroism a daily habit and discovered in the absence of authority the limits of authoritarianism. They are the chorus of extraordinary women, such as Consuelo Romo, Dr. Chiringas, Victoria Munive, and Evangelina Corona, as well as the Good Samaritans from Las Lomas and Santa Julia who boiled water, cared for the injured, fed others, and forced the members of the brigades to wash their hands. They are the clear voices of the boys of La Ibero and La Anáhuac, suddenly forming a brotherhood of cohesive action and political indignation with the chavos banda, the students of the Colegio de Ciencias y Humanidades [a public high-school system] and the Boy Scouts. They are the testimonies of doctors and nurses from the Medical Center, of firefighters mourning the death of Jesús Vitela Valdés, an engineer who died while doing rescue work. They are the actions of the volunteers from all parts of the world.

Nada, nadie is, above all, the voices of the victims of Tlatelolco, of the organizations from the tenements, of the brigade members, of the seamstresses, of those who overcame official ineptitude, taking back their rights, imposing obligations, and beginning to form, perhaps without realizing it, a new social pact, a new nation. For example, in subsequent pages of *Nada, nadie* José Luis Vital relates that "when I arrived at the General Hospital and turned toward the place where Gynecology used to be, it was as if it had never existed; I saw a pile of rubble and, excuse me, I said, 'Oh, shit.' I'm not rich or anything, but that day I was wearing new boots and I hesitated a moment, thinking 'my boots!' and then I said '¡Que viva México!' because if I can save a life it will be more than worth it."

Printed Images

It makes sense that there was a pause in Elena's literary production after the earthquake; the only book she published between 1985 and 1988 was a collection of verbal sketches of several authors entitled *¡Ay, vida, no me mereces!* (1985)(Life, You Don't Deserve Me!). Her essays about writers such as Juan Rulfo, Carlos Fuentes, Rosario Castellanos, José Agustín, Gustavo Sáinz, and others call to mind the style of literary syncretism that is so much her own, in which the subjective and the objective dissolve to engender something peculiarly "Hellenic." In her review of the work, entitled "¡Sí que no la mereces, vida!" (Truly, Life, You Are Not Worthy of Her!) and published in the book supplement of *La Jornada* on February 6, 1986, Tununa Mercado underscores some of the literary characteristics of Elena's work:

> Sketch, commentary, literary entertainment, personal impression—Elena Poniatowska's most recent book, *¡Ay, vida, no me mereces!*, resists being pigeonholed in a genre. Very far from academic pretensions and the rigors of academia, the texts about Carlos Fuentes, Rosario Castellanos, Juan Rulfo, and their so-called "de la onda" [new wave] literature are, according to the author, "images in print" of personalities within Mexican cultural life. "Its substance has nurtured me," she adds. "They have given me life and strength. It is not a repayment of old debts nor criticism, it is not even an essay: it only attempts to be a gesture of love toward the men and women who are very dear to me."
>
> When discussing Mexico's leading writers, Elena Poniatowska reflects, between the lines, on the role such intellectuals have played and the interrelationships they establish within their milieu. Their own ideas, therefore, are intertwined in their texts, and that is perhaps what is most interesting to emphasize.
>
> In the first place, I would say that Elena Poniatowska merges with the object of her discourse, puts no distance between herself and the author she is writing about, and melds with the work she is analyzing. Thus, there are no barriers between

the "I" of the observer (herself), the writer, the character she creates, and the narrator. . . .

The idea of a literature that brings to life this fusing-merging philosophy is completed with another phenomenon, that of absorption: the writer, be it Fuentes, Rulfo, Rosario Castellanos, or Elena Poniatowska herself, absorbs reality, incorporates it, swallows it, segregates it as if it were food being digested before going out to the light of words. This capacity of absorption-exteriorization which embodies the act of writing assumes an ethical and even political direction: to reflect reality, to set forth its naked glory or misery, would be to denounce it. Fuentes or Rulfo, made one, in turn, with the material they write, have assimilated what surrounds them, which enables them to "carry the voices" of those who suffer or relish that reality. Responding to a particular destiny, the writers are converted, more than anything, into transmitters of themselves.

Such acute perception and transmission have targets indicating where they should land, and their purposes include presenting perspectives on Mexico and its intellectuals, defending an idea of justice, claiming a truth, in an exemplary manner provoking a reaction in the face of individual mistakes—in sum, defending their causes. Once more, with characteristic freshness and incisiveness—qualities that in this case are complementary—Elena Poniatowska puts herself at the service of her "characters"; she makes them speak, she interprets their exploration of areas unknown even to themselves, and she fleshes out images that allow them to be better understood. In this sense, her writing is an act of discovery, and she succeeds in extracting what she glimpses—isn't the interview one of her most precious resources? Hers is a daring and peculiar invention: protected behind "reality," she produces fiction by using the devices of imagination, and she gives herself up to the vertigo of words, because she could not—even at the cost of any "reality"—sidestep her essence as an artist.

Literary Therapy

In a sort of literary escapism, Elena took refuge in her own childhood memories, sweet images that she perhaps used to block out
those she had faced while writing her chronicle of the disastrous
earthquake. While rummaging through drawers, scrutinizing
long-forgotten texts, and reviving the happiness and innocence of
her youth, Elena discovered a novelistic project buried under the
testimonies of missing students and squatters in Cuernavaca. Ever
faithful to her self-confessed workaholism, Elena converted this
into a literary exercise. She returned to a novel conceived in the
mid-fifties with a grant from the Centro Nacional de Escritores
that she and others—including Héctor Azar, Emilio Uranga, and
Juan García Ponce—had received in 1957:

> La "Flor de Lis" is a novel of youth. In those days I began to
> feel the need to write useful books, books for my country,
> which made Carlos Fuentes exclaim, "Look at poor little Poni,
> there she goes in her VW Bug to interview the head of the
> slaughterhouse . . . " The prices of onions and tomatoes, as
> well as reports of evictions and land takeovers, were much
> more important to me than the often-fleeting ideas of the con-
> temporary literary vanguard. The second part of La "Flor de Lis"
> slept like Sleeping Beauty until last year, when I was working
> on the book about the earthquake. That book's testimonies
> were atrocious, so for a change, I took the novel Naranja dulce,
> limón partido (Sweet Orange, Sliced Lemon)[4] out of the drawer.
> I rejuvenated it, adding the first 150 pages or so, and changed
> the name. I called it La "Flor de Lis" after the shop that sells
> tamales in the Colonia Condesa as well as because the fleur-
> de-lis is closely related to France.

Chronologically, the second part of this novel was written
right after the publication of Lilus Kikus, in 1954, the small book
that relates the witticisms and concerns of an extremely curious
young girl who—following in the author's footsteps—is sent to
a convent in the United States at the end of the book. There,
she would learn everything that a well-brought-up little girl would

need to know to become a good wife, mother, and member of privileged society. Although this book contains some undoubtedly autobiographical episodes, the author herself insists that they are only starting points for the creation of an exceptional character, the little girl Lilus Kikus. The author similarly draws on her own experiences in creating La "Flor de Lis," a novel about a middle-class girl named Mariana who arrives in Mexico from France with her younger sister, Sofía, and their lovely mother, Luz, after the Second World War. They discover—among other things—their own Mexican identity, long lost in their genealogy. In fact, their mother's forebears were longtime owners of haciendas such as La Llave in Querétaro and San Gabriel in Morelos.

Up to this point, La "Flor de Lis" is an autobiographical novel or memoir. Later, the author introduces characters and situations that were not present in her adolescent life, such as the odd priest Teufel, whose name means "devil" in German. According to Elena, she was inspired by the prêtres-ouvriers (worker-priests) of France, who abandoned the clergy after coming into contact with the working classes. Teufel is based on an actual person but is transformed into a memorable literary character by Elena's daring pen. Furthermore, Father Teufel becomes an indispensable tool in terms of the narrative, as he permits the author to stand apart from her own subjectivity in order to observe, document, and criticize the life of the protagonist.

According to José Cueli, the author of "La aristocracia de Elena" (Elena's Aristocracy), an article published on April 8, 1988, in La Jornada, Elena manages to isolate an "observational 'I' in the figure of Father Teufel, allowing her to criticize herself and her world, represented principally by her mother Luz." In contrast, in his article entitled "La bondad del padre Teufel" (The Goodness of Father Teufel), published in La Jornada on April 1, 1988, José Joaquín Blanco—an original reader and critic of the book manuscript—discovers something more than mere narrative technique in the figure of Father Teufel. He argues that the extraordinary priest constitutes an ideological starting point for his neophyte Mexicans, who will soon contemplate a world away from the rosary, catechism, and confession, one full of injustice and indolence:

The goodness of Father Teufel consisted in his intelligence and his conflicted sincerity; he sincerely preached destabilization, something in which he shared and suffered a good part of the disaster. In exchange, he helped spark criticism and thought in those intelligent and profound consciences made lethargic by well-being and distracted by bourgeois frivolities. From such demoralized beings springs true morality. The more unstable and full of incongruities and faults he turns out to be, the more reliable his doctrine and his presence become, because the experience he radiates and suffers from, is as a result that much more authentic. La "Flor de Lis," says Elena, is more than anything, fiction and reality. All literature is a bit autobiographical. Even Octavio Paz writes autobiography, since he participates fully in the events he describes. Such is his Pasado en claro; such are his love poems to the woman he adores. La "Flor de Lis," named for the tamale shop at 19 Huichapan Street, is the history of spiritual retreats led by a priest who comes from France and whose new ideas shake the whole French expatriate community, whose members originally lived in the town of Barcelonette and whose young converts meet on Jalapa Street in Mexico City to attend his spiritual retreats.

A Book of Memoirs

In the text written for the foreword of La "Flor de Lis" and published later in La Jornada on April 30, 1988, Antonio Lazcano Araujo comments on the author's presence in the novel. Her role, apparently that of the protagonist, dissolves in a universe of literary characters that emerge from other works of hers and come to life and inhabit their own narrative space after passing through the sieve of Elena's literary imagination and being combined with autobiographic features.

La "Flor de Lis" is not a book of memoirs, but it is not difficult to see in Mariana the same rétroussé nose, the sky-blue eyes with the same expression of candor, the same innocence combined with a devilish curiosity and an acute intelligence we see in

Elena Poniatowska . . . Where did La "Flor de Lis" spring from? Every book hides autobiographic elements among metaphors and paraphrases. In this new book, characters sketched many years ago merge and are reincarnated in stories such as "Castle in France," "De Gaulle in Minería," and "The Inventory." These are characters that Elena Poniatowska has woven together through the invisible stitches of her writing in order to form a novel, to invent a life for Mariana, to relate part of her autobiography, and to explore the Federal District of the fifties, when it was still possible to meet a young white-gloved duchess in a red "Colonia del Valle–Coyoacán" public bus.

For their part, reminiscent of the enthusiasm provoked by the publication of *Hasta no verte Jesús mío*, several critics discovered in *La "Flor de Lis"* qualities that come to light when the novel is separated from the real life of the writer—a difficult feat for the writer and for many critics, who insist on pointing out what is essentially autobiographic, or at least self-referential, in all feminine artistic expressions. From the sonnets of Sor Juana Inés de la Cruz to the painful self-portraits of Frida Kahlo to the egocentric poetry of Guadalupe Amor, these representations can be considered confessional to a certain point, but that does not diminish their artistic quality. In this case, Elena's work contains qualities that merit critical attention and thwart any attempt to define her as a writer of intimate texts.

One of the innovations in *La "Flor de Lis"* is the creation of a feminine literary world. Because of this, the book fills an important gap in the history and tradition of Mexican novels, especially because it is not a history of poverty and marginalization or of disinherited *soldaderas* and abandoned women artists, but of a privileged society in full decadence. As Antonio Lazcano Araujo writes,

> The book *La "Flor de Lis"* immediately evokes *The Leopard*, the splendid novel by Prince Giuseppe di Lampedusa, which also painted from the inside—and with precise and subjective strokes—the fall of the aristocracy, their *adieu* to the past, and the final aria of a period and a class of which only tatters remain. From within this universe, which slowly closes upon

Consecrated author, 1990.

itself and which had not been described in Mexican literature until now (except through books that one can do without, such as *Los de arriba* by Eduardo León de Barra), Elena Poniatowska has discovered the existence of a still deeper world, the innermost feminine world that Mariana moves within, but always in the shadow of her mother, Luz, an unreachable woman whose beauty is as dazzling as her name, but always distant.

José Joaquín Blanco, author of such original works as *Mátame y verás* (Kill Me and You'll See) and the provocative essay "Ojos que da pánico soñar" (Eyes That Cause Panic to Dream) reiterates Lazcano Araujo's observation:

The concept of the "feminine" novel, on the other hand, is closer to *La "Flor de Lis,"* in the sense that it is not only a novel by a woman about other women, but it is also about the long life *in gineco* [among females] . . . The fact that it joyously addresses the closed world that women make to protect themselves, love themselves, enjoy themselves, and learn from one another is a great contribution, as this world remains like an "age of shadows" in feminine biographies, which only illuminate women's dealings with men. This world of mothers, daughters, grandmothers, aunts, nurses, maids, vulgar little friends, and quarrelsome and envious sisters becomes a sort of Eden in La "Flor de Lis," until a masculine lout, dressed in a cassock, appears and breaks some pieces of the fine crystal that abounds.

A less specific and therefore more universal vision is presented by poet Ethel Krauze, who glimpses in Elena's work a meditation on the subject of the Mexican psyche—nothing new in itself. Nevertheless, in La "Flor de Lis" Elena approaches this national obsession from the perspective of Mariana, a little girl who realizes her dramatic difference from Mexico and Mexicans and fights to reaffirm her own place in a closed society that looks on foreigners with suspicious or deceitful eyes. Here, the subject truly is totally autobiographical, especially when Elena recalls the phrase her ancestors repeated: "We don't belong." Krauze's review of La "Flor de Lis" was published in Excélsior on April 21, 1988:

> With all this, Poniatowska succeeds in delving into one of the most characteristic aspects of Mexican culture: denial. That is, the denial of the Mexican pretension to aristocracy, because what is Mexican is seen only as synonymous with the Indian servant. It is paradoxical for the typical Mexican to deny Mexicanness "to the white man with the strange last name"; you're a foreigner with blue eyes, don't speak, you have no rights, you aren't from here. Then nobody is Mexican. Or who is the true Mexican? "And I," Mariana asks, "Where am I from?" The whole book gives the answer: I am the product of this accumulation of contradictions, and that makes me entirely Mexican.

8   From Earth to Heaven

Tinísima

During the early 1980s, Elena discovered in a roundabout way an extraordinary woman who, like herself, was Mexican at heart, and whose artistic and political contributions to postrevolutionary Mexico are splendid examples of militancy. In a curious case of parallel lives, Tina Modotti also came with her family to the Americas, albeit under very different circumstances. Whereas Elena, her sister Kitzia, and their mother came to Mexico City in 1942, fleeing the war in Europe, Tina and her family moved to San Francisco, California, from Udine, Italy, around the turn of the twentieth century, in search of the American dream. Along with many other immigrants of the time, Tina labored in the infamous sweatshops, where the working conditions were deplorable and the hours eternal. Through acting in Italian-language plays in San Francisco, Tina found work as an actress in the silent movies that were then being made in Hollywood, inevitably being relegated to roles such as the lynx-eyed Latin femme fatale with a dagger between her teeth. In Los Angeles, Tina met Edward Weston, with whom she traveled to Mexico in 1923. They arrived in a country jubilant at the triumph of the revolution, and where the best artists were employed by the government under the patronage of Secretary of Public Education José Vasconcelos.

Thanks to Vasconcelos' initiative, many teachers traveled to the remotest villages in Mexico, providing the inhabitants with a basic education, which under the Porfiriato had been available only to the upper classes. In this atmosphere full of great expectations and partly inspired by her new partner, Cuban revolutionary Julio Antonio Mella, Tina discovered her true calling: that of militant photographer devoted to the international Communist Party. She was mentored in photography by Edward Weston and hired by the Mexican communist daily *El Machete*, where Tina had the opportunity to showcase her photographic talent in a political context of great social change.

From Screenplay to Novel

Through her activities and attitudes, Tina was the role model who helped Elena better understand her own place in the world at large. As with Josefina Bórquez and Angelina Beloff, chance led Elena to Tina when the acclaimed Mexican filmmaker Gabriel Figueroa commissioned her to write a screenplay for a movie about Tina's life. The movie was never made, but Elena had already invested a great deal of time and energy in the project by the time she learned that it had been abandoned. She realized that through her numerous interviews with key individuals of the period, including Manuel Álvarez Bravo, Vittorio Vidali, Pablo O'Higgins, Guadalupe Marín, Yolanda Modotti, and others, she had accumulated an enormous amount of material. In fact, she had enough for a literary project that would become a comprehensive mural of postrevolutionary Mexico, comparable to the imposing imagery of Rivera, Orozco, and Siqueiros, and a record of an era that, according to Elena, was truly unmatched in the twentieth century. The novel, named *Tinísima* in honor of the superlative dimensions of its subject and especially of her times, is a true epic of Mexican culture and politics in the twenties and thirties. The story follows the protagonist's path through the bohemian middle class of Los Angeles; Mexico City; the Russia of Stalin, Lenin, and Trotsky; and civil war–torn Spain, where Tina fought alongside "Commander Carlos." In a November 2, 1992, interview with the magazine *Proceso*, Elena speaks of this challenging literary project and its genesis:

"Why did you choose [to profile] Tina rather than the life of a society debutante, as you had said on occasion you would do?"

"No, I have never wanted to write the life of a society girl. Tina actually was commissioned by Gabriel Figueroa. He told me that he urgently needed a script about Tina Modotti because two movies were going to be made, one about Antonieta Rivas Mercado, by Carlos Saura, and another about Tina Modotti, which never materialized. I had already done interviews for the script and it seemed very unfair to disappoint these individuals. Besides, it seemed unjust to judge Tina Modotti through her lovers, so I began to conduct more and more extensive interviews with Fernando Gamboa, María Luisa Lafita, Pablo O'Higgins, Lola Álvarez Bravo, Manuel Álvarez Bravo, and finally, with Vittorio Vidali in Trieste, Italy, which is the most crucial of my interviews and is more than three hundred pages long.

"Writing about Tina came about totally by chance. Of course I already knew old communists such as Rafael Carrillo, Miguel Ángel Velasco, and Fausto Pomar, all the people I later interviewed and who served my investigation well. I did not know that I was going to write a novel about Tina, but when the movie project was dropped, I immediately thought about how disappointed many old communists would be. I was mostly seduced by the epoch, not by Tina herself. I was deeply moved by the period of the 1920s in Mexico; it seems to me not only a unique moment in our history, but an unsurpassable one as well. It seems to me that personalities like Diego Rivera, Siqueiros, Orozco with all his bitterness and his bad temper, Manuel Álvarez Bravo who resembled a little bird, Lola Álvarez Bravo, Dolores del Río, and Emilio Fernández, along with so many other characters, will never be seen again because they are unique. The whole muralist movement was extraordinary. It's like the vulcanologist 'Dr. Atl' [Gerardo Murillo], there's never been anyone like him again. Besides these figures, there were all the people active in Mexico at that time: Edward Weston, Tina, Hart Crane, Langston Hughes,

Katherine Anne Porter, Frances Toor, Anita Brenner, Chabela Villaseñor, Gabriel Fernández Ledesma, Mireya and Germán Cueto, Frida Kahlo, María Izquierdo. Also María Asúnsolo, Adelina Zendejas, and if you include the forties and fifties, there is Elena Garro, another figure who has not been surpassed. These are mythical, legendary women. Much can be said about Rosario Castellanos, and to a certain extent the same may be said about Pita Amor, only Pita Amor at times ran dangerously close to losing her mind. There are no longer great figures in Mexico; women are more conformist and are less original in their viewpoints. Besides, this city has become gigantic, and now nobody knows what anybody else is doing; there are no longer places where people come together. The only one I can see who stands out is the actress Jesusa Rodríguez, because she has an exceptional destiny. She is also a thinker, a member of the political opposition, a cutting-edge social critic, and when all is said and done, a true creator."

Social Realism?

In her interview with Javier Molina, published in *La Jornada* on September 20, 1992, Elena feels obliged to contemplate the genre of *Tinísima*, as many critics still insisted that her narrative was purely historiographic and ignored its obvious literary qualities:

"Do you consider [*Tinísima*] a historical novel?"

"I don't know how to categorize like that. Fernando del Paso says that his book *Noticias del imperio* (News from the Empire) is a historical novel, but I don't want to make the same mistake as the textbooks that want to turn the current presidency into national history."

"[The book] may be historical, political, social, a chronicle of the culture of an era but, above all, it is a novel; it is literature. Can you please comment on this?"

"It is a novel in which I tried to turn exposition—words taken from my interviews—as well as what I read in the newspapers, into literature. If the book's language echoes old-fashioned Spanish, that is because as the years went by I began to internalize my subject, Tina Modotti, and I brought her forth with the greatest of ease. She made me grow and through this novel I learned a lot. During the fall of the Soviet Union, the Persian Gulf War, the radicalization of Castro's regime . . . and many other things that affected me, I began to change as well. Of course, the earthquake influenced my chapters on the Spanish Civil War because here in Mexico we also know about the destroyed houses, the losses, the pain, the overflowing hospitals . . . Daily life formed part of the novel as well."

"It has been said that many parts read like social realism."

"That may be. I was informed by the newspapers of the time: *El Machete, El Universal Ilustrado, Excélsior*. The individual who had the greatest impact upon me was José Pérez Moreno, a great journalist who is still not given his fair due. He covered very important stories in the thirties . . . "

In this interview, a result of Elena's attendance at the presentation of her novel at the Casa del Risco, in San Ángel, Molina reproduces part of the comments Carlos Monsiváis made about *Tinísima*, which he called mere "impressions of a reader," but impressions that led him to express a very positive opinion of the literary qualities of the book: "I believe that *Tinísima* is a great book, and I believe that by saying this, I am anticipating only by days or weeks the judgment of its assuredly numerous readers." In his presentation, Monsiváis enumerates four main points about the novel:

One. *Tinísima* serves various functions. It is at once a historical novel, a cultural and political chronicle, a portrait of a period, and the life story of a woman who, in her forty-six years, moved from middle-class bohemian to militant communist to fanatical Stalinist. It represents, in particular, a kind of literature that re-creates the historical and moral impetus that produced unwavering solidarity.

Two. The focal point of the narrative is the exceptional woman who lived an extraordinary life, as the first half of the twentieth century forced many to do. She is a second-

Elena portrayed as the Venus of Botticelli, a photomontage created in honor of her sixtieth birthday. (Photomontage by Jesusa Rodríguez)

rate Hollywood actress, the partner of photographer Edward Weston, a protégé of Diego Rivera, the lover of communist painter Xavier Guerrero and of the Cuban leader Julio Antonio Mella, the victim of moral lynching by the Mexican right wing, and an outstanding photographer (one of her photographs was purchased in New York for more than a hundred thousand dollars). Passion permits her to widen her horizons and also reduces her to the condition of a caricature of her ideology. She abandons photography and lets herself grow old, living only for her duty to the party. Elena Poniatowska neither patronizes nor castigates her character, for there is always narrative discipline in her work. She re-creates the essence of the period exactly as it was: Stalinism was monstrous, but from 1917 to 1956 at least, many saw it as the achievement that gave new meaning to history. Tina threw herself into the cause, which reduced her to the level of becoming a spy and caused her to be condemned by those who had been her comrades only moments before. The writer shows respect for the vitality of the character, and she leaves it to the readers to determine their ultimate sentiments about Tina Modotti.

Three. It is also a succession of dazzling ambiances: San Francisco, Mexico City, Hitler's Germany, Republican and then Franco's Spain, the Mexico of Cárdenas and Ávila Camacho. The characters are both the sons and the parents of their moment in history.

Four. Tina Modotti was a great photographer, a woman of evident sensuality, and a personality who almost always lived life to the limit. [Here Monsiváis identifies the great tragedy of the protagonist: she learned to see, in the deepest sense of the word, and then learned to abandon seeing through her compulsive militancy.]

An Intimate Mirror

In her review of *Tinísima*, which she published in *Excélsior* on December 16, 1992, author Ethel Krauze describes the "intimate mirror" that Elena's novel creates; it is the manifestation of personal and political convictions, of the carnal and humanistic desires of its protagonist and, to a certain extent, of its author. Although Krauze does not acknowledge the importance of the personal—almost intimate—link between Elena and her subject, she sees in the novel a collective history of women. Her view was more generous than that of Octavio Paz, who chided Elena for writing a novel based on the life of a Stalinist, while Doña Paulette lamented that her daughter dedicated the novel to her because it was the biography of a communist. Krauze declares

Tinísima is much more than the biography of Tina Modotti— the Italian photographer who lived in our country and became the scandal of the era: a liberated woman, a professional, and a militant communist. It is the intimate reflection of a woman who struggles between her social ideals and her need for individual expression, her importance and her courage, her love for men and her love for others, her austere discipline and her wish for aesthetic contemplation. It is the timely journey of any woman who discovers her own intelligence and searches for her identity in order to make sense of her own existence.

Moreover, it is a fragment of our country's history and its fascinating characters. The portrait of Diego Rivera is excellent and human. But the Lupe Marín of *Tinísima* is quite simply a work of art. Politicians, artists, social activists, terrorists, assassins, and intellectuals parade by. We enter their dialogues, their parties, their fights, their bedrooms, and their secrets, thanks to the sensibility and talent of the author, who enters into the forbidden territory of the country's official history with passion and no reservations.

Consequently, *Tinísima* fills us at once with pride, sadness, and bemusement: to see what we were, what we could have been, and what we have become. The refreshing courage; the explosion of artistic, political, and social expressions; the commitment to turning words into actions gave way to bureaucratization, apathy, mercantilism, mediocrity, mass production, and political rhetoric . . . From revolution to corruption, and in between a tale of love, a tale of death, a history of art, a history of struggle—the history of a woman so unique that she can speak for all women.

Tinísima earned Elena Poniatowska the Mazatlán Prize for the second time; she had already received the award in 1971 for *Hasta no verte Jesús mío*, also a biographical novel giving voice to another woman, Jesusa Palancares. This prize arrived at exactly the right time for its author, in that Elena had run into a number of rather serious obstacles while researching the novel about Tina. For instance, in her dealings with Irish writer Margaret Hooks, Elena had provided the former with a considerable amount of original material (interviews, notes, and documents—her entire book manuscript) for a biography about Tina that Hooks was writing.

Hooks' biography appeared in 1993, before *Tinísima* was released, and enjoyed great international success; in fact, Mick Jagger, lead singer of the Rolling Stones, wanted to make a movie based on her book. Still, the publication of *Tinísima* generated enough buzz to interest the New York–based publisher Farrar, Straus and Giroux, which, in 1996 released a (greatly abridged) English translation of the novel.

The Zapatistas

After the success of *Tinísima*, Elena returned to her journalistic and literary endeavors. These included interviews with Mexico's cultural celebrities, including Manuel and Lola Álvarez Bravo, Juan Soriano, and Gabriel Figueroa, and appeared in *La Jornada, El Nacional,* and *El Financiero* throughout the nineties. These interviews, among the more than 10,000 that Elena has done since 1953, are contained in the compilation entitled *Todo México* (All of Mexico), whose first volume was published in 1991 by Editorial Diana.

To everyone's great surprise, on January 2, 1994, Mexico awoke to two political events that accentuated the contradictions of postrevolutionary society. On the one hand, the North American Free Trade Agreement was approved, thanks to the efforts of neoliberal president Carlos Salinas de Gortari. According to the president, this continental accord would earn Mexico a place in the elusive—and until then exclusive—first world. On the very same morning, while the Institutional Revolutionary Party (PRI) was dreaming of a modern Mexico that enjoyed the unconditional support of the Mexican people, a group of black-hooded Indians rose up in San Cristóbal de las Casas, Chiapas, led by a charismatic revolutionary: Subcomandante Marcos. His political organization, the Ejército Zapatista de Liberación Nacional (EZLN) (Zapatista Army for National Liberation), rallied around the slogan "land and liberty," coined in 1910 by Emiliano Zapata and forged out of decades of abuse and indifference toward the indigenous population of Chiapas. In the late twentieth century, the heirs of the extraordinary Mayan civilization still inhabited a semi-feudal world where powerful hacienda owners cultivated the land and controlled their laborers through intimidation and hunger. As Carlos Fuentes correctly points out in his *Nuevo tiempo mexicano* (New Time for Mexico), "The revolutionary movement initiated in 1920 that so radically transformed the economic and social structures of Mexico (and to a lesser degree its political structures) did not reach Chiapas, where oligarchic practices not only have failed to return the land to the farmers, but have also benefited cattle breeders, large landowners, and loggers who treat Chiapas like a colonial preserve for their own gain" (116–17). In their "Declaración de la Selva Lacandona" (Declaration from the Lacandón Rain Forest), dated January 2, 1994, the EZLN, headed by Subcomandante Marcos, addressed the people of Mexico and condemned the deplorable conditions in which the majority of its native population lived:

> **Fellow Mexicans:**
>
> We are the product of 500 years of struggles: first against slavery during the War of Independence against Spain, headed by the Insurgents. Later, we fought to prevent our being absorbed by U.S. expansionism, to promulgate our Constitution, and later still, to expel the Empire from our homeland. Finally, when the dictatorship of Porfirio Díaz denied us the fair application of the Laws of Reform, the people rebelled, following leaders including Villa and Zapata, poor men like us, to whom the most elemental education had been denied. We are thus more easily used as cannon fodder, and they can more easily plunder the wealth of our country without caring that we are dying of hunger and curable diseases, without caring that we have nothing, absolutely nothing, not even a proper roof over our heads, nor land, nor work, nor health, nor food, nor education. We lack the right to elect our authorities freely and democratically, to gain independence from foreign powers, [we are] without bread or justice for ourselves or our descendants . . . But today we say ENOUGH!

Almost immediately, the EZLN enjoyed great popularity among even the most moderate left-leaning intellectuals, artists, students, and politicians, and Elena was no exception. Thanks to the Zapatista movement, she realized her dream of directly participating in a revolution where her journalistic work would have the power to help change a despicable reality, as Tina's work in *El Machete* had done so many years prior.

A Singular Invitation

On July 14, 1994, Marcos invited Elena to visit him at his headquarters somewhere in "the mountains of southeast Mexico." In a letter of invitation undoubtedly inspired by Cervantes, the subcomandante makes a literary allusion to Elena's being known by her European acquaintances as the Princesse Rouge, that is, the "Red Princess." The letter of invitation she received from Marcos, along with the chronicle of her trip to Chiapas with her children, appeared in *La Jornada* on July 30, 1994, under the seductive title "Invita Marcos a Poniatowska a posar su rubio pie sobre las rebeldes tierras" (Marcos Invites Poniatowska to Set Her Tender Foot upon Rebel Lands):

> May your beauty receive multiple and spectacular reverences. Let the military bands fall silent in their awkward greeting. Let my mare Rocinante approach the sill of thy window and my intrepid daring reach up to thy balcony so that I might, with the awkward danger of falling to the ground (On what floor is your fair Excellency's abode? Couldn't we negotiate a ground floor? No? And how about a swimming pool at a prudent distance? A fluffy pillow of soft feathers? At least a bunk bed?), formally invite you to condescend to place upon these rebellious and threatening lands the tender sole of thy foot. We could converse on many subjects and, more important, silence many others. Or, if not, we could gaze at each other with a distant and serious air. From afar I shall see that my tender warriors provide you with a thousand and one courtesies. What is the probable date for angels to land in this land of demons (Prigione *dixit*)? They say it is said that the stars, the moon, the tides, the military checkpoints, and the evictions might come into a favorable conjunction on the twenty-third

day of this uncertain month of July. Place, time, and probable agenda for such a fortunate event? It comes from the mouths of the kind envoys of my missive. If the date we suggest is not convenient, not to worry, transgressors have no set schedules; we work piecemeal, that is, full time, throughout the duration of the "sabbatical" which we traded in years ago for our truly "jungle existence."

So be it, keep well, and bring one of those uncomfortable sleeping bags, because here, besides being full of dignity, our ground is hard.

From the mountains of southeast Mexico,
Insurgent Subcommander Marcos
Mexico, July of 1994

Moving Inland

Elena—visibly excited—made all the preparations for the trip to Chiapas: she purchased plane tickets for herself, her children, and the scientist Manuel Fernández; she went to Sanborn's to buy tobacco for the subcomandante, whose pipe was the symbol that linked him to other Latin American revolutionaries such as Che Guevara and Fidel Castro; and gathered other items that she would be sure to need in the dense jungles of Chiapas. During the weeks following the uprising in Chiapas, Elena's house had been converted into a small warehouse for the books destined for the library built by the Zapatistas (which already had a computer and a printer), among other things collected for later transport by caravan to southeast Mexico. In contrast to her previous experience with Josefina Bórquez, on this occasion Elena was not alone in her zeal to help these people; her children, Felipe and Paula, were also devoted to the Chiapas cause, and their home vibrated with emotion and activity as young people arrived with loads of clothes, school supplies, and food for the rebels. As Elena documented in her chronicle, published in *La Jornada* on July 30, 1994, the road to Chiapas was a hazardous one:

It is not easy to reach Subcomandante Marcos. It is necessary to make contacts, connections, to become submerged in
an ocean of codes and symbols. The trip from San Cristóbal
de las Casas to Guadalupe Tepeyac is supposed to take five
hours, but as this is the rainy season, it takes longer and even
then is only possible provided you acquire a special vehicle:
only Jeeps, pickups, and the occasional VW bug that does not
fear the bumps in the roads can get through. All of this without taking into account the military checkpoints that begin in
Tuxtla Gutiérrez and upon deplaning at Terán Airport . . . At
the last military checkpoint, Lieutenant Colonel Juan Daniel
Lara Capuchino is more courteous than the director of proto-
col at the Ministry of Foreign Relations, and this must not be
easy in the midst of the mud and solitude interrupted only by
khaki tents and the steely muzzles of the guns.

When they finally arrived at Guadalupe Tepeyac, the closest
town to EZLN headquarters, they hunkered down in an empty
hospital that the Zapatistas had converted into a shelter. There
they waited again to be called to begin the last lap of the road to
Marcos. While they waited, Elena wrote in her notebook: "the
day is spent waiting and despairing. One never knows when the
little man in the black hood will come and say 'NOW.'" When the
day agreed upon for the meeting was almost over, Elena received
another message signed by the "Sup," again full of oblique compliments but written in an enigmatic tone:

> The sound of thousands of trumpets resounds in valleys and
> ravines. Could it be the aspiring candidate from some official
> party of some country in some imminent election process?
> No! It is your arrival being announced and the cortège being
> formed; the sound of military bands may be heard, the bells
> are ringing. My boots are still torn, and I rush, I rush the Com-
> mittee, the Committee rushes me, an assembly is held and a
> vote taken on whether or not to hurry. The Committee rushes
> the vote. And in a rush wins the vote. And yes, in full consen-
> sus, we all rush to form a line that goes toward the free zone
> where thy beauty relieves thy fatigue. But it so happens that,

Face-to-face with Subcomandante Marcos. (Photo by Felipe Haro)

notwithstanding the rushing haste and all that, it will take us hours, perhaps days (months and years if the wind blows against us) to arrive at your side. Patience is the virtue of warriors but not of writers, so I have thought of sending thee a hasty blossom amidst our hurried approach, and thus to try to hold thee back sufficiently that we can succeed in organizing our haste (which the way things are going will take place around the year 2013), and we will all arrive (still trying to get our helmets on straight in the midst of our hurry) before thy presence, literally falling (for surely someone will undoubtedly stumble due to the rust on his suit of armor) at your feet. I cannot appear until the clock at Buckingham Palace strikes twelve (I have not the vaguest idea what time that may be, but the part about "Buckingham" certainly sounds veeeery elegant), for until that hour I must endure a horrible curse that for many years has condemned me to be a pumpkin by day; a lovely pumpkin, assuredly, but a pumpkin nonetheless. I find it doubtful that your Excellency would consider it prudent to interview a pumpkin, especially if the pumpkin is wearing a black hood, so I beg of you to wait out the improbable hour of the improbable clock, within the improbable palace of the improbable "Buckingham" (is that proper way to spell it? . . .)

So be it. Health and a magic potion of the sort that turns dragons into frogs and princes into official candidates . . . Isn't that the way it goes? Well, perhaps wishing you simply good health . . .

From the mountains of southeast Mexico
(that is to say, very close by)
The Sup, or graduate pumpkin, in the process of rolling
down the hill.
Mexico, July of 1994

At last the long wait came to an end, and Elena and her children were led to Marcos' tent, where he entertained them for several hours with his well-known sense of humor and vast knowledge of culture. The long conversation resulted in an extended interview published by Elena in two parts on July 30 and 31, 1994, in *La Jornada* and considered to be one of the most outstanding interviews with the charismatic revolutionary.

During the more than ten years that have passed since Elena's revealing interview with Subcomandante Marcos, the resourceful insurgent has not vanished from Mexico's cultural and political scene. On the contrary, in 2005, at the onset of Mexico's 2006 presidential elections, Marcos founded *la otra campaña* (the other campaign), of which he considers himself *delegado cero* (delegate zero). Although the EZLN does not actively sponsor political candidates, as would a traditional political party, it does insist on a new constitution that prohibits, among other things, the privatization of national resources, such as electricity and oil, while demanding autonomy for an estimated sixty indigenous communities throughout Mexico. More than nine hundred organizations have joined Marcos' "other campaign" since its inception. Perhaps surprisingly, though, it is not even remotely aligned with left-of-center presidential candidate Andrés Manuel López Obrador, of the PRD (Party of the Democratic Revolution) who, according to the Sup, will only continue the disastrous neoliberal model established by Carlos Salinas de Gortari, Mexico's notorious president from 1988 to 1994, an economic program that has further enriched the minuscule upper class while leaving the destitute majority more disenfranchised and impoverished than ever before.

Homage to Mexico

On her sixtieth birthday, Elena was crowned "Queen of Mexican Intellectuals" by her dear friend, actor, and political activist Jesusa Rodríguez. As she looked back upon her life, both personal and professional, Elena discovered a chorus of voices, the product of her interviews with hundreds of personalities of the Mexican cultural world, some by now old friends. As she revisited the vast number of interviews she had accumulated over more than forty years of work—carefully saved by her mother in numerous scrapbooks—Elena decided to organize and publish this material in a series of volumes entitled *Todo México*: "I wished to honor my country," the writer explains, "and I decided to gather the interviews I had conducted throughout my entire professional life. That is why these volumes are called 'All of Mexico.' But I do not pretend to be the biographer or the chronicler of Mexico; this is simply one part of my work."

In addition to this impressive collection of interviews, Elena also published an illustrated edition entitled *Luz y luna, las lunitas* (Light and Moon, the Little Moons) in 1994, which contains photos by Graciela Iturbide, Rosa Nissán, and Paula Haro. The book contains six essays that range from an elegy to her soul mate Jesusa Palancares, aptly entitled "Vida y muerte de Jesusa" (Life and Death of Jesusa), to "Las señoritas de Huamantla" (The Young

Ladies of Huamantla), an essay full of folklore and "local color" which describes the traditional fair of Huamantla, a village in the state of Tlaxcala, as well as its magic mushrooms, which survived the rigors of the Conquest and the imposition of a new religion.

An Acquired Profession

A literary example of how Elena returned to her formative years during the nineties may be seen in her novella *Paseo de la Reforma*. This venerable avenue, designed by Maximilian's architect so that Empress Charlotte could observe her husband from the terrace of their bedroom atop Chapultepec Hill on his daily trips to the National Palace, has witnessed the epic history of modern Mexico. In the fifties, Elena lived with her grandmother and twenty dogs on Berlin Street in the Colonia Juárez, just a few steps away from the elegant boulevard, which is an imitation of Elena's beloved Champs-Élysées in Paris. Writer Adriana Malvido, the author of *Nahui Olin: mujer del sol* (Nahui Olin: Woman of the Sun) chatted with Elena about the fortunate genesis of *Paseo de la Reforma*, which came into being at the request of publisher Juan Guillermo López, of Plaza y Janés. This interview was published in *La Jornada* on December 17, 1996:

> "I had nothing planned," the author insists. "I spent several days thinking, What can I write about? I threw myself into it, and less than four months passed between the moment I started and the novel's completion. It was a pleasure, because I enjoyed myself as I had never enjoyed writing books before; they had always been a sort of punishment, a sacrifice, because I take everything tragically: love, politics, everything. Besides, I'm very unsure of myself."

The final product was a lyrical narrative illustrating that Elena, now a mature woman with more than forty years in Mexico's cultural milieu, had not wasted her years of experience. The novel tells the story of Ashby Egbert, a young aristocrat from Mexico City, and his relationships with two very different women: Nora, his wife, and Amaya Chacel, who has a very individual attitude toward life. According to José Cueli, in his review of the book published in *La Jornada* on November 20, 1996,

> Elena Poniatowska lost her bearings when she wrote *Paseo de la Reforma* and managed to stir up her ghosts. Her characters (Ashby and Amaya) go through life never quite ready for it. They would like something more. Desperate, they live with a different concept of time, of space, and of the speed of events. *Paseo de la Reforma* slips into another galaxy, different from that of the rest of her work, and exists in a time measured by a clock without hours. The writer's seductiveness is permissible thanks to her acquired skill of stretching minutes and slight or nonexistent periods, and linking them to images that she allows her characters—Ashby, Amaya, and Nora—to inhabit. A fatality that overflows when she does not adapt to the conventional life that is represented by Ashby and his aristocracy. A presence out of bounds, out of the norm, on the margin, on the margins themselves, in the unknown regions that are absence itself.

Roman à Clef?

In the previously mentioned interview with Adriana Malvido, Elena also explains the singular feature—a novelty for her—that defined the writing of this novella: its composition was a "delight from beginning to end." During the four months that it took her to write the book, Elena enjoyed, invented, and played with enormous freedom. Malvido inquires,

> "Do you attribute your delight to this freedom?"
> "I believe it is due to the fact that the work is pure fiction. I did not have to consult anything; I never opened a book to check a date. I invented the situations, or perhaps I already had them inside of me, memories of real situations that I have lived through or that I had been told about many years back, and I proceeded to incorporate them all into these two characters: Ashby, who is very close to me and with whom I greatly

With Octavio Paz, 1987.

identified, and Amaya Chacel, who is very surprising and most unexpected."

"Who is Ashby Egbert? Who is Amaya Chacel? Who is Nora? These are questions that undoubtedly go through the mind of the reader of *Paseo de la Reforma*, especially because they exist side-by-side with real characters. Elena begins to list them one by one and analyzes them minutely."

"All my life I have observed women, their movements, their attitudes, their gestures, their manner of walking, of laughing, or of moving their heads, and they remain recorded like mental notes that reappear when I write and merge them together in one character."

"Who is Amaya Chacel based on?"

"She is a composite of traits of people I have known over time and who have impressed me greatly. For example, there is Rosario Ibarra de Piedra, who is a very assertive woman, one of those who speaks the truth to politicians straight out. I also recall that when I was very young and beginning to work in journalism, I was greatly impressed by Elena Garro. On one occasion I went with her to see the journalist Elvira Vargas—who also inspired this character a bit—at Ahuatepec, in the state of Morelos. And there are also bits of Rosario Castellanos and Celia Chávez—the wife of Jaime García Terrés and my childhood friend—in the character of Nora, Ashby's wife. But I don't know if they recognize themselves or not, and perhaps they are not pleased, but there are things about them that impressed me and which I have retained almost unconsciously, like some of Rita Macedo's postures or traits of Ana Cecilia Treviño, Bambi, which will some day come out . . . "

Upon being questioned by Malvido about the male protagonist of her book—as none of her previous literary works have had male protagonists—Elena confesses that she identifies with "Ashby for his capacity to pull himself away from his own circumstances, his capacity to break away from his 'caste,' as those of his social class would put it, his capacity to love the streets and see others with an infinite curiosity. This happens after his sojourn at the Hospital Obrero, for although he had been close to death before, he had never opened himself up completely to others . . . "
    Malvido continues,

Through the imaginary jaunt with Elena Poniatowska we see all the novel's characters—those with whom Ashby interacted in the hospital and who changed his life—parade before us. The writer pauses to comment on them:
    "When you are writing, with your motor running, you include even the people you pass in the street. I was working at that time with an extraordinary Swedish journalist, Kent Klich, and we often went out to chat with homeless children at the places they hung out. There was one called El Calimonstruo, another was El Todomenso, and at another gathering place we found El Gansito. I spent ten days with them, and then I transformed them a bit in order not to hurt them."

At the end of her interview with Elena, Malvido asks about another project that Elena had begun working on years back; four years later, this book would change Elena's professional life: "She continues writing," Malvido mentions, "a novel that has to do with the meaning of science in a third world country, described through the life of a young scientist." This enormous literary endeavor would culminate in 2000 with the publication of her most significant novel since *Hasta no verte Jesús mío*. Her magnum opus, a novel inspired by the life and discoveries of her estranged husband, Guillermo Haro—who passed away in 1988—was at the time enigmatically titled "T. Tauri," in reference to a group of stars discovered by the extraordinary Mexican astrophysicist. Contemplating this project and others, Elena, in a rare moment of self-reflection, confesses that "I have less and less time, and I must hurry up before my time comes. Imagine, I have to turn in twenty books of *Todo México*, and if I don't hurry, I will have to throw in the towel before they are finished. But I am also aware that it is a bit neurotic to carry a typewriter around one's neck like some sort of anchor. I want to be with friends, to write better books and less of this avalanche of articles."

Intertwined Lives

In explaining her reasons for publishing an important collection of her interviews in *Todo México*, Elena denies that she aspires to become the chronicler or biographer of Mexico. Nevertheless, at the end of the nineties, she became a biographer—not of Mexico, but of two great creative figures of the twentieth century: Octavio Paz and Juan Soriano. She interviewed both for the first time in 1953, initiating a long series of interviews that are proof of her fruitful friendship with both (the two men were also friends themselves). In 1998, these longstanding relationships bore two important fruits: *Octavio Paz: las palabras del árbol* (Octavio Paz: The Words of the Tree) and *Juan Soriano: niño de mil años* (Juan Soriano: Child of a Thousand Years). Both works were based on information gleaned from the interviews Elena had accumulated over nearly half a century of work, along with her own research on the life and work of these two personages of Mexican cultural life. In an interview with Javier Aranda Luna, published in *La Jornada Semanal* on January 24,

1999, Elena admits to an important shortcoming in her book on Mexican Nobel Prize laureate Octavio Paz:

> The book seemed a bit weak to me because I was not sufficiently critical. But the point of the book is that everything included in it is something I told Octavio to his face. I told him, for example, that the way he had treated Carlos Fuentes was despicable, and perhaps because I told him face-to-face, he did not get angry. I would frequently ask him, "Have you seen Carlos Fuentes?" Finally, his wife said, "Why don't you pick up the phone and call him?" Octavio read *Las palabras del árbol* a year before it was published, and he allowed me to say impertinent things that he would not have permitted from anyone else. His corrections were minimal and basically related to the correct spellings of the names of foreign writers.

Although in her comments about Paz's biography she denies any personal tension in their friendship, it had been the strongest in the sixties and seventies and had waned since then. Recall that Paz wrote the foreword to the English translation of *Massacre in Mexico*, but he distanced himself from Elena after she published *Tinísima*, which was the biography of a communist who, according to Paz, knew about and accepted Stalin's crimes.

The painter Juan Soriano was an entirely different matter, for, until his death in 2006, he had been Elena's constant friend and, according to her, was a jovial and tranquil man, not at all solemn or overbearing. The idea of writing a biography of Soriano came up when the artist participated in the launch of *Las palabras del árbol* and afterwards Elena remarked offhand, "Oh, and maybe I'll do a book about you!" Soriano's answer was that yes, he would like that very much. According to Elena, her biography of the Jalisco-born painter is written in the first person in order to eliminate her presence and allow the readers to approach Soriano more closely. The biography is the product of many hours of conversation with Soriano and many shared experiences dating from August 1953, when Elena published her first interview with him in *Excélsior*, entitled "Trece vidas al margen del tiempo" (Thirteen Lives on the Margin of Time). In her conversation with Ángel Vargas, which appeared

With Gabriel García Márquez. (Photo by Pedro Valtierra)

in *La Jornada* on November 29, 1998, Elena reveals her fervent devotion to the painter, which was born forty years prior:

> Actually, it is a devotional work, but also full of *fleurs du mal*, because Juan Soriano says many things that are sometimes sort of diabolical, somewhat terrible. He is my little saint, to whom I have prayed for many years, because to me he possesses a knowledge others lack, the type of knowledge that is able to contemplate life. Everything he has told me throughout my life has been like spiritual guidance; it has always helped me. From Juan Soriano I have received only good things; he has always been good to me.

When asked what is original in this biography, Elena's answer is surprising: Soriano "speaks very freely about his homosexuality . . . this is what is new in the book. If anyone can talk about homosexuality it's Juan, precisely because he is a seventy-eight-year-old man. Besides, he is a man of enormous intelligence, a great wit, a big heart, and great sensibility. Therefore I think that he, in a certain way, is the person to speak on this subject and dispel its tragedy, its drama."

At the end of the interview, Elena mentions another biographical project that she still had not completed in late 2002: "Sometime soon," she insists, "in two or three years, I would like to write a book about Carlos Monsiváis, if I don't die first." Only the future will reveal whether Elena, with her multiple commitments to write forewords, interviews, and articles, will accomplish this living homage to "Monsi," her dear friend and guardian angel.

Collective Lives

Three projects that Elena completed at the turn of the millennium are also biographical in nature, but instead of being histories of the lives of individual illustrious Mexicans, they are collective biographies devoted to various groups of women in Mexico's history and its present. The first of these works—published by ERA in 1999, in cooperation with the National Institute of Anthropology and History—is entitled *Las soldaderas* (Women Soldiers [of the Mexican Revolution]). According to the author, her text was based on the accounts of participants in the Mexican Revolution, such as her mentor Josefina Bórquez; it was illustrated with photographs that are now part of the vast collection owned by the Fototeca Nacional (National Photographic Archive) in Pachuca. Elena's book explores and documents the role of the women in the Mexican Revolution

> [who] in their percale skirts and white blouses, with freshly washed faces, eyes lowered to hide their embarrassment, their innocence, their modesty, their brown hands holding a shopping bag or getting ready to pass a Mauser to their partner— they do not resemble the foul-speaking and vulgar beasts described by the authors who write about the Mexican Revolution. On the contrary, although always present, they stay in the background. They never challenge. Covered with their rebozo, they carry their child or the ammunition with equal ease. Standing or sitting next to their man, they have nothing to do with the grandeur of the powerful. On the contrary,

they are the very image of weakness and resistance. Their smallness, like that of the Indians, allows them to survive.

Very different women are collected in a slim volume entitled *Las siete cabritas* (The Seven Little Goats), published in 2000 and dedicated to Elena's "three graces": Carlos Monsiváis, José Emilio Pacheco, and Sergio Pitol. Elena came up with the odd title after a conversation with her daughter Paula, who upon being asked what would be the most appropriate title for the book, answered with a mischievous smile, "The Sweet Kitty-Cats" or "The Fine Fillies." When Elena rejected these two suggestions, arguing that these women were much more fearless than submissive and that years ago the fine fillies had studied at the exclusive Colegio Francés, Paula got angry and told her mother that she would never again try to come up with titles for her mother's "measly books." Finally, Elena opted for *Las siete cabritas* because all these women were "considered mad," perhaps crazier than goats, and because they "shine like the Seven Sisters of the celestial dome." Through revisiting her own experiences, memories, interviews, research, and family references, Elena explores the inner worlds of Frida Kahlo, Nahui Olin, Guadalupe Amor, Rosario Castellanos, María Izquierdo, Elena Garro, and Nellie Campobello. The final product complements the series of interviews in *Todo México*, where many of these women speak for themselves.

The last in this cycle of three books devoted to exploring the female world is entitled *Las mil y una: La herida de Paulina* (2000) (The Thousand and One: Paulina's Injury). It is an extended essay of indignation written after the horrible rape of a thirteen-year-old Mexican girl. It is also a strong denunciation of hypocrisy and religious backwardness, which still dominates certain sectors of Mexican society in the early twenty-first century. Paulina, who lived in Mexicali with her mother and brothers, was raped by a burglar who broke into the house to take what little they owned. Paulina became pregnant as a result of the rape, and when she wanted to abort the baby—whose father turned out to be a heroin addict as well as a criminal—she was denied an abortion. Doctors and religious associations seeking an injunction won their case based on a mere technicality.

Elena pictured as Frida Kahlo. .

Elena wrote this book because she was moved by Paulina's indignation that in a country where abortion is legal when the preg-
nancy is caused by rape, it would be denied to a thirteen-year-old
girl. "How dare the religious groups interfere in the life of others?"
Elena demanded. "Paulina entered my days without my asking it of
her or planning on it. I was astounded by her ability to express her
indignation as well as her strength, for she was then only a four-
teen-year-old girl. I put Paulina's indignation on paper. I showed
the support men, women, and groups gave to a younger sister in
the face of this outrage."

International Heritage

On March 7, 2001, Elena received a telephone call from Marcelo
Uribe of the ERA publishing house, congratulating her on having been awarded the fourth Alfaguara Prize for Literature for her
novel *La piel del cielo* (*The Skin of the Sky*). Elena, dressed in sweat-

pants and on her way out to the gym, was barely able to exclaim, "I never thought I would win! I entered the contest feeling very unsure of myself. I did not even want to use my own name, so I used Dumbo as a pseudonym." (This is the same alias Elena had wanted to use as a byline on her first articles, to match Bambi, the name Ana Cecilia Treviño used in *Excélsior.*)

News of the award came at a difficult time in the writer's personal life, as her mother, Doña Paulette Amor de Poniatowski, had been hospitalized with serious bronchial pneumonia. She passed away on March 22 of that year, at age ninety-two. Doña Paulette's reaction to the news of the award was not at all surprising to those of us who knew her well: "Good, now you won't be writing any more!" she quipped, with her still very noticeable French accent. According to Elena, her mother believed that writing so much over so many years had taken up time that Elena could have devoted to more important things, such as spending time with her family and friends as well as taking care of herself: "All you do is write. Whatever for?"

"I have always felt guilty," Elena confesses:

It is part of my inner self; it is a vocation that I cultivate and one that causes me pain. Although I work a lot, I feel that I do not give all of myself. I tried to make my mother see things my way. The last two weeks of her life coincided with the arrival of the Zapatistas in Mexico City. She identified greatly with the Indians and their demands. It was what she always chose to watch on TV. And when I had to go to Cuicuilco for a rally, having been invited by Subcomandante Marcos, she insisted from her hospital bed, although she had great difficulty in speaking due to the pneumonia, "Go, you must go, go ahead." And I left heartbroken, but was warmed by the greetings from the comandantes, especially from Zebedeo, and I loved listening to Carlos Montemayor speaking in Tzotzil. "Does he speak it well?" I asked myself. I also recall two faces, those of Carmen Castillo and José Saramago. Upon my return to the hospital, my mother's condition had worsened, but I refused to accept it. I denied her death, even after it had happened. I thought, "What is wrong with everybody? Why do they keep on expressing their condolences?"

Before the jury's decision came out, it was rumored that the winner of the Alfaguara Prize was a Mexican woman writer, and at five o'clock in the afternoon Madrid time, the rumor was confirmed by the Casa de América. Elena was the second woman and the first Mexican to receive the award, estimated at 25 million pesetas (approximately $175,000), and her book was chosen from among 596 manuscripts submitted by authors from all over the Spanish-speaking world. In previous years, the award had been given to the Cuban writer Eliseo Alberto, to Sergio Ramírez from Nicaragua, and to the Spaniards Manuel Vicent and Clara Sánchez. In the words of jury president Antonio Muñoz Molina, the youngest member of the Academy of the Spanish Language, Elena's novel deals with "a character searching among the possibilities of science for an explanation of the world and of life, and who, in the process of this search, finds the challenges of love. It is a biography that encompasses contemporary Mexican history." As to the narrative talents of the author, which impressed the jury very strongly, he points out that "Elena Poniatowska's writing is extraordinarily clear and of great precision, with a narrative rhythm which continually moves forward." The novel was originally entitled "T. Tauri," too arcane a title for a book that would assuredly become a best seller, because according to Elena, the point of the award is to sell at least $175,000 in books in order to cover the prize. The author, who never learned to say no, renamed her novel with a more promising and assuredly more marketable title: *La piel del cielo*. According to Elena, her novel was "written with her heart and also with her feet, for I'm certain that I made hundreds of mistakes. One of the objectives of this book is to vindicate science in a country where it does not exist," she explains. "I wanted to give voice to the men of science. Since writers sometimes act like divas, I think we should make the most of our opportunity to do so." In an interview with her good friend César Güemes published in *La Jornada* on March

7, 2001—the day she learned about the prize—Elena speaks about the genesis of her novel:

> "We had no news of this novel," Güemes comments, "except for a fleeting remark you made some time back: When did you write it?"
>
> "I started it two years ago. The fact is I'm always doing newspaper work, giving conferences, and writing forewords to other books. This takes up a lot of my time. Two years ago, realizing that I'm no longer a spring chicken, I finally set myself the challenge of devoting myself seriously to writing a novel."

On being asked about the prize and what it means to her as a woman and as a journalist, Elena responded,

> "It must make us journalists very happy, because I have always been told that I'm a paltry journalist. As if this weren't enough, when you are out reporting, you have no control over whether the interviewee treats you well or not, or whoever is in charge of the layout chops off your work, or whoever is responsible for the issue in fact publishes it. It is a job that teaches you humility every single day . . . It is also a prize for women, of course. It gives me pleasure, because I feel very close to women's causes. As to the novel's prose, well, it passes the gender test, because the jury never suspected that the author was a woman."
>
> "As you point out, not much attention has been paid to the protagonist, Lorenzo. Is this always the plight of Mexican scientists?"
>
> "That's true, so in that sense the novel is a very strong criticism of the policies of the country and the PRI. It is incredible that our scientists are not given any support, and for this reason, many remain abroad after obtaining their doctorates. If our Nobel Prize winner Mario Molina had stayed in Mexico, he would never have attained that recognition. I engage the backwardness of third world countries and the protagonist's

sadness and anger that the government devotes no resources
to education or science. What does science mean in a nation
like Mexico? Nothing. We depend upon the United States.
The fact is that our science, except in the area of astronomy,
is always lagging behind."

Toward the end of their conversation, Elena speaks of her future
projects "such as the novel about Demetrio Vallejo, which I started
years ago, and the one about Lupe Marín, which is also pending."

The Skin of Elena

I learned of *La piel del cielo* one day when I climbed the stairs to
Elena's studio and found her, as always, sitting at her computer,
looking intensely at the screen, lost in thought. We spoke of current politics, her beloved Zapatistas, and her family. It was 1998,
and Mexico still dreamed of true democracy. That day Elena asked
me to help her keyboard some documents on the computer, something I had done previously on several occasions. This time, however, the material seemed quite unlikely. They were not the letters
that her father had sent her mother during the Second World War
nor quick notes jotted down in florid handwriting, an imperish-
able reminder of her formative years at the Convent of the Sacred
Heart, but rather some truly incomprehensible scientific treaties
full of theories, equations, and symbols that I did not understand
at all, least of all how they could be turned into literature. Months
went by and Elena continued with her reading: astronomy, physics, and astrophysics. Galileo, Kepler, Hubble, Einstein, and
Hoyle were the authors of many of the books that were piling up
in an enormous basket on the floor of her studio. Only later did
I discover the reason for this interest; at first I thought that Elena
might be composing a sequel to Sor Juana's *First Dream*: "Pyrami-
dal, funereal, of the earth born a shadow . . . " But, no, it wasn't
that. Elena was working on a novel inspired by her husband, astrophysicist Guillermo Haro, and her elder son, Mane, a physicist
and head of the laboratory at the Universidad Autónoma Met-

ropolitana (UAM). Nonetheless, as Elena confesses, if Guillermo were to read the novel, "his hair would stand up on end inside his tomb, because I attribute to him a bunch of love affairs that he didn't have." Several years passed, and I never saw the scientific treatises again, so I thought that she had abandoned the project. I was very surprised when I discovered that Elena had won the Alfaguara Prize for her novel *La piel del cielo* (a literary approach to a difficult subject: the legacy of astronomic research in a country such as Mexico). Suddenly, I recalled that in an interview with Elena in 1998, I had asked her about her current literary projects, and she explained that she was working on a novel concerning science in a third world country. Undeniably, the novel encompasses much more than that. It is a bildungsroman that recounts the intellectual and emotional development of its main character, Lorenzo de Tena, a precocious child brought up by his mother in the utopian orchard of San Lucas, in Coyoacán—formerly no more than a hamlet—among cows, hens, donkeys, and horses. When his mother dies, the spell of childhood is broken and the young man finds himself immersed in a hostile world. His father, who had been absent until then, reappears and takes Lorenzo and his four brothers to live with one of his aunts in a decrepit mansion dating from the Porfiriato. The house is reminiscent of the Ancien Régime of France, but its inhabitants and visitors—Braniff, Escandón, Iturbe, Creel, Amor, de la Torre, Rincón Gallardo—have fallen on hard times thanks to that "monster" Zapata who, years back, had taken their pulque, sugar, coffee, and henequen haciendas. Lorenzo and his siblings are baptized "the orphans" by the aunt, Doña Cayetana, who speaks French at the table "á cause des domestiques" and is indignant at the orphans' bad manners. In this milieu, so difficult to assimilate into, Lorenzo meets Dr. Carlos Beristáin, who will soon stimulate the young man's growing intellectual interests. Along with mathematical formulas and scientific calculations, Lorenzo discovers other mysteries, those of the flesh, through a romance with an old friend of his aunt, the intriguing spinster Lucía Arámburu y González Palafox. In addition, Lorenzo must take care of his siblings, especially Leticia, who is left alone and pregnant, and whose life will go in directions that he will never quite understand. During his high-school years, he meets José Revueltas and works for the journal *Combate*, an experience which opens his eyes to the injustices suffered by the great majority of his country's inhabitants.

Nonetheless, the greatest change in Lorenzo's life and fortunes takes place when he meets Luis Enrique Erro, who also is a member of the League for Political Action. In addition to being a great public speaker despite his progressive deafness, he is an amateur astronomer who has set up a small observatory on the roof of his house. One day he invites Lorenzo to observe the constellations, and from that decisive moment on, Lorenzo becomes a man possessed by the celestial spheres and the heavenly dome. For him, "the heavens were his skin, his bones, his blood, his breath, the only thing for which he would give up his life." In the meantime, on earth Lorenzo is tormented by his fellow humans who "came and went with an infinite complacency, devoted to their small affairs, without questioning what was happening in the heavens." His obsession with astronomy softens one day when a fascinating woman, Fausta Rosales, appears in the Tonantzintla observatory— the place of Tonantzin, a goddess transformed into the Virgin of Guadalupe—and leads Lorenzo through different galaxies where he will learn the meaning of life on this earth. In *La piel del cielo*, Elena Poniatowska has created a true universe of planets, whose inhabitants embody human constellations, that simultaneously reveals her interminable zeal for knowledge and her enormous narrative abilities. With *La piel del cielo* Elena has certainly created a firmament where human dignity shines in all its colors.

A "Mexican Offertory"

Let us hope that *La piel del cielo* will not suffer the same fate as *Tinísima*, a novel that, according to literary critic Christopher Domínguez Michael, has been praised more than it has been read. On the Internet I found an article by Julio Ortega, a professor of Latin American literature at Brown University, whose "Canto Amoroso de Elena Poniatowska" (Loving Praise to Elena Poniatowska) appears on the Web site of *Verbigracia*, the literary supplement of the Caracas daily *El Universal*. According to Ortega,

> *La piel del cielo*, the novel by Elena Poniatowska that was awarded this year's Alfaguara Prize, is a Mexican offertory to the promises of the twentieth century. It possesses the emotional clarity of an act of thanksgiving and the emotion of a narrative of discovery. It has a fortunate narrative dynamic, which does not disappoint, as well as the rare authority of sympathy. Its limpid prose shines through in a mature, transparent astonishment. Soon the reader pauses in the midst of that uncertain intimacy. Its perspective is a reconstruction, but it is not only an evocation, because the past flows into the present, and the character lives not the *dénouements*, but the dilemmas of the present. The tempo is thus sustained on the page, in the very line that we read, and places us among its true characters. As a fable, it recoups the past with the conviction of a future to be won by creativity. Seldom does a novel develop as a ritual of what is genuine, asking itself for the horizons of what has been lived. Rarely does it come to pass that the novel succeeds in communicating the nobility of the greatest demand.
>
> A sum of historic lessons and family chronicle, of scientific memoir and spiritual biography, the novel reconstructs the past like a promise of what is to come. It is a novel possessed by the classic notion that life owes itself total fulfillment. This Faustic view develops in the biographic fable, in the vital project forged within the possibilities of the environment and its times, and tests the adventure of knowledge, which is capable of exceeding the media and transcending its own times, in order to stretch its limits to the fullest. That is why this is a novel about the passionate strength of creativity. This vocation to learn and do, to discover and teach, contaminates this history of the century during its time of gestation, as if its narrative was an open project for a life shared, that does not cease to begin again. In this sense, *La piel del cielo* is faithful to

its innermost motivations: it is an exemplary memorial of its times, a daughter of the century it depicts. It is as much the saga of knowledge, which is constructed through the chronological progression of the narrative as well as by the faith in a narrative capable of articulating life and history in their mutual elaboration. And this demonstrates the profoundly Latin American character of this novel: it is the allegory of creative identity and of a creative nationality.

9 Elena: An International Treasure
(A Conclusion of Sorts)

Export Quality

The Alfaguara Prize made Elena Poniatowska and her literary work known throughout nearly all corners of the Spanish-speaking world—in her words like some sort of "saleswoman promoting a new brand of soap." The globalization of her work had begun decades before, however, in the seventies and eighties, when researchers from universities in the United States—nearly all of them women—began to publish interviews, translations, reviews, and interpretations of the writer and her growing literary corpus.[1] In turn, nonspecialized but widely distributed publications with diverse readerships, including the *Evergreen Review*, published several interviews with Elena, who was the author of two major but at that time not yet translated books: *La noche de Tlatelolco* and *Hasta no verte Jesús mío*. Over the years, and for good reason, these two titles would become the focus for U.S. literary critics, both inside and outside academic circles, in English and in Spanish.

One of the first pieces devoted to Elena, her work, and her ideas on literature in general was her 1974 interview with U.S. academic Beth Miller, in which Elena answered the questions that have intrigued her readers from the beginning of her career and that are addressed in this book: Do you consider yourself a writer or a journalist? Is it difficult to combine your role as wife and mother with your literary career? Which Mexican women writers do you most admire? Why did you decide to write *La noche de Tlatelolco* and how did you write it? What was the creative process for *Hasta no verte Jesús mío*? The interview appeared one year later, in 1975, in the *Latin American Literary Review* published by Carnegie Mellon University in Pittsburgh.[2]

Family Resemblances

In addition to U.S. academics' expressed interest in Elena Poniatowska's narrative works, her cultural and linguistic heritage explains her close connection with the United States. Recall that Elena's paternal grandmother, Elizabeth Sperry Crocker, was born in the United States. Elena's unquestionable linguistic talent—she is completely fluent in French, English, and Spanish—was decisive in her first career objective. After giving up her ephemeral dream of becoming a physician, Elena enrolled in a typing school, planning to become an executive secretary. Through her friendship with María de Lourdes Correa—Maú—her classmate at Eden Hall, Elena had her first journalistic opportunity. She began her career with an interview (in English) with Francis White, who was the U.S. ambassador to Mexico at that time. Numerous conversations with other cultural and political figures soon followed, some translated from French or English, but the great majority in Spanish. As a multilingual writer, Elena has always translated from English and French into Spanish. Such was the case of *The House on Mango Street*, by Sandra Cisneros, which Elena translated with Juan Antonio Ascencio in 1994. In 1998, Elena also translated her mother's autobiography, *Nomeolvides* (Forget-Me-Nots), into Spanish (it was originally written in French and English).

Social Consciousness

Elena's childhood and adolescence, along with her emerging social and political conscience, is the subject of Bell Gale Chevigny's foundational article, "The Transformation of Privilege in the Work of Elena Poniatowska," published in the *Latin American Literary Review* in 1985. In her analysis Chevigny—like the majority of later critics of Elena's work—centers her attention upon *La noche de Tlatelolco* and *Hasta no verte Jesús mío* in order to illustrate an important contradiction—or metamorphosis—in the person and work of the writer:

With Mexican American writer Sandra Cisneros in Texas.

For Poniatowska's social roots are aristocratic and her political antecedents are conservative. Generations of exile from reform and revolution in Mexico and Poland produced in France Poniatowska's parents and Poniatowska herself. Against such a background, Poniatowska's two most celebrated works stand in high relief; they delineate the dual trajectory of her career. In *Hasta no verte Jesús mío*, she journeys to the opposite end of woman's world of social possibility and, in *La noche de Tlatelolco*, she journeys to the alternate pole of political possibility . . . The particular force of Poniatowska's work derives from the emptiness she found in her position as a woman of privilege and from her using that position to cultivate a readiness of imagination and spirit; when this readiness met with vivid exposure to the dispossessed, she converted equivocal privilege into real strength. Such an evolution would make her links to the dispossessed a continuing necessity (5).

The "Tlatelolco Novel"

Although somewhat critical of U.S. foreign policy, Elena has cultivated her connections with that country and gradually earned a place—both academically and editorially—in its academic and literary communities. In 1976, Elena made her U.S. literary debut with her chronicle of the student demonstration and massacre at the Plaza de las Tres Culturas. Its English title, *Massacre in Mexico*, is more prosaic than the original, *La noche de Tlatelolco*, but the work soon became the prototype of a literary subgenre documenting the social revolutions of 1968, a definitive year that also witnessed the Soviet invasion of Prague, student uprisings in Paris, and numerous rallies and protests in the United States incited by the Vietnam War as well as the growing civil rights confrontations between blacks and whites in large urban centers. *Massacre in Mexico*, translated by Helen R. Lane, includes a lengthy foreword by Octavio Paz—at that time, the most internationally renowned Mexican writer—who attempts both to describe the event, which he compares to a Greek tragedy, in universal terms, and to place it within the historical context of Mexico. Elena's chronicle, originally published (in 1975) by Viking Press and reprinted nearly twenty years later—in 1991—by the University of Missouri, was praised by U.S. critics and is now included with *Biography of a Runaway Slave* by the Cuban writer Miguel Barnet and the works by Oscar Lewis as a classic of Latin American testimonial literature.

Massacre in Mexico—whose structure Elena describes as a collage—immediately attracted the attention of U.S. critics specializing in Latin America and its cultural production. In her book *Politics, Gender, and the Mexican Novel, 1968–1988: Beyond the Pyramid*, Cynthia Steele describes Elena's formal technique as one that

> juxtaposes the voices of numerous participants in and observers of the movement, thus enhancing the dialogic dimension of the novel and focusing on the community—Mexico City— as literary and political protagonist. In doing so Poniatowska is working in the highest tradition of Mexican fiction; one might say that she has replaced the apathetic, defeated peasant community which is the collective protagonist (the very

literal ghost town) of Juan Rulfo's *Pedro Páramo* (1955) with an assertive, forcibly subdued, yet not defeated urban community. (29)

Steele also sees *Massacre in Mexico* as an example of female solidarity because, in her view, Elena was inspired to write the book by the testimony of women who lost their sons and daughters in the bloodbath. To illustrate the transcendence of this work and others like it, Steele points out that in the 1970s "the Novel of Tlatelolco would displace the Novel of Revolution and the Novel of the City as the principal genre of Mexican fiction" (9). Furthermore, she recognizes Carlos Monsiváis and Elena Poniatowska as the authors "responsible for converting the testimonial novel and the social and political chronicle into the quintessential narrative genre of the seventies and eighties; at the same time, they have perpetuated José Revueltas' model of the committed writer as public figure" (11).

In enumerating the thematic characteristics of Elena's work, Steele presents the image that people in the United States have of her, distinguished by "a commitment to representing powerless, marginalized, and oppositional members of society who lack access to self-representation in print and the media: the handicapped, AIDS victims, earthquake victims, women artists and writers of the past, political performers, political prisoners, trade-union organizers, opposition leaders, servants, garment workers, Indian women" (11–12). After quoting several literary critics and theorists, Steele concludes that "the *testimonio* is a narrative genre unto itself, neither biography nor autobiography, fiction nor journalism" (34), a fact well understood by any reader of the U.S. "new journalism," which includes the neorealist works of Tom Wolfe and Truman Capote.

In his study *The Postmodern Novel in Latin America: Politics, Culture, and the Crisis of Truth*, Raymond Leslie Williams argues that the year of Tlatelolco was the starting point of Mexico's postmodern era, which ended in the mid-nineties with the uprising of the EZLN in Chiapas. *Massacre in Mexico* is for Williams a work representative of the Mexican "postmodern condition," in that "many postmodern novels question the very concept of the individual subject, [and] many testimonios emphasize the community over the individual. Rather than novels, testimonios are closely aligned to postmodern ethnography" (122). Yet paradoxically whereas "in general, the different variants of postmodern fiction have in common distant and subversive positions toward truth; testimonio tends to seek veracity and truth" (121).

Epistolary Genres

In 1986, eleven years after the U.S. release of *Massacre in Mexico*, Pantheon Books published Katherine Silver's translation of *Querido Diego, te abraza Quiela*, under the shortened title of *Dear Diego*. Now, Elena's English-speaking readers could appreciate her genuine literary talent in addition to her ability to give social testimony. In her slender book, Elena turns the tempestuous relationship between Diego Rivera and his Russian lover, painter Angelina Beloff, into an epistolary novella. Like so many of Elena's other stories, it is a blending of fact and fiction, as it was inspired by the distraught letters Beloff sent Rivera from Paris. The book enjoyed great success in the United States because it was short and dealt with Mexico's most internationally recognized painter, best known in the United States for his controversial (and obliterated) mural at Rockefeller Center, as well as for the frescoes that adorn the interior courtyard of the Detroit Institute of the Arts. In an illustration of how Elena has profited from her multilingualism in all aspects of her literary production, she discovered the raw material for what would later become *Dear Diego* in the pages of Bertram Wolfe's well-known English-language biography of the painter, entitled *The Fabulous Life of Diego Rivera*.

In her book entitled *Textured Lives: Women, Art, and Representation in Modern Mexico*, Claudia Schaefer devotes one chapter to updating the "epistolary canon" while analyzing the unique discursive structures of *Dear Diego* and *Gaby Brimmer*. In both of these works—as Schaefer demonstrates—Elena acts as a *bricoleuse* who reassembles already existing signs or objects into new discourses and who speaks to and through others' letters, using former constructs for her emergent creations, [and] establishes personas for Beloff and Brimmer. The new personas contribute potentially hidden, publicly unacknowledged, subconsciously latent, or even purely fabricated aspects of these characters, whose "masks" or "voices," rather than being figures of authority, exhibit elements of contradiction not reconciled by Poniatowska . . . In thus filling the interstices of both women's letters, it appears that Poniatowska proposes to subvert any idea (or accusation?) of direct mirror identification between literature and history, the supposed representation or reflection of objective reality, by offering in its place subjective interpretation. The reader is left with no doubt that this is a mediated discourse whose "rules" are those of fictional narrative. (66–67, 68)

Schaefer's methodical analysis of the discursive world Elena invented characterizes both the literary and ideological depth and the rigor of interpretations of Elena's work in the United States, a country where more than one hundred monographs in dozens of literary publications have been devoted to her. Schaefer concludes with a critical analysis of the complexity of the literary universe Elena invented, using as an example the general model she employed in her two aforementioned works:

[This] epistolary genre makes available to Poniatowska a repertoire of certain characteristic elements or formulas that she can exploit to construct new textual possibilities for the exploration of women's egos within these two examples of very different discourse. Several of these conventions are especially pertinent to a study of the texts under consideration—the function of the letter as an attempt to recover a loss or absence, for example, and the idea of reciprocity or "correspondence" (69).

"Engaging Dialogues"

Second to the English translations of several of her works, the next most important attempt to introduce Elena's oeuvre to U.S. readers was the publication of Beth Jörgensen's 1994 monograph *The Writing of Elena Poniatowska: Engaging Dialogues*, a critical study based partly on the "dialogic" ideas of the Russian theoretician Mikhail Bakhtin and initially written as Jörgensen's doctoral dissertation. The book is divided into four chapters: the first, "Face to Face," contemplates Elena's trajectory as interviewer and how her first articles "pay tribute to the prevailing social and gender hierarchy, while also posing a limited challenge to the authority of her prominent interviewees" (xiv). "Creative Confusions," the second chapter, is a critical reading of the novel *Here's to You, Jesusa!*, the work through which Elena "achieved increasing notoriety and a greatly expanded reading public in Mexico and abroad . . . this novel has sparked an ongoing debate over the status of authorship and referentiality in a literary text which blends the documentary and the fictional into a seamless narrative" (xvi–xvii). The two last chapters are "Chronicles of the Conquered," which explores issues of authority and history in *Massacre in Mexico*, and "Intimate Conversations," which analyzes three "privileged pieces of fiction": *Lilus Kikus, La "Flor de Lis,"* and *De noche vienes* (You Come by Night).

In her assessment of Elena's works and of the idea of the author as subject, Jörgensen analyzes Elena's main themes, stating that "in all cases, Poniatowska's work offers a critical—and self-critical—perspective on contemporary Mexican reality by recuperating previously silenced versions of events and by scrutinizing her own considerable stake in the status quo" (xii). With regard to the forms employed in her books, Jörgensen points out that, because she is "never bound by an adherence to established genres, Poniatowska frequently creates hybrid texts by combining the discourses of fact and fiction and by utilizing many linguistic registers and literary forms. These formal innovations correspond to the exigencies of her investigation into class, gender, and ethnic difference, the struggle of women and the poor for economic and social justice, and the mechanisms of repression of that struggle" (xii). In conclusion, Jörgensen summarizes Elena's literary history, which is essentially "the story of her encounter with Mexico, and her texts inscribe the ever-changing relationship between her voice and the voices of her diverse compatriots" (xix). Regarding the undeniable originality of Elena's work, the investigator points out that it is the product of the "dialogue that she has actively sought, first from a position as a cultural outsider, and then from a position of increased cultural rootedness and authority within Mexico. The dynamics of reciprocity and mutual influence between speakers in a conversation make it an ideal forum for the exploration of self and of other which is central to Poniatowska's work. On another level, she encourages a dialogue between conventionally distinct modes of writing by connecting the practices of journalism and imaginative literature in her work" (xix).

Notwithstanding the prestigious places occupied by the aforementioned titles, Elena's most ambitious literary project was the publication of *Tinísima*, the biographical novel based on the life of Italian American militant Tina Modotti. Originally published in 1992, this work is in its fifth edition in Mexico and earned the author the Mazatlán Prize for the second time, thus making her the only woman to have received it twice. A much shortened version translated by Katherine Silver was published in 1996 by Farrar, Straus and Giroux with the same title and was published by Faber and Faber in the UK three years later. Although *Tinísima* did not receive the same attention from critics as some of Elena's other works, the novel generated questions regarding the biographical genre and the relationship of visual media—in this case, photographs—to the documents more traditionally employed as and considered legitimate sources for the literary reconstruction of a lifetime. These are some of the issues taken up by Beth Jörgensen— the most prolific U.S. critic of Elena Poniatowska and the author of the only book devoted entirely to Elena's work—in her chapter entitled "Light-Writing: Biography and Photography in *Tinísima*," which appears in the excellent book *The Other Mirror: Women's Narrative in Mexico: 1980–1995*, edited by Kristine Ibsen and published in 1997 by Greenwood Press. In this chapter, Jörgensen points out that *Tinísima*, "like many of the Mexican writer's works . . . , is a hybrid text that moves across the fluid boundaries between fictional and factual discourses. Specifically, it invites a reading as both biography and novel, as Elena Poniatowska's own commentary suggests" (57). Her analysis of *Tinísima* also "examine(s) the texts as a biographical novel using recent feminist approaches to biography in order to analyze the construction of its historical and fictive subject" (58). Jörgensen concludes with a discussion of "the relationship between the photographic record left by Tina Modotti, including both the photos that she took and those for which she modeled, and the verbal image of her created by Poniatowska" (58), in order to "address how Elena Poniatowska used photographs as a 'source' for her vision of Modotti and how photographic reproductions are an integral part of the published book" (58). In order to achieve this goal, Jörgensen takes three factors into account: "(1) The nature of her sources, (2) Poniatowska's relationship to these sources, and (3) the conjunction of the biographical (Tina Modotti) and the autobiographical (Elena Poniatowska) in *Tinísima*" (66). Jörgensen concludes that "tensions are present throughout the novel and that they may be attributed to a complex interplay of factors: the nature of the written and oral sources employed by Elena Poniatowska, her respect for those sources, the photographs, and the intersection of the biographical and the autobiographical" (71).

Another of Elena's books was translated to English in the same year, but its circulation has been limited almost exclusively to academic circles; *Nothing, Nobody: The Voices of the Mexico City Earthquake* documents the 1985 natural catastrophe that triggered a frantic rescue and reconstruction effort while unmasking the corruption and disorganization prevalent in the Mexican government, especially with regard to the often corrupt issuance of building permits. Originally published in Mexico in 1988, *Nothing, Nobody* was splendidly translated into English by Aurora Camacho de Schmidt and Arthur Schmidt in 1995 and published by Temple University Press.

Matters of Genre

As previously mentioned, of Elena's five books translated into English, two stand out for the number of commentaries generated by U.S. critics: *Massacre in Mexico*, already considered in this chapter, and *Here's to You, Jesusa!*, translated by Deanna Heikkinen and published by Farrar, Straus and Giroux in 2001. Despite the fact that it was not available in English translation for more than thirty years after its original publication in 1969, the novel is analyzed by Cynthia Steele in *Politics, Gender, and the Mexican Novel*, where she argues that "along with *La noche de Tlatelolco*, *Hasta no verte Jesús mío* is Poniatowska's masterpiece to date. It fulfilled the same function of advocacy for the urban poor that *La noche* did for the politicized middle class" (31). In Steele's words, *Here's to You, Jesusa!* constitutes

> a model for testimonial fiction and other literature that strives to represent non-hegemonic subjectivities, including those of poor women, female artists, and political dissidents. It reproduces popular Mexican dialects and ideology, just as Fernando del Paso and José Emilio Pacheco incorporate the language and liberal humanism of the intellectual, urban middle class that came of age during the 1940s, and José Agustín textualizes the irreverent countercultural perspective of sixties youth culture. Poniatowska's works constitute the novel as collaborative process or dialogue (25).

In her highly influential book entitled *Plotting Women: Gender and Representation in Mexico*, Jean Franco also devotes herself to an exegesis of *Here's to You, Jesusa!*, pointing out that "this text raises important questions about genre and directly challenges the kind of ethnographic discourse represented by Oscar Lewis' *The Children of Sánchez*. More importantly, it confronts the deep rooted assumptions of those literary and intellectual institutions that had excluded everyday life as trivial and had insisted on literature's transcendence of social praxis" (176).

If there is one thing that represents Jesusa Palancares, she continues, "it is what Gayatri Spivak has termed 'the loneliness of the gendered subaltern.' Poniatowska's 'novel' cannot claim the typical-ity of ethnography, nor does it transcend everyday life in the manner of history or literature. On the other hand, since the book is not a transcribed tape recording, but Poniatowska's recreation of Jesusa's voice, I have chosen to consider it as a compositely authored work, which, because it is composite, avoids the problem of the hierarchical alignment of writer and informant, writing and voice" (178).

Required Reading

As we have seen, following the translation of some of her most representative works, Elena became a literary presence in the English-speaking world. Yet the impact her Spanish-language works had already had in U.S. universities should also be mentioned. Her novels and chronicles appear in the syllabi of hundreds of courses and seminars devoted to Mexican testimonial literature and women's literature, besides forming part of any bibliography of Latin American literature in general. To date, twenty-four doctoral dissertations have analyzed her work, either exclusively or along with works of other authors—a number that compares favorably with the number of dissertations devoted to other contemporary Mexican writers such as Carlos Fuentes (70), Octavio Paz (53), and Rosario Castellanos (33). Elena herself has been the keynote speaker at academic conferences such as the Modern Language Association meeting and has guest lectured at various universities in the United States, including the University of California at Davis and Florida Atlantic University, in Boca Raton. In addition, she has been honored with three honorary doctorates, from Manhattanville College (2001), Florida Atlantic University (1995), and the New School for Social Research (1994).

Although a book such as this must come to an end, the same is not true of the subject of my biography. Since *Elena Poniatowska* was first published in Spanish in 2003, Elena has continued to work persistently on various literary projects, in particular a book of eight short stories entitled *Tlapalería*, published by Ediciones Era in 2003. Here, through the use of what at first appears to be rather unsophisticated dialogues, the author's observational talents conspire with her skill for writing deceptively simple prose to produce a collection of brief accounts that reflect the lives and loves of diverse inhabitants of the multicultural urban jungle that is today's Mexico City.

More significantly, however, in 2005 Elena finally completed her long-awaited novel about Demetrio Vallejo, the leader of the striking railway workers of the 1950s, entitled *El tren pasa primero* (The Train Passes First). According to the author, she set this book project aside more than forty years ago, because when she read passages of the original manuscript to the novel's protagonist, who was at the time a prisoner in the Palacio Negro de Lecumberri, he would promptly doze off in his cell.

Nevertheless, as with *La "Flor de Lis,"* Elena reworked this manuscript that she had set aside long ago, in this case converting it into an engaging novel about a decisive chapter in Mexico's political life. These railroad workers, whose massive 1959 strikes paralyzed the country, were an inspiration to those who took to the streets in 1968 to protest the military's involvement in the affairs of UNAM. Once again, we bear witness to the fact that Mexico's history relies on the works of Elena Poniatowska as much as the author depends on the country's twentieth-century experience for the basis of her narratives, an exceptional oeuvre that blurs the boundaries between literature and journalism, testimony and the novel. The completion of *El tren pasa primero* constitutes yet one more star in a literary universe that was born nearly fifty years ago in the pages of *Excélsior* and, like the heavens, continues to expand infinitely.

In recognition and celebration of Elena's extraordinary literary and journalistic vocation, in late 2006 she will receive the Lifetime Achievement Award from the International Women's Media Foundation. She is the first Mexican to receive this illustrious prize, which "recognizes a woman journalist who has a pioneering spirit and whose determination has paved the way for future generations of women in the media." Clearly, Elena Poniatowska is an outstanding choice for this award, as her career has inspired many younger journalists for whom she has been a role model, while her weekly writers' workshop has been the breeding ground for more than a few of Mexico's most promising female literary talents of the twenty-first century.

Annotated Bibliography

Principal Works of Elena Poniatowska

All works are listed in chronological order according to date of first publication. English translations, where existing, are listed under the Spanish-language entry. Translations to other languages are noted, but no bibliographic data are provided.

Narrative

Lilus Kikus. México: Los Presentes, 1954.

Los cuentos de Lilus Kikus. 2nd expanded ed. México: Universidad Veracruzana, 1967.

    3rd ed. México: Grijalbo, 1982.

    4th ed. Illus. Leonora Carrington. México: Ediciones ERA, 1985.

Lilus Kikus and Other Stories. Trans. and intro. Elizabeth C. Martínez. Illus. Leonora Carrington. Albuquerque: University of New Mexico Press, 2005.

Hasta no verte Jesús mío. México: Ediciones ERA, 1969. (45 editions)

    Madrid: Círculo de Lectores, 1984.

    Madrid: Alianza Editorial, 1984.

    Lecturas Mexicanas, 2nd series. México: Secretaría de Educación Pública, 1986.

    Havana: Casa de las Américas, 1991.

Here's to You, Jesusa! Trans. Deanna Heikkinen. New York: Farrar, Straus, Giroux, 2001. Translations to French, Italian, and Flemish.

Querido Diego, te abraza Quiela. México: Ediciones ERA, 1976. (20 editions)

    Madrid: Alianza Editorial, 1978.

Dear Diego. Trans. Katherine Silver. New York: Pantheon Books, 1986. Translations to Dutch, Polish, Danish, French, and German.

De noche vienes. México: Grijalbo, 1979. México: Ediciones ERA, 1985. (10 editions)

La *"Flor de Lis."* México: Ediciones ERA, 1988. (10 editions)

Tinísima. México: Ediciones ERA, 1992. (5 editions)
Tinisima. Trans. Katherine Silver. New York: Farrar, Straus, Giroux, 1996.

Paseo de la Reforma. México: Joaquín Mortiz, 1996.

La piel del cielo. México: Alfaguara, 2001.
The Skin of the Sky. Trans. Deanna Heikkinen. New York: Farrar, Straus, Giroux, 2004.

Tlapalería. México: Ediciones Era, 2003.

El tren pasa primero. México: Editorial Alfaguara, 2006.

Theater

Melés y Teléo, apuntes para una comedia. Panoramas 2 (Summer 1956): 135–299.

Interviews

Palabras cruzadas, Ediciones ERA, México, 1961.
Domingo Siete, México: Océano, 1982. (3 editions)
Todo México, vol. 1. México: Editorial Diana, 1991. (5 editions)
Todo México, vol. 2. México: Editorial Diana, 1994. (2 editions)
Todo México, vol. 3. *Gabriel Figueroa: la mirada que limpia.* México: Editorial Diana, 1996.
Todo México, vol. 4. México: Editorial Diana, 1998.
Todo México, vols. 5–7. México: Editorial Diana, 1999.

Chronicles

Todo empezó el domingo. Illus. Alberto Beltrán. Special volume in the Vida y Pensamiento de México series. México: FCE, 1963.
    Reprint, México: Océano, 1997.

La noche de Tlatelolco: testimonios de historia oral. México: Ediciones ERA, 1971. (54 editions)
Massacre in Mexico. Trans. Helen R. Lane. Foreword by Octavio Paz. New York: Viking, 1975.

Fuerte es el silencio. México: Ediciones ERA, 1980. (10 editions). Translated to German.

Nada, nadie: las voces del temblor. México: Ediciones ERA, 1988. (7 editions)

Nothing, Nobody: The Voices of the Mexico City Earthquake. Trans. Aurora Camacho de
    Schmidt and Arthur Schmidt. Philadelphia: Temple University Press, 1995.

Essay Collections

El último guajolote. México: Martín Casillas and Secretaría de Educación Pública,
    1982.
*¡Ay, vida, no me mereces! Carlos Fuentes, Rosario Castellanos, Juan Rulfo, la literatura de la
.   onda.* México: J. Mortiz, 1985.
Luz y luna, las lunitas. México: Ediciones ERA, 1994.
Las soldaderas. México: Ediciones ERA (CONACULTA/INAH), 1999.
Las siete cabritas. México: Ediciones ERA, 2000.
Las mil y una: la herida de Paulina. México: Plaza y Janés, 2000.

Biographies

Gaby Brimmer. México: Grijalbo, 1979. (15 editions)
Juan Soriano: niño de mil años. Mexico: Plaza y Janés, 1998.
Octavio Paz: las palabras del árbol. México: Plaza y Janés, 1998.
Mariana Yampolsky y la bugambilia. México: Plaza y Janés, 2001.

Correspondence

Cartas de Álvaro Mutis a Elena Poniatowska. México: Alfaguara, 1998.

Works about Elena Poniatowska

Ascencio, Esteban (interviewer). *Me lo dijo Elena Poniatowska: su vida, obra y pasiones/
    contadas por ella misma.* México: Ediciones del Milenio, 1997.
Jörgensen, Beth. *The Writing of Elena Poniatowska: Engaging Dialogues.* Austin: Uni-
    versity of Texas Press, 1994.

Principal Guides to Poniatowska's Work (English)

Bassnett, Susan, ed. *Knives and Angels: Women Writers in Latin America.* London: Zed
    Books, 1990.
Franco, Jean. *Plotting Women: Gender and Representation in Mexico.* New York: Co-
    lumbia University Press, 1989.
Ibsen, Kristine, ed. *The Other Mirror: Women's Narrative in Mexico, 1980–1995.*
    Westport, CT: Greenwood Press, 1997.

Kaminsky, Amy. *Reading the Body Politic: Feminist Criticism and Latin American Women Writers*. Minneapolis: University of Minnesota Press, 1993.

Meyer, Doris, and Margarite Fernández Olmos, eds. *Contemporary Women Authors of Latin America*. Brooklyn: Brooklyn College Press, 1983.

Neubauer, John, and Helga Geyer-Ryan, eds. *Gendered Memories*. Amsterdam: Rodopi, 2000.

Schaefer, Claudia. *Textured Lives: Women, Art, and Representation in Modern Mexico*. Tucson: University of Arizona Press, 1992.

Steele, Cynthia. *Politics, Gender, and the Mexican Novel, 1968–1988: Beyond the Pyramid*. Austin: University of Texas Press, 1992.

Williams, Raymond Leslie. *The Postmodern Novel in Latin America: Politics, Culture, and the Crisis of Truth*. New York: St. Martin's Press, 1995.

Index

About the Author

Michael K. Schuessler received his Ph.D. in Hispanic languages and literatures from the University of California, Los Angeles, in 1996, with a specialization in the literature of colonial Spanish America. He is the author of various articles devoted to the interpretation of Latin American literature and culture, as well as two books and one anthology: *La undécima musa: Guadalupe Amor* (1995), *Elenísima: ingenio y figura de Elena Poniatowska* (2003), and *El universo de sor Juana* (1995), the last coauthored with Perla Schwartz, and all published in Mexico by Editorial Diana. In the fall of 2006, Diana published his critical edition of *Peregrina: mi idilio socialista con Felipe Carrillo Puerto*, which will be published in its original English-language version by the University of Texas Press in early 2007. Currently, he is completing a book entitled *Artes de fundación: teatro evangelizador y pintura mural en la Nueva España*, which will be published by Mexico's National Autonomous University (UNAM). Schuessler is an independent scholar residing in Mexico City.